20TH-CENTURY
ITALIAN WOMEN
WRITERS

Dacia Maraini   (137: society responsible for women's status

86   The Silent Duchess compared to The Leopard
94-99 The Silent Duchess (La lunga vita di Marianna Ucria)

20TH-CENTURY
ITALIAN WOMEN
WRITERS

The Feminine Experience

Alba Amoia

Southern Illinois University Press

Carbondale and Edwardsville

Copyright © 1996 by the Board of Trustees,
Southern Illinois University
All rights reserved
Printed in the United States of America
Designed by Chiquita Babb

99 98 97 96   4 3 2 1

Library of Congress Cataloging-in-Publication Data

Amoia, Alba della Fazia.
    Twentieth-century Italian women writers: the feminine experience / Alba Amoia.
        p. cm.
    Includes bibliographical references and index.
        1. Italian fiction—Women authors—History and criticism.
    2. Italian fiction—20th century—History and criticism. I. Title.
    PQ4174.A48   1996
    853'.91099287—dc20   95-22079
    ISBN 0-8093-2026-6 (cloth). — ISBN 0-8093-2027-4 (paper)   CIP

The paper used in this publication meets the minimum requirements
of American National Standard for Information Sciences—Permanence
of Paper for Printed Library Materials, ANSI Z39.48-1984. ∞

CONTENTS

PREFACE

The structural organization of feminism in Italy and its development within a strong leftist cultural-political context distinguishes it from the British or American feminist experience. The originality of Italian feminism lies in the fact that women, caught up in new social movements, shared in the debate on the very nature of the political process at the same time that they were conceiving a new awareness of their inner selves. Even as they battled openly for equal representation in Italy's society, they were expanding their personal visions and dreams and searching for fulfillment. Those who were inclined to write took up their pens to illustrate the split between how women appear in male-authored texts and what their "I" really is like. Through fiction, drama, essays, and "literature of memory," they expressed their malaise in a patriarchal society that has always dictated female behavior. The novel proved to be the best vehicle to trace the stages of women's development and to define their role not according to society's ruling principles but according to the dictates of their own minds and sensitivities.

The strength of Italian feminism lies in its openness to diversity, which is manifest within both fiction and nonfiction. The eleven novelists and journalists whose oeuvre I analyze in this book have articulated their individual and sometimes contradictory points of view in diverse ways, illustrating that there is no intrinsically female subject, style, or literary approach. Yet all the writers have focused in some way on the inner world of the female and have broached the issue of sexual difference. The lives and literary careers of all the writers are examples of the feminine "anxiety of authorship."

The first two chapters of this book deal with two women who, in the early twentieth century, were prey to feelings of guilt arising from the conflict between crippling traditional values and a thirst for freedom. Nobel Prize winner Grazia Deledda was compelled to flee her island of Sardinia and its society that provided no models for women writers. Sibilla Aleramo, whose evolving concepts of self helped her to escape the imperatives of a male-dominated society, gave witness to her experience in a novel, *Una donna*, that had a decisive influence on twentieth-century women's literature.

Chapter 3 examines the novels of a stylistic master, Gianna Manzini, who explores the mental and emotional states of her characters and finds release from her own physical pain and psychic discomfort through the process of writing. Chapter 4 deals with the works of Lalla Romano, whose autobiographical motifs stress the domestic aspects of "literature of memory."

Chapter 5 is devoted to a supreme anticonformist, Elsa Morante, one of the world's outstanding twentieth-century writers. Her novels, predicated on the necessity to disrupt traditional patterns of thought and expression, contain completely new visions of the real and of the surrealistic. In chapter 6, I discuss Natalia Ginzburg's prescription for a new lifestyle and look at her approach to language and literature, which was fashioned by masculine criteria even while her sociocultural values and concerns remained strictly feminine. Chapter 7 traces the movement toward a new language and a new vision in the works of Rosetta Loy, an illuministic author who has broken free from the confines of traditional structures and language and has redefined, refined, and extended the scope of the novel.

In chapter 8, I discuss feminist visions of liberated sexuality and female transcendence in the novels of Dacia Maraini. Her works represent the fullest development of female-ordered language and cultural forms, as well as the most complete assimilation of the female into the concept of the warrior.

Finally, chapter 9 is devoted to three Italian women journalists, but with no attempt to set them up as models of a "female journalism," which critics agree does not exist. Matilde Serao, a woman of fierce willpower, knew that society's laws did not permit happiness to women; Oriana Fallaci, a pugnacious reporter and an author of best-selling novels, has spent much of her life in the midst of wars; and Camilla Cederna, a courageous, justice-seeking observer of the Italian sociopolitical scene, has challenged her contemporaries for half a century, using irony and truth as her chief weapons.

While my choice of prose writers in this book is representative, such a limited study can make no claims to be exhaustive, but it will, I hope, provide some indication of the reasons for the growing number of studies on the presence of women on Italy's literary-cultural scene.

CHRONOLOGY

1856	Matilde Serao born in Patras, Greece.
1871	Grazia Deledda born in Sardinia.
1876	Sibilla Aleramo born in Alessandria.
1881	Italian realism (*verismo*) and regionalism prevail on the literary scene.
1883	*Fantasia*, Matilde Serao's first novel, published.
1890	*Stella d'Oriente*, Grazia Deledda's first novel, published.
1896	Gianna Manzini born in Pistoia.
1906	*Una donna*, Sibilla Aleramo's first novel, published. Lalla Romano born in Demonte (Cuneo).
1912	Elsa Morante born in Rome.
1916	Natalia Ginzburg born in Palermo.
1921	Camilla Cederna born in Milan.
1922	Beginning of eighteen-year fascist regime in Italy.
1925	Women obtain the right to vote in local elections only.
1926	Nobel Prize for literature awarded to Grazia Deledda.
1927	Death of Matilde Serao.
1928	*Tempo innamorato*, Gianna Manzini's first novel, published.
1930	Oriana Fallaci born in Florence.
1931	Rosetta Loy born in Rome.
1935	Gianna Manzini receives prize of encouragement from the Royal Academy of Italy.

1936	Death of Grazia Deledda. Dacia Maraini born in Florence.
1937	Fascist anti-Semitic laws passed in Italy. *Cosima*, Grazia Deledda's autobiographical novel, published posthumously.
1941	Italian neorealism begins to define itself. Elsa Morante marries novelist Alberto Moravia (the couple becomes estranged in 1963).
1942–44	Many Italian women, some of them writers (Natalia Ginzburg, Oriana Fallaci, Lalla Romano, Camilla Ravera, Marina Jarre, Iris Origo, Renata Viganò, Marina Sereni), are active in the antifascist resistance movement during World War II.
1942	*La strada che va in città*, Natalia Ginzburg's first novel, published.
1943	A group of women (Ada Gobetti, Rina Picolato, Lina Merlin, Elena Dreher, etc.) belonging to the antifascist parties found women's "defense groups" in Piedmont and Lombardy.
1944	Three months after the liberation of Italy, the Unione Donne Italiane (UDI) is officially constituted in Rome on 15 September.
1945	Italian women gain general franchise. Neorealism firmly established in Italian literature and cinema. Gianna Manzini's *Lettera all'editore* published.
1948	*Menzogna e sortilegio*, Elsa Morante's first published novel, awarded Viareggio Prize.
1950	First law passed for protection of working mothers.
1952	Natalia Ginzburg's *Tutti i nostri ieri* published.
1956	Gianna Manzini's *La Sparviera* awarded Viareggio Prize.
1957	Law passed granting "equal rights for equal work." Elsa Morante's *L'isola di Arturo* published.
1960	Death of Sibilla Aleramo.
1962	By law, "paternal" authority is replaced by "parental" authority within the family. *La vacanza*, Dacia Maraini's first novel, published.

1963   Law gives parents parity of decisive powers in certain family, business, and residence matters. Law grants access by women to all public offices and possibility for full career in public administration. Natalia Ginzburg's *Lessico famigliare* awarded Strega Prize.Elsa Morante's *Lo scialle andaluso*, a collection of twelve stories, published in book form.

1966   Elsa Morante's *L'isola di Arturo* (published in 1957) awarded Strega Prize.

1968   Students' and workers' "revolutions" give impetus to the feminist emancipatory movements that proliferate in the 1970s. Elsa Morante's *Il mondo salvato dai ragazzini*, a collection of poetry, published and highly acclaimed (awarded Zafferana Prize).

1969   Lalla Romano's *Le parole tra noi leggere* awarded Strega Prize.

1970   Divorce established in Italy.

1971   Law passed for subsidy by national government of nursery schools. Second law passed for protection of working mothers. Gianna Manzini's *Ritratto in piedi* awarded Campiello Prize.

1973   Protective legislation passed for women in cottage industries. Gianna Manzini's *Sulla soglia* published.

1974   Popular referendum results in decisive defeat of papal and Christian-Democrat attempts to annul divorce law. Elsa Morante's *La Storia* published. Rosetta Loy's first published novel, *La bicicletta*, awarded Viareggio Prize. Death of Gianna Manzini.

1975   World Conference for International Women's Year and Declaration of Mexico City has significant repercussion in Italy.

1978   Voluntary interruption of pregnancy legalized, but full application of law still lacking today.

1979   Oriana Fallaci's *Un uomo* published.

1982   Elsa Morante's last novel, *Aracoeli*, published.

1983   Natalia Ginzburg's *La famiglia Manzoni* awarded Bagutta Prize. Suicide attempt by Elsa Morante.

1985	Death of Elsa Morante.
1988	Rosetta Loy wins both the Campiello and the Viareggio Prizes for her novel *Le strade di polvere*, published in 1987.
1990	Dacia Maraini's *La lunga vita di Marianna Ucrìa* wins the Campiello Prize.
1991	Death of Natalia Ginzburg.
1993	Dacia Maraini among Strega Prize finalists for her autobiographical *Bagheria*.
1994	Dacia Maraini's *Voci* published.

20TH-CENTURY
ITALIAN WOMEN
WRITERS

ONE

GRAZIA DELEDDA

The Scandal of a Woman Writer

ike her American contemporary Willa Cather, who was also a "regional" writer, Grazia Deledda (1871–1936) struggled to emerge from the constricting life and stifling effects of small-town society. Deledda refused to submit to the local behavioral codes of her native Sardinia, and deviating from the common model, she became a writer. In nearly fifty novels, she describes the passions smoldering in the hearts of her island's primitive and often violent shepherds, peasants, and mountaineers. Harking back to Sardinia's archaic Barbary civilization, she evokes her people's animistic beliefs, their religious attitudes toward life and destiny, their rites, their myths of supernatural justice, and the rituals that govern the peacemaking between warring families.

Deledda's sources are Sardinian history, biblical and pagan credences, legends, customs, and traditions. She gives resonance to the silence and solitude of the island's vast *tancas* (stretches of fenced-in grazing land), where shepherds and flocks live out the cyclical course of nature and time. She writes of brigands and of treasures buried deep inside *nuraghi* (Sardinian stone towers). She frames thwarted loves in a stratified society headed by austere patriarchs and somber matriarchs.

She describes how the singing of Sardinian women washing clothes in a stream blends with the sound of the water "on the same melancholy and monotonous note";[1] how at home the women wash their men's feet "with affection, in fact a sort of religiosity: because the man walks for the good of the family"; how the women prepare medicine with herbs, salt, and holy medals; how peasants bathe ritually in the river on the eve of the feast of Saint John "in order to be baptized anew." Victims of tarantula bites are buried in the ground up to their necks while around them "seven widows seven wives and seven virgins dance until the earth sucks out all the poison,"[2] writes Deledda, with an unusual (for her time) omission of commas, which helps to replicate the chanting quality of the magic formula.

From remote myths about male strength, honor, reputation, and revenge for offense, Deledda learned about Sardinia's proud and scornful masculine figure—the famous and infamous *padre/padrone* (father/master). Many of the male characters in her future novels would come to symbolize those undefiable paternal and communal laws on which the authority of the *padre/padrone* rested.

Deledda's early writings treat sentimental themes from folklore. They reveal a pessimistic view of life and a preoccupation with evil and death, as well as a concern for Sardinia's downtrodden. The style of these works is a somewhat rough-and-tumble mixture of the late nineteenth-century literary trends and regional verism, if, as she wrote, "verism is a portrait of life and humans as they are, or better, as I know them."[3] Her conception of Sardinian psychology resembled Giovanni Verga's idea of the Sicilian peasants, and although she looked to D'Annunzio for literary inspiration, she carefully went about preparing her own distinctive evocations of regional life. She delved into anthropological studies and the folklore of her island: proverbs, prayers, magic and Christian formulas for exorcising evil spirits, propitiatory rites, lullabies, and the customs of the Mediterranean people who had gone to Sardinia as conquerors of the past—these were her "living documents." The works of her mature period constitute a veritable Sardinian saga in which vivid characters appear and reappear in a narration woven with sympathy and understanding of the human tragedy.

Deledda's character delineations reveal her compassion for Sardinia's miserable peasants living in subhuman conditions in hovels. Helpless victims of social injustice, with no hope of recourse, they are also slaves of their eternal passions, jealousies, and hates. "Siamo nati per soffrire" [we are born to suffer] is their constant lament. In their defense, Deledda writes:

> The man of these mountains is still primitive. . . . Segregated from the rest of the world, engaged in a constant struggle with his similars—often his own relatives, his own brother . . . he believes he has the right to take justice into his own hands, by whatever means he can: physical strength, cunning, slander. . . . And he does have this right, because far-removed society remembers him only when it wants to exploit him; it demands taxes of him, obliges him to do military service, protects him neither from his enemy nor from thieves; it does not help him when the bitter winter kills off his cattle; nor does it defend him against those who bear false witness when he is accused of some crime.[4]

Sumptuous and affecting nature descriptions are another hallmark of Deledda's work. Her canvases of Sardinia's churning sea or of its mountains, forests, *tancas,* and isolated villages capture the ruggedness of the island's terrain and the diversity of its ancient Mediterranean vegetation. Characters' moods are reflected in variegated landscapes, and often nature's chromaticism becomes the very expression of human psychology. The colors of nature, for example, are absorbed by a brooding female character: "the grayish sky appeared suffused in the ashes of a fire whose final flames were smoldering in the west . . . and down behind the crumbling churchtower the pomegranates were stained with red. Noemi felt all this gray and red inside herself."[5] Here Deledda frames in referents of nature both the poverty of the village and the moral misery of her character.

Nature's sounds, sights, and colors are living presences, participating in the desires, pain, and crimes of her personages. The lush perfume of the island's eucalyptus, asphodel, arbutus, mastic trees, myrtle, and wild roses arouses the islanders' senses to love and passion. Men covet rich green farmland almost as though it were a woman. At the same time, a stretch of cleared mountain forest conveys the idea of a cemetery: "the tree stumps looked like tombs and crosses and the rocks like funeral monuments: and families of humble plants . . . still trembling in terror, gathered around the dead giants, like survivors of the destruction. . . . This wild place was populated by men with melancholy faces but who wore gentle expressions despite their arms of axes and knives" (*Il nostro padrone*, 44). Stressing their animistic and religious beliefs, Deledda writes that these men fear "not men, but the occult forces of nature and the arcane means at the disposal of the offended Divinity to chastise men for their sins" (104). On a moonlit night, a whispered exchange between two of them near "rocky steps that looked like Jacob's ladder suspended between the mountain and the sky" is closely paralleled by nature's lugubrious sounds: "the trees, even without stirring, uttered a deep sigh . . . and two owls hooted, one raucous and sad, the other slow and almost sweet, carrying on a kind of melancholy conversation" (96).

Deledda grew up in close contact with nature, which powerfully influenced her childhood imagination. She was born and raised in the central Sardinian town of Nuoro, the third daughter in a family of six children. Schooling was permitted through the fourth grade only for girls, while boys could continue to higher studies. She describes her land as one "where the woman was considered according to oriental standards, and therefore confined to the home with the sole assignment of working and procreating," and herself as "dark-complexioned, diffident, and a dreamer, like a bedouin peeping out of her tent [to catch] a glimpse of golden mirages on the desert horizon."[6] Physically unattractive ("Grazia" only in name, she writes tongue in cheek),[7] she consoled herself with the thought that all great women writers were ugly.

Her somber mother, who never set foot outside the home and who dressed always in the local costume of Nuoro, which has remained unchanged since ancient times,[8] inculcated in her children the only doctrine she knew: all religion and austerity. Grazia learned from her mother that her role as a woman was to be rigorously linked to the home, a good marriage, the bearing of many children to increase the family's "wealth," and the good administration of small domestic businesses, such as selling dairy products, wine, and olive oil to local neighbors.

Typically patriarchal, the Deledda family submitted to masculine authority, which was beyond discussion. The father, in accordance with the community's traditional principles, was responsible for the economic well-being and the moral uprightness of his family. He decided the fate of his children, commanded their respect rather than their love, and enforced the "religion of the home"—that is, the cult of sacred memories and traditional values, and fidelity to the family's laws of honor. The death of the father demanded, in accordance with tradition, a long and severe mourning period: for two or three months the women of the household remained sealed inside the house with the windows closed, after which the wearing of a sad countenance over a four- to five-year period was de rigueur.

As a *signorina per bene* (a young lady of good social standing), Deledda rarely mingled with the people about whom she wrote, except at the oil press, during the grape harvest, or at religious feasts. Yet she felt as one in spirit with the peasants, shepherds, and mountaineers; she appreciated their sense of honor and of hospitality; she listened to their endless dramas of hardship and misery; and she developed a keen feeling for the austerity of their lives. She was also intrigued by their religion, a mixture of devout Roman Catholicism, superstition, witchcraft, and fatalism, as well as by their dreams about ancient mythical events and primitive symbols.

What Deledda learned from the islanders was quite different from the knowledge she gained from books. Her voracious but disorganized readings ranged from the Bible, Edmondo De Amicis, and the early Ada Negri, to mainland and foreign romantic and realistic writers, to the great Russian novelists—Turgenev, Gogol, Gorky, Tolstoy, and, later, Dostoyevsky. Deledda would even aspire to become one day for Sardinia what Tolstoy was for his people: the observer and epic singer of his country. But her early, solemn and rigid Sardinian stories met with nothing more than surprise and curiosity from her mainland readers, who considered Grazia Deledda to be anomalous and insufficiently "regional" to have any impact on the scene.

Her first short story, "Sulla montagna" (On the mountain, 1888),[9] written when she was only seventeen, is a lyrical description of Sardinia's rugged landscapes. Both the writing of the tale and its submission to a Rome magazine were carried out secretly and in fear, because she was defying her society's rules for feminine conduct. Its acceptance for publication convinced Deledda of her vocation as a creative writer. "Sangue sardo" (Sardinian blood, 1888),[10] the story that followed, is a tale written in dialect on the risqué topic of love and revenge. It enraged her fellow townspeople. Fearing they would be identified with the characters and become subjects of ridicule, they anathematized her and spitefully denied her the island's usual guarantees of protection for young women. Writing about purely Sardinian characters,

Deledda thought she was doing honor and giving pleasure to her compatriots, but they only flung insults at her and accused her even of having a ghostwriter. Another young woman writer might have balked; Deledda simply renewed her literary efforts: "I must be strong and calm to accomplish the duty I have set for myself . . . to do good for Sardinia, my, our, beloved Sardinia."[11]

Her own family and relatives grew increasingly fearful that "with her passion for books [she could not] become a good wife."[12] Grazia's two illiterate, acidulous spinster aunts burned the pages of the magazine in which "Sangue sardo" had appeared, uttering the worst prophecies for the budding writer. Even her brother, who had initially encouraged her creative efforts, urged her to discontinue writing love stories. All of these circumstances help to explain why her first novel, *Stella d'Oriente* (Star from the East, 1890), was published under the pseudonym Ilia di Saint-Ismael.

Deledda also felt constrained to give a feminine pseudonym (Countess Elda di Montedoro) to the male editor of the Rome periodical that was publishing her later short stories, with whom she corresponded regularly from 1891 to 1900. Her letters describe her *éducation sentimentale* and the stages of her inner growth and development. At the young age of twenty-one, she writes: "O, Elda! You've said it: I know deeply the human heart, and even though I'm very young, perhaps I have nothing further to learn about it: the characters of my story [*Fior di Sardegna*, Flower of Sardinia, 1892] never existed, but the passions I've described are almost general in all people, and I did nothing more than study what was around me, inside me, in the book of life."[13]

In the same year, she scolds him: "You tell me to get myself a husband! . . . But don't you know this is the ugliest, most prosaic thing you could wish me? I don't believe in love. I believe in friendship, affection, esteem, gratitude . . . everything that is noblest and holiest on earth, but I don't believe in love."[14] Her protest probably stemmed from her observations of Sardinian forced marriages as well as from the quashing of her own early inclinations of the heart. Her family insisted that she target a doctor, lawyer, or engineer; but she was attracted to writers, poets, and journalists, and she rejected the advances of a local schoolteacher, so determined was she to break all ties with the island.

Love between men and women is rarely a pure sentiment for Deledda, and she describes passion-love as a primitive, upsetting force. She preferred to discharge her repressed energies in the physical act of writing.[15] To the early Sicilian *verista* (realistic writer) and critic Luigi Capuana, she wrote in 1897 that "the guide I lacked in my first [literary] attempts I now feel within myself." She confessed that she heard "an intimate inner voice indicating something to me—something high and pure and very luminous."[16]

Synonymous with sin, passion-love conflicts with all that is "high and pure and very luminous." Its temptations and promises of pleasure are deceiving; its evil effects are devastating; and the guilt associated with it must be expiated. Deledda's creations of passionate characters in love are crystallizations of tales she heard in her childhood, which depicted such lovers as possessed of an animal-like strength in their impetuosity and violence. Deledda believed that a frightful destiny is in store for women who become victims of fatal love.

Eighteen ninety-nine was to be the author's decisive year: she was invited to Cagliari by Maria Manca, the editor of the magazine *Donna Sarda*, to which Deledda had earlier contributed. In the Sardinian capital, she met, and married, the government civil servant who would take his bride to Rome, where Deledda spent the rest of her life except for brief visits to the island. She had long dreamed about the civilization of the "Continent" (mainland Italy), convinced that only there could she realize her literary ambitions. Rome also represented her social and aesthetic point of reference: Gabriele D'Annunzio, whose works had introduced Deledda to an enchanting, evil world full of "poisonous flowers and forbidden fruits," where voluptuous women clad in billowing veils contrasted with Sardinia's sickly, sad-faced women, "yellow and black in visage as well as in vestment" (*Colombi e sparvieri*, 200).

Now comfortably distanced from her stifling, suspicious society and her enemy islanders, she began writing her best novels, adjusting her outlook to the new cultural milieu and the mainland Italian reading public. Her one political experience, in 1909, gave her enemies an opportunity to take their revenge. Deledda allowed her name to be entered on the Nuoro slate of candidates of the Radical Party, which championed women's rights. She was roundly defeated by scandalized Sardinians who exercised their vote against women and, especially, against a woman writer. Her courageous public declaration on the subject of divorce, which she defined as a painful but indispensable step in cases of incompatibility, won her the declared enmity as well of Matilde

Serao (see chap. 9), the antifeminist opposed to both divorce and the woman's right to vote. Deledda's actress friend Eleonora Duse, however, who in her only film (1916) played the heroine of the author's novel *Cenere* (1904; *Ashes: A Sardinian Story*, 1908), incarnated the model of the "new woman" as conceived by Grazia Deledda: "courageous, self-assured, free to love, and free to express herself through art."[17]

Never shirking her family duties, Deledda continued to write regularly and prolifically in Rome, disclaiming any merit except to recognize that through her efforts she could assure her children a better education than a civil servant's salary would allow. She was innately shy, and it was almost against her will that she became famous both in Italy and abroad. To the critics' mind, this woman writer who was so little inclined to follow literary fashion had gained the reputation of being a classic. The atemporal dimension of her works likewise lent them a measure of classicism. Formal international recognition came in 1926, when she received the Nobel Prize for literature.

Deledda called her early story *Fior di Sardegna* an "intimate" novel that describes "faithfully our original and bizarre customs."[18] The novel gives a true-to-life picture of a bourgeois landowning family at the end of the nineteenth century. At the same time, it narrates romantically the legends connected with Sardinia's mountains as well as pilgrimages to those high places where trees and rocks take on symbolic value. Simmering hatred and a thirst for blood direct the plot on its course, dividing the family of a young girl from the family of the young man she loves.

Similarly, hatred of God stirs in the souls of characters hardened by a harsh life of deprivation, whose "religion" is revenge, in *Racconti sardi* (Sardinian tales, 1894), a book of short stories that illustrate the islanders' religion fed by pride, hatred, and blood feuds. But the harshness of these tales was offset by a "rosy" novel, *Anime oneste* (Honest souls, 1895), a family romance about two cousins in love.[19] Here Deledda observes and exalts simple, daily life in the countryside to underpin a doctrine of natural religion.

The most important work of her first period is *La via del male* (The path of evil, 1896), which served as the model for all her subsequent works. Deledda had by this time turned to the great Russian novelists for inspiration.[20] She interweaves themes of passion, guilt, remorse, repentance, and need for expiation, and she stresses, as does Dostoyevsky in *Crime and Punishment*, purification and redemption through sorrow and suffering.

The "via del male" is the path that leads to crime. The lowly Pietro Benu is driven by some "dark passion" and "mysterious power" into the arms of the mistress of the house, Maria Noina, but because of class differences, their love affair is destined to end in tragedy. Maria marries a rich young man, but she continues her love affair with Pietro and is constantly tormented by a deep sense of sin. Pietro sharpens his ambitions to reach middle-class status and begins the struggle for "possession" that is in every Sardinian peasant's blood. He feels the "primitive man" stir within him, and a painful need for "blood and tears." Formerly humble and tender in his love for Maria, he undergoes a personality change during a three-month prison sentence he received for having shared in a supper of stolen mutton. In a revolt reminiscent of Raskolnikov's in *Crime and Punishment*, Pietro inveighs against society's evils and feels the need to take justice into his own hands. Later in the story, Maria's husband is found dead. Pietro asks for and receives the widowed Maria's hand in marriage. After the wedding, Maria learns that Pietro was one of her husband's killers, his motivation being his uncontrollable, savage love for Maria. Deledda does not, however, describe the crime melodramatically as one of revenge; rather, she emphasizes the horror and guilt felt by Maria and that character's awareness of a sin to be expiated together with Pietro. A catharsis must follow the catastrophe: instead of handing the criminal over to the forces of justice, Maria, filled with a vague sense of complicity, resigns herself to expiating at Pietro's side "il loro male" [*their* crime].

Luigi Capuana saw in *La via del male* a thematic and stylistic improvement over the earlier *Fior di Sardegna*, which he had considered a not very promising endeavor by the young writer. Capuana wrote that Deledda did well in not going beyond the boundaries of her native Sardinia, and he praised her for not straying in the directions of verism, symbolism, idealism, and cosmopolitanism—all the "isms" that, in his opinion, were contaminating the writings of his male literary contemporaries.[21]

Deledda was now moving away from her earlier concerns about specifically Sardinian problems. She was more interested in plumbing her characters' minds and showing the workings of their souls. During her best period (1900–1915), she began toning down her somewhat laden descriptions of landscape and atmosphere to stress symbol and myth, so that her works took on universal connotations. With the symbolic *Il vecchio della montagna* (The old man of the mountain, 1900), she showed the tragic effects of temptation and sin on the conscience and consciousness of primitive human beings, capturing their more generic human characteristics. Nonetheless, she remained faithful to the roots, traditions, and memories of her island, and when she described tragic, solemn, and archaic Sardinian traits, it was her way of defining and accepting the human condition.[22] Her insistence on the home and hearth, on the humble objects in the hovels of peasants and shepherds, effectively supports her concept of the existential condition and clarifies her attitudes toward evil and affliction.[23]

In *Dopo il divorzio* (1902; *After the Divorce*, 1905; title of Italian edition changed in 1920 to *Naufraghi in porto* [Shipwrecked in the harbor]), the woman protagonist lives out remorse and expiation for her "sins" during the remainder of her already miserable life. She is a victim not only of her own errors but of those inherent in the social structure and the judicial system. The novel is essentially about an innocent man, whose heart and soul are intimately probed by Deledda. First he is unjustly condemned for a crime he did not commit, and then he is rightly sentenced for a crime that must be seen as a self-fulfilling prophecy. The novel is also the story of the devastating effects that a woman suffers because of poverty, injustice, and ancestral guilt buried deep in her conscience—one of Deledda's recurring themes.

Considered by many as her masterpiece, *Elias Portolu* (1903) enacts the struggle of a weak man torn between pleasure and holiness, between temptation and the desire for good. It is the story of an ex-convict in love with his brother's bride, whom he refuses to marry when she becomes a widow, deciding to consecrate himself to the priesthood. Deledda describes the love of the mystically inclined shepherd Elias Portolu for Maddalena, his brother's bride, as intoxicating but desperate, thrilling but paralyzing. He dares not confess his love either to his mother or to his brother, and he sinks into somber feelings of perdition. Love, far from being a positive force, hardens, rather than softens, Elias. He feels a need "to harm someone."[24] Counsel sought from the wise old island shepherd Zio Martinu does not reassure him. Martinu understands that Elias's decision to enter the priesthood is but a senseless abdication in the face of a difficult situation, not a real vocation, so he attempts to dissuade him. Lack of resolution causes a tragic split in Elias Portolu's personality, further cleaved by the conflicting advice he receives from those around him.

The part given to self-awareness is represented in the novel by Zio Martinu, a gigantic being with "yellowing hair and a thick gray beard, [solemn as] a prehistoric man" (211–12), whose hard life has taught him that one's only salvation is facing up to situations, not running from them. The part given to insincerity and artificial solutions is represented by Prete Porcheddu, the priest who relentlessly goads Elias into the seminary with no regard for the shepherd's true vocation. Maddalena represents the pragmatic feminine approach to problems arising from Elias's wavering resolve, but as in most of Deledda's works, the woman is shunted aside so that the man's decisions may prevail. Once again, Deledda stresses human weakness in the face of blind passion, and she offers Elias Portolu as a symbol of the human condition: he is forced to undergo a long calvary before resigning himself to cruel and absurd fortune.

Elias Portolu is the novel in which Deledda perhaps expresses most eloquently the call of the wild and the enchantment of her island's archaic past: "Oh, pale nights of Sardinia's solitude! The loud call of the horned owls, the wild fragrance of thyme, the sharp smell of mastic, the distant murmur of lonely forests blend in a monotonous and melancholy harmony that brings a sense of solemn sadness to the soul, a nostalgia for ancient and pure things" (183). But it is also a novel that gives readers a good flavor of the language spoken by Sardinia's villagers and mountaineers. On the one hand, Deledda replicates their euphemistic speech: "disgrazia" [misfortune] refers to Elias's arrest and imprisonment; "quel luogo" [that place] means "jail"; and "fra cento anni" [in a hundred years] expresses the hope that it will never happen again. On the other hand, she gives readers a sharp taste of the harshness and violence of the language spoken by the ignorant shepherds, faithfully transcribing their savagery in her dialogues. Elias's father says to his son: "If you're feeling sick, either get well or die; I don't want weaklings around me" (225); Maddalena's husband repeatedly tells his wife and his mother-in-law, "I'm the boss, and if there's anyone around here who wants to give orders, I'm ready to crush her the way we do locusts" (242); Elias thinks, "I'll cut him to pieces, and then I'll lick the blood from the knife" (247).

Another tormented relationship, this time between a mother and her illegitimate son, is described in *Cenere*, in which an illegitimate son causes his "superfluous" mother's suicide. *L'edera* (Ivy, 1908) also ranks among Deledda's best works, offering one of the most powerful feminine portraits in all her oeuvre. It tells of a woman servant in a small shepherd village who kills to save her master, whom she loves, from financial ruin, and who later finds in marriage with him nothing but punishment for her sin. In this novel, Deledda plays up her weak male and strong female characters. The ambiguous master, Paulu, with his "gentle eyes slit wide,"[25] is loved by others for his natural charm. Although he is tempted to kill the rich old man who can resolve his situation, it is the woman, Annessa, who commits the crime on the night of a terrifying storm that both encourages her to act and adds to her terror. Paulu's guilt in the murder is comparable to that of Dostoyevsky's Dmitry and Ivan Karamazov, who only *desired* their father's death. But whereas the brothers Karamazov accepted their responsibility in the crime, Paulu does not. Instead, he shifts the entire burden of guilt to Annessa's shoulders. She is stronger, more capable of sacrifice, more faithful, more deeply involved in their love affair. Through her strength and willpower, and because of her driving passion for Paulu, she provides all his needs—but at the cost of spending the remainder of her life exacerbating her own remorse and self-punishment.

Canne al vento (Reeds in the wind, 1913) was Deledda's preferred novel and is undoubtedly among her best works. It is about the decline and fall of the once powerful Pintor family, now lonely and destitute. The title's reeds in the wind symbolize nature's lullaby and prayer for Efix, the family's humble servant, in whom are reflected the devastating effects of prejudices, superstitions, and differences in the social scale. Efix works the tiny plot of remaining land from which the three Pintor sisters—bearing the biblical names Ruth, Esther, and Noemi—eke out a living. Efix resignedly serves the three women, without recompense, depriving himself of basic necessities, and tolerating every humiliation and offense. Why? Because he is atoning for his still undiscovered crime—his unintentional murder of old Don Zame Pintor, the violent and cruel father of the three sisters. Deledda describes the sisters' infernal existence under the patriarchy:

> Don Zame keeps the four girls closed up in the house like slaves until husbands worthy of them come along. And like slaves they had to

work, bake bread, weave, sew, cook . . . and above all never raise their eyes in the presence of men, or allow thoughts of men to enter their minds unless they were destined to become their husbands. . . . Woe to them if he caught them looking out of the windows onto the street, or if they left the house without his permission. He would slap their faces, heap insults on them, and threaten to kill any young men who happened to pass by twice in a row. (*Canne al vento*, 557–58)

Don Zame's haughtiness and jealousy of family honor, compounded by traditional class distinctions, has forced the peasant Efix to keep secret his illicit love for Lia, the fourth sister, who flees to the mainland, marries, and dies after bearing a child. Deledda's example of a girl of noble birth who flees the paternal home is stunning, but the oppressed woman, having liberated herself from a tyrannical father only to die tragically after childbirth, illustrates the author's pessimistic conviction that freedom comes only with death.

Efix is fully analyzed in his psychological simplicity and complexity by Deledda, and his superstitious beliefs are related in fairy-tale style. On a moonlit night, when nature seems to be filled with mysterious presences, Efix kneels to recite "seven prayers to Our Lord and to Our Lady," but strange sounds reach his ears: "the *panas* [women who have died in childbirth] doing their laundry in the river, beating the clothes with the shinbone of a dead man." He thinks he sees "the *ammattadore*, that goblin with seven caps that contain a treasure, jumping here and there under the almond trees, pursued by vampires with tails of steel." Still other strange spirits come to life in Efix's imagination: he sees "those unbaptized babies, white spirits that flew around in the sky changing themselves into little silver clouds behind the moon; and dwarfs and *janas*, little fairies who stay inside their houses in the rocks during the day to weave golden cloth on golden looms [and at night] dance in the shadow of the big *filirèa* bushes." After evoking these tiny creatures, Deledda calls forth "giants [that] appeared among the moonstruck rocks, holding the reins of big green horses that only they knew how to mount." From high places, the giants look into the deep valley below to "see whether down there among the stretches of poisonous euphorbia there was not some dragon in hiding or if the legendary serpent *cananèa*, which has been alive since the time of Christ, was not crawling about in the sands around the swamp." Efix believes that humans must not disturb these creatures, writes Deledda, "so it is time to retire and close one's eyes under the protection of the guardian angels. Efix makes the sign of the cross and rises from his knees" (553–54). In this passage, Deledda vividly conveys the fusing of pagan and Catholic beliefs in the minds of her people, and she demonstrates how susceptible the islanders are to myths associated with nature.

Efix is a fragile creature, under the constant burden of a sense of sin. Like an oppressed biblical personage, he finally goes off with the poor and the blind, begging, penetrating ever more deeply into the religious meaning of life. He is the archetype of the Deleddian wandering hero, whose adventures are a metaphor for the spiritual path. He finally returns to society as a "bringer of life," and then he dies, having attained to an integrated physical and spiritual maturity. He is reminiscent of Dostoyevsky's old, itinerant pilgrim-serf Makar Dolgoruky in *A Raw Youth*, who similarly puts his life into the hands of God, but who enters into union with obscure and mysterious presences in nature and is able to dissipate all tensions arising from a rigid master-serf relationship.

Perhaps the best known of Deledda's novels revolving on the theme of forbidden love between master and servant is *Marianna Sirca* (1915). The rich *padrona* is irrepressibly drawn into a love-hate relationship with a handsome peasant and outlaw in whom a "wild beast" lies dormant. Love as sin and love as remorse are the themes of this work, in which the lovers are brought together and separated like "reeds in the wind." Deledda again emphasizes the moral and social difficulties that plague a forbidden love because of class distinction. But more important are her descriptions of the existential condition of both the lone outlaw in his wilderness and the lonely mistress forever awaiting his return.

L'incendio nell'uliveto (Fire in the olive grove, 1918)—which reveals the author's traditionalism and conservatism—as well as *La madre* (1920; *The Mother*, 1928; also translated as *The Woman and the Priest*, 1922)—the tragedy of a mother who realizes her dream of making her son a priest but then sees him yielding to the temptations of the flesh—mark the beginning of Grazia's Deledda's literary decline. However, her autobiographical *Cosima* (1936, published posthumously in 1937) is a storehouse of invaluable poetic and existential thoughts. The novelized diary, written in the third person singular, is that of a talented woman writer handicapped by her inherent primitive characteristics as well as by the double standards set by her society for the education of young women.

Grazia Deledda had the courage to rebel against the irrationality of the patriarchal system. She rejected her islanders' feelings of religious-existential guilt, which she nonetheless captures so successfully in her novels. She opposed her nineteenth-century insular society, whose traditions and customs denied women the right to write. She lived out a myth of supernatural justice by becoming Italy's first and, so far, only woman recipient of the Nobel Prize for literature. The Swedish Academy recognized in her work "her power as a writer, sustained by a high ideal, who portrays in plastic forms life as it is on her lonely native island, and who treats problems of general human interest with depth and warmth."[26]

TWO
SIBILLA ALERAMO

A Woman at Bay

A poet, a novelist, and an essayist, as well as a prolific letter writer, Rina Pierangeli Faccio (1876–1960) used the pseudonym Sibilla Aleramo. *Sibilla* (sibyl, prophetess) was the "name of mystery" given to her by one of her many lovers as she "whispered her ecstasies" to him during "an ambiguous and magic hour" in the pinetum of Tivoli.[1] Aleramo's intense love life (she has been seen as a female Don Giovanni for her erotic vitality), her sociopolitical insights, and her prophetic voice as a writer combine to make her the premiere literary feminist of the early twentieth century.

Aleramo was born in Alessandria (Piedmont) but was raised both in Milan (where she received elementary schooling to the fifth grade only) and, from 1881, in a small town in Le Marche, the central Italian province bordering on the Adriatic, where her father managed a glass factory. She refers in her diaries to "the extreme sensitivity" of her mother, from whom she inherited an aesthetic sense and a romantic melancholy, but with whom she had no meaningful relationship. For her father she felt "unlimited adoration," favoring his "authoritarian will" over her mother's femininity. A learned atheist, her father inculcated in Rina—

his firstborn—traditionally male ideals of courage, virility, love, and heroism, as well as a "human religion combined with a pantheistic . . . awareness of all things."[2]

Shunning home chores, Aleramo worked as a bookkeeper in her father's factory. On the one hand, she developed a work ethic as well as an awareness of the problems of the working class through readings of Dumas, Hugo, Manzoni, Giusti, Aleardi, De Amicis, and other writers. On the other hand, she cultivated a love for nature, silence, and meditation, which led to her moral isolation and spiritual loneliness.

The unhappy marriage of her parents culminated in her mother's suicide attempt, insanity, and eventual confinement when Aleramo was still an adolescent. Her father progressively neglected, and ultimately abandoned, his family, having taken a woman factory worker as his secret mistress. Outraged by his deceit, Aleramo now looked in horror at the man she had blindly adored, and she perceived life as hideous and incomprehensible.

At seventeen, she was raped with cunning intent by one of her father's employees. That crime was shabbily mended by a marriage that took place in 1893, which was followed by ten years of unhappiness. She was forced to live in undesired intimacy with an unloved husband. Confined to her husband's home, her only social activities were those approved by him; he gave her a son but left her alone with the child and carried on with his own life. She rebelled, but she also blamed women in general for their cowering acceptance. A good mother should not be "a simple creature of sacrifice," she wrote, but "*a woman*, a human being."[3] She had seen her own mother sacrificed. She did not intend to remain the resigned female. Her only outlet during this period was reading. She read such authors as Whitman, Emerson, Nietzsche, Amiel, and Ibsen. One book, Guglielmo Ferrero's *L'Europa giovane* (Young Europe, 1897), aroused her desire to accomplish some broad social mission in life. But though she had grown intellectually, she felt that no humanitarian work could replace love in a woman's heart.

During a brief period in 1900, when her husband was unemployed and "allowed" his wife to work, she directed a review, *L'Italia Femminile*, in Milan, a city that vibrated with cultural and artistic activity. Her return to deadening provincial life in Le Marche when her husband assumed the management of her father's factory marked a turning point in Aleramo's life. Although she succeeded in having some of her socialist- and feminist-slanted articles published, her overriding concerns were the feminine condition and her need for total independence. Denouncing the marriage institution as the enslavement of women, she committed an "unmotherly crime" with calculated determination in 1901: she fled her home. She was, of course, desolate at leaving her son behind, but unlike so many women writers of her day (Neera's retrograde ideas on motherhood especially come to mind), she refused to play the traditional mother role. Rather, she gave priority to individual, personal choice. She also regretted leaving behind the many pages she had written in a state somewhere "between sleepwalker and prophetess" (*Dal mio diario*, 23), which had cost her so much effort and which her husband would certainly destroy.

Over and over again in her writings is heard the leitmotiv "non era per amore di un altro uomo ch'io mi liberavo: ma io amavo un altro uomo" [not out of love for another man did I liberate myself: but I did love another man] (*Il passaggio*, 35). The man Aleramo loved when she left her husband and son was the now forgotten poet Guglielmo Felice Damiani, whom she soon left for the editor of *Nuova Antologia*, Giovanni Cena, also a poet, who fed her ideas of becoming a writer. With Cena she moved to Rome in 1902. There, with his encouragement, she wrote her first and best-known novel, the autobiographical *Una donna* (1906; *A Woman*, 1980), published during the heyday of reformist socialism. It was, however, still a period when feminine consciousness was submerged and inarticulate, and the call for divorce and liberation was subversive.

Una donna was a prophetic novel of conscience, and on it hinges early twentieth-century feminism. Its protagonist served as the principal model for Italian women writing between the two world wars. Such authors as Gianna Manzini (see chap. 3) and Fausta Cialente (b. 1900) considered Aleramo their most authoritative predecessor. Translated into seven languages shortly after its publication, *Una donna* became a landmark in the struggle for equality of the sexes and women's liberation; it was hailed also by such illustrious male writers as Maksim Gorky, Anatole France, Alfredo Panzini, and Stefan Zweig, and by the critics Arturo Graf and Georg Morris Brandes. Aleramo would later describe her work as containing the best of her spirit and the most of her own future.[4]

After moving to Rome with Cena, Aleramo set up a clinic for the poor sponsored by the Unione Femminile, gathered earthquake relief for Sicily in 1908, and organized the distribution of aid to prostitutes. She was associated with Cena for about eight years in the setting up of schools for migrant workers in the malaria-ridden Roman and Pontine plains, even as the couple lived out their inexhaustible need for love.

Leaving Cena in 1910, but continuing to live in Rome, Aleramo took frequent trips to Florence searching for liaisons with notable figures of both sexes. She was fully aware of her own duality and recognized in herself the imprint of both male and female characteristics. She knew that she was both angelic and diabolic, and that her writing was split between reason and instinct. In her novel *Amo dunque sono* (I love therefore I am, 1927), she "prophesies" the type of being that will eventually inhabit the earth: a "liberated hermaphrodite . . . inviolable . . . never entirely possessed by a man."[5] Her liaisons with Lina Poletti, Giovanni Papini, Umberto Boccioni, Salvatore Quasimodo, and others, although referred to as "amorous nomadism,"[6] may in fact also be seen as so many rites of passage in Sibilla Aleramo's life—personal crises followed by artistic and cultural maturation.

Unlike Grazia Deledda, who considered passion-love as sinful, Aleramo saw in physical love a triumph of the senses. She actively went in search of love, refusing all conventions in her determination to set up a model of rebellious lifestyle. Scandalously, she engaged in free love well into middle age, causing her contemporaries to heap reprobation on her name. But her audacity was rewarded; she succeeded in imposing her rebellion on Italian society, even though, as she writes bitterly, "no one has ever sacrificed anything for me . . . and no one has ever killed himself or killed anyone for me" (*Il passaggio*, 193–94).

After what she referred to somewhat archly as "il tempo di Cena, 1902–1910" [the Cena period, 1902–1910] (*Dal mio diario*, 68), Aleramo took another lover (the poet Vincenzo Cardarelli) in 1911, but she duly deserted him the following year, taking refuge in a small village on the island of Corsica. Quite alone, she began writing lyric poetry, which was to become her preferred artistic form.

Despite an already tempestuous and tormented life, Aleramo, nothing daunted, plunged into a passionate, albeit short-lived, liaison, as famous as it was turbulent, with the mentally unstable poet Dino Campana—"the Italian Rimbaud." It began in the summer of 1916 and lasted only until the winter. During their relationship, he beat her frequently and boasted publicly of the bruises he had inflicted on her. He drank heavily after their separation, forcing her to hide from him in fear.[7] Going through a breakdown and in financial difficulty, Aleramo turned to friends for help.[8]

At the end of World War I, she established permanent residence in her Via Margutta attic in Rome, distancing herself from the feminist movement in which she had earlier so actively been involved,[9] preferring to live alone and to cultivate D'Annunzio's elegant, sensual poetic style. After a thirteen-year hiatus, she published her second novel, *Il passaggio* (The passage, 1919), written during sojourns in Corsica and Capri. In her preface to the 1932 edition, she wrote that she had poured "the most intimate essence" of her spirit into this novel (xvi), but though it was well received in France,[10] it did not receive the recognition she thought it deserved in Italy. She expressed the hope, in a 1951 radio broadcast, that posterity would do justice to *Il passaggio* (*Confessioni di scrittori*, 12).

Aleramo was also embittered by the failure in Italy of her only published play, *Endimione* (1922). Parisian spectators at the Théâtre de l'Oeuvre had applauded the dramatic poem in three acts during the winter 1922–23 season, but audiences in Turin and Rome booed it in 1924 and 1925. Aleramo did recognize, however, that although her entire life was mirrored in *Endimione*, the work was a theatrical mistake (*Confessioni di scrittori*, 11).

Three collections of Aleramo's prose writings, however—*Andando e stando* (Going and staying, 1920), *Gioie di occasione* (Occasional joys, 1930), and *Orsa minore* (Ursa Minor, 1938)—earned praise from her friend, the eminent critic Emilio Cecchi, who bracketed her name (inappropriately) with Colette's for these nonfictional pieces (*Confessioni di scrittori*, 12).

Aleramo's declared intention in writing her third novel, the epistolary, autobiographical novel *Amo dunque sono*, was to define, in feminine terms, the very essence of woman. Narcissistically identifying herself with her character, she offers her readers an image of a spiritualized woman writing a long, lyrical confession in a series of unanswered love letters. The virtuous heroine is awaiting the return from his spiritual retreat of her beloved (an ambiguous figure inspired by Giulio Parise, with whom Aleramo was actually painfully involved). Meanwhile, she writes the novel of their love—that is, the novel of preparation for perfect love by the chosen woman awaiting the mysterious lover to whom she has sworn sexual abstinence until his return.

Il frustino (The riding-whip, 1932), again autobiographical, is based on her love affair with the writer Giovanni Boine. Appearing as the personage of Caris di Rosia, a genial and apparently "perfect" woman musician, Aleramo contrasts herself with a jealous woman of the people. The man who is the object of both women's desire rejects Caris di Rosia's superior, transcendent love, ceding to the earthiness of the plebeian.

Aleramo's last great love affair, with the poet Franco Mattacotta, began in 1926, when she was sixty-four and he was in his twenties. The couple went to Greece in 1937 and then to Capri, where by way of sanctioning their "five years of [total] communion" (*Dal mio diario*, 83–84), she filled diaries with the story of their "tender" relationship (83), which ended in forced separation because of the outbreak of World War II. The war, she lamented, prevented her from writing and drove her into a state of "mysterious inertness" (9). She imputes war to human, and especially male, barbarism. Imagining Hitler looking at a rose, she writes in her diary: "A woman . . . in the presence of a rose could never plan a war, or want war. (Times of the matriarchy, my distant desire!)" (36).

Aleramo was eclectically involved as a socialist, a fascist, and a communist, according to Italian political winds. World War II drove her into the arms of communism—at first only ideologically, but from 1946 on as a militant and a parliamentarian of the Italian Communist Party. At the age of seventy-five, she gave readings of her poetry in factories, mines, and at other large gatherings of the "common people," who, to her delight, were sensitive to her verses and understood them thoroughly. This, her last "social mission," renewed her hopes for a more brotherly future generation through "the miracle of poetry" (*Confessioni di scrittori*, 13).

In 1956 the eighty-year-old Aleramo met her last protégé, the budding twenty-year-old poet Elio Fiori, to whom she wrote over one hundred letters.[11] Her stormy life ended in 1960, when she was eighty-three. Her affairs of the heart had resolved themselves disappointingly, but she felt that the "elect," of which she was one, were called on to suffer and to lead humanity forward.

The novel on which Aleramo's fame rests, one that shook the age-old foundations of feminine submission, is the autobiographical *Una donna*. The work traces the *éducation sentimentale* of a prototypical woman through the figures of her father, her mother, and her husband, none of whom is named. Thus the story may be taken emblematically as repre-

a Gianna Manzini,
che alcune di queste pagine
ha già deplorate,

e ad Enrico Falqui,
che probabilmente
non ne approverà nessuna,

la rassegnatissima

Sibilla Aleramo

con gli auguri
per il Natale
1945

Autograph dedication of *Dal mio diario: 1940–44* by Sibilla Aleramo. Courtesy of the Biblioteca Nazionale Centrale di Roma.

sentative of all women marked in childhood by a hard, contemptuous father and a humble, submissive mother and in adulthood by an unloved tyrannical husband. Aleramo re-creates her life story in an effort to associate *a woman* with Everywoman.[12]

The heroine of *Una donna* enacts the drama of her entrapment within the historic feminine condition and of her escape into personal, social, and literary self-fulfillment. She sees both her mother and herself in the slave-chain of women oppressed by institutionalized mother-hood: "Why do we idealize sacrifice in mothers?" she demands to know. "Where does this inhuman idea come from, that mothers should immolate themselves? For centuries, mothers have handed down to their daughters this bondage, which is now a monstrous chain that fetters them" (193). Whereas previously she was a submissive and fatal-istic victim like her mother, she now understands that there is no slavery without a willing slave—her domineering husband could not take his sadistic pleasure in browbeating and humiliating her if she were not somehow compliant. This realization is the point of departure for her liberation. Like Aleramo, the heroine flees her home, leaving her son behind, thus destroying the feminine model and exorcising the mater-nal mystique.[13] Her escape into the night is an irrevocable act of dignity by a woman fully conscious of the gravity of her desertion. She prefers to offer her son a more dignified mother, albeit in absentia,[14] and the novel fittingly ends with an invocatory prayer for her child.

Although Aleramo wrote in a style typical of the late nineteenth cen-tury, *Una donna* retains its vitality and does not seem dated. Describ-ing a woman's choice between family and career, it fits into the more modern genre of "literature of memory." Even though the novel is a dra-matic and bitter denunciation of the female lot, Aleramo transforms her protest into poetic and communicative prose. The work has a personal, musical tempo that beats out the rhythms of her anger, her aspirations, and her revenge: the woman dreams of writing "a book, *the book* . . . that would show the world the modern female soul . . . and for the first time would make the male soul throb with remorse and desire" (121). Through the act of writing, she is convinced, she will give shape and form to her tangled self as well as to the complex "female soul." But words often elude her as she tries painfully to name each element of her "dark inner world"; personified words rise and fall in her conscious-ness; what she does not succeed in expressing in writing "drop[s] forever into the abyss from which it had emerged for an instant" (117). She links reading and writing to active human association, self-awareness, and ca-tharsis: reading and writing allow her " 'I' . . . along with [her] misery" to disappear (106). But to this miserable "I" Aleramo juxtaposes her heroine's "deep and authentic 'I'," which is repressed and masked. As she goes about caring for her child, the realities of mothering are described in accumulations of negative words and phrases—"incapacity," "insufficiency," "moral fatigue," "physical fatigue," "dissatisfaction with [herself]," and so on. The heroine's biology having become her destiny, she is forced to follow society's fixed gender rules even though "the better part of myself reproaches me." She recognizes that "in me, the mother was not integrated with the woman" (69). When she finally flees her home, the emergence of her "deep and authentic 'I' " is conveyed in symbolic terms: she boards a train in the darkness of the night and then begins a new day as "the sun begins to clear away the fog."

Aleramo excels in portraying in lifeless imagery women's entrapment and lethargy. The face of the heroine's mother is "indistinguishable among the pillows and blankets" (22); her own face in the mirror, after her marriage, reveals the "half-asleep expression of an old child" (49), signifying her psychological and intellectual regression. Her outer world and physical surroundings have shrunk; she is reduced to literal and figurative domestication. "My flannel robes," she recalls, "confirmed at every moment that I was indeed *a married woman*, a serious person whose existence was specifically defined" (44). Only after her liberation is she able to redesign this conceptual framework.

Aleramo uses series of infinitives and exclamatives not only to emphasize the heroine's rebellion but also to move her first-person-singular identity away from herself to include Everywoman: "Leave, leave for ever. Never again resort to lies. . . . Suffer all—be separated from [my son], be completely forgotten by him, die but never again feel disgusted by myself . . . !" (195). Another peculiarity of her style is the shifting from present to past through recall ("around the age of eight, I had a sort of strange fear that I did not possess a 'true' mommy" [5]) or through apostrophe, the present narrating "I" shifting to the subject "I" of the past ("Oh, daddy, daddy! Where was our superiority, of which I was so proud until yesterday?" [44]). Sometimes the apostrophe in the present moves to the future: "My son! . . . the last torment of my life will have been the writing of these pages" (195). A double shift in time occurs in her series of rhetorical questions after the rape: "So now I belonged to a man? I accepted this after I don't know how many days of nameless confusion. . . . Suddenly my existence, already shaken by my father's desertion, was . . . being tragically transformed. What was I now? What was I going to become?" (35). Here, Aleramo's technique effectively wraps up her heroine's pondering of society's equation of the sexual act with possession, as well as her future as a female object.

In the novel that Aleramo felt did not receive the recognition it deserved, the poetic *Il passaggio,* she gives her own name, Rina, to the
heroine-narrator, and she once again takes up the plot of *Una donna*,
weaving it into a long prose poem that actually should be read in paral-
lel to the earlier novel. *Il passaggio* does not relate facts; rather, it describes an unending search for spiritual consolation and comfort; and
the author herself admits that it is "not an easy book" (1932 preface, xv).

Written in the midst of personal and world conflicts, during World
War I, Aleramo expresses her own surprise that she was able to orches-
trate her "most intimate essence," persist in her search for "accord with
mystery," and complete "the passage from larva to myth" (1932 preface,
xvi). The larva that she was in her early form, fundamentally unlike her
parents and still awaiting metamorphosis, is destined to develop into a
womanhood of mythical proportion. Aleramo refers to herself in her
diaries as "a living poetic myth" (*Dal mio diario*, 31), theorizing the
genesis of a "myth of the feminine spirit" that parallels "a religion . . .
of poetry" (353–54).

Searching beyond herself and venturing into cosmic realms, Aleramo listens to the voice of her unconscious. But she needs a lover to
"put his ear close to her to hear her grow" (*Il passaggio*, 91). Long before
Luce Irigaray, she defines a couple's love based on sexual difference.
Harmonious communion with her lovers unleashes libidinal force; she
achieves a new faith in life, which she calls her "hymn to life"; love is
"the reason for [her] existence and for the existence of the worlds" (41–
42). Reaching an inner spiritual level through sexuality, she seizes her
visions in an oneiric world of erotic meanderings and makes them her
poetic creations.

Aleramo wrote in her 1932 preface that *Il passaggio* is comparable to
"works of certain mystics, of a Novalis, perhaps" (xvi)—works, that is,
that join mysticism to an allegorical explanation of nature. In analytical
psychological terms, Aleramo, like the Novalis of *Hymns to the Night*
(1800), went in search of psychic equilibrium, plumbing her inner
depths and looking for her mystical center, where the creative élan is experienced. *Il passaggio* is a poetic reenactment of mythical birth, death,
and dismemberment rituals, explaining, perhaps, why an unprepared
Italian reading public did not accord it sufficient recognition.

Psychoanalytically, the novel describes first a *regressus ad uterum*, a
return to the prenatal condition, where the poet contemplates an as yet
unlived experience. She is bathed and cradled, knows preconscious ex-

istence, and experiences, in Novalis's words, "Unending life [that] swells grandly in me."[5] She considers herself—her parents' firstborn, the fruit of their joy—to be the fusion of two flames who were in love with each other because they were different from each other and because everything in the one fascinated the other. The force of their love gives her a sense of well-being in this preexistent state where she experiences a link with her ancestral and primordial past.

Then, retreating into a dream world, she relives her childhood memories. She is able to admire her father differently—to remove him from the cerebral domain—and to find a new understanding of herself: "But if I had never known my father?" she asks. She would be different from what she is had he been different from what he was (18–19). She would not have become a "donna libera" [liberated woman] (67) desirous of self-realization and worthy of mingling with the All (14).

She had been brought into the world as "l'Innominata" [unnamed, nameless]: "A woman, among so many women: a human being in the great flow of humanity" (33). Her own child was born to her before she herself was completely born and named, before she had completely blossomed. She was not complete when he was born, because she had not been a woman during her marriage—not even when she delivered and breast-fed her baby. Until she desired the love of a man, until her spirit needed a man, and until she could transform her lover into poetry, she knew neither her own raison d'être nor that of the world (35–36). The son that was born to her was not a fruit of love, as she had been for her parents. He was not the son of "tutta me" [all of me] (42). She was "all herself" only when awaiting her lover's letters and his visits, only when she felt the poetic ecstasy of their first kisses. Her love for her lover was "her child."

But she would leave her lover, just as she had left her son. She crawled out from under that crumbling conjugal roof because she wanted to combine flesh and intelligence. Legal ties do not exist for her, but the poetry of her son's voice does. It reaches her ears in her sleep, in "the dream of a dream" (31). When she recalls her son's letters expressing his yearning to be with her, she hears "the weeping of the sea" (62), although she walks under the pines of Rome.

In specifically feminine writing, she compares her written words to blood oozing from her breasts, her readers to babes at suck. Holding open her "wounds of love," she finds sweet, intense pain in reliving sex by writing about it (14). Unplaiting her braids, she uses them as stinging words "to lash [her] perpetual impossible dream" (195). Throughout *Il passaggio*, Aleramo adopts feminine variants of the life/poetry cycle, directly transposing "pain," "blood," and "work" in a transmutation process that moves from feeling, to word, to poem.

Love, for Sibilla Aleramo, is more important, more disinterested, more ecstatic, than the perpetuation of the species. For this, she is able to stir the reader with her highly poeticized description of a voluptuous lesbian relationship in an allegorical setting. In evocations paralleling those of Novalis, she experiences "all the realms of the world" as graceful forms infiltrate the arcadian landscape, azure images sparkle and shimmer, and the sun gazes down to observe the embrace of the two women—the blooming of a "perfect flower" (115).

The death of one of her male lovers leads her into the darker, more somber recesses of her poetic consciousness. She feels "amputated" when a love experience ends, but she accepts death as part of a cosmic process leading to the mystery of being. Her own arduous death comes as a dismemberment by raging male forces ("lo spirito maschio" [220]). But death itself takes on poetic beauty: "Cosa di perla anche la morte, compenetrata di luce" [Death, too, is a pearly thing, permeated with light] (223).

Aleramo's "secret laws of rhythm" and "awareness of all things" cry out in her writings. She believed that woman must "create herself" by seeking her own aesthetic laws within herself. She is both the subject and the object of her novels—the absolute heroine who aspires to elevate a man to a superior life. She found herself enmeshed in many painful relationships with "lo spirito maschio" because she was unable to exist for herself alone. Both for her numerous love affairs and for her passionate protest against social conventions that bind a wife to her husband against her will, Aleramo shares notoriety with George Sand, with whom she declared her spiritual affinity.

THREE
GIANNA MANZINI

Parental Imagoes

The place of Gianna Manzini (1896–1974) among Italy's leading women novelists is undisputed. She is the author of twenty-four volumes of novels and short stories written in the refined stylistic tradition of art for art's sake. Using an imaginative shorthand language, Manzini suggests, rather than develops, her aphorisms. Although a few of her works have been translated into various European languages, only one short story has been rendered in English,[1] perhaps only one because her style and syntax defy rhythmic translation into the English language.

As a child, Manzini was happy only when she had a pen in her hand.[2] Though frail and ailing, she was remarkably tough-minded—a trait probably inherited from her father—and she imposed on herself a strict writing regime that apparently lessened her constant physical pain. Writing also relieved the trauma caused by her parents' death. She would find her father and mother again by virtue of the pen—that is, by tracing in words a platonic idea of paternal and maternal entities.

Her chronic respiratory illness, which she imparted to some of her characters, became a tangible expression of her femininity: "A woman is really a woman when she is sick," she wrote in 1929;[3] and in her last novel, *Sulla soglia* (On the threshold, 1973), written a year before her death, she wrote that "illness is richness. . . . Life is never so ardent, so lavish, so coveted as in illness. A thousand perspectives, with a thousand crossings and a thousand probabilities, are opened up by illness."[4] Manzini's relationship to sickness resembles that of Flannery O'Connor, who suffered but accepted incurable lupus erythematosus, declaring herself satisfied as long as she had enough energy to write.

Perhaps Italy's best representative of the experimental approach to "literature of memory," Manzini defines the "true novel" as one that "lies at the meeting point between the plot and episodes of [the novelist's] own life."[5] Accordingly, she kept a diary of her life, which she used imaginatively for her plots, confirming a widespread idea that "autobiographies, as much as novels, depend on narration, provide explanations, and insist on the comprehensibility of life."[6] A novel is a "point of perspective with relation to the world," declares Manzini's alter ego, the novelist-protagonist of *Un'altra cosa* (Another thing, 1961): "It is an explanation" (166).

One of Manzini's general concerns was women's rights. She sought an explanation for the feminine tendency toward self-abasement. One of her female characters is "satisfied and liberated by her own image of humiliation,"[7] while another is convinced that inherent in womanhood is "ancestral slavery."[8] Manzini herself conformed to middle-class convention, and her mother was an exemplar of the sensitive, harrowed woman ensnared by sociohistorical restrictions: caught up in a cruel social conflict, she vacillated between love and admiration for her anarchic, freedom-loving husband on the one hand and, on the other, deference to her bourgeois family's demands for conformity and economic security. As Manzini's writing evolved, however, she wrote less about the angelic feminine self-humiliation that characterized the protagonist of *Tempo innamorato* (Time in love, 1928) and focused more on women's cultural and educational choices, which were stymied by the *"presumed privilege of female slavery."*[9]

Manzini's parents were opposites. Leonilda Mazzoncini was weak and self-renouncing; Giuseppe Manzini was a forceful, anarchical atheist who, in his daughter's words, "died, all alone, for [the cause of] antifascism,"[10] having suffered a heart attack after being ambushed by a group of fascists.

Born in Pistoia, Manzini lived her first literary period in Florence, where Giuseppe Prezzolini's *La Voce* (1908–16) held sway. This literary journal was famed for its contributors' incorporeal representations of reality in lyrical prose "fragments." Though influenced by Joyce, Proust, and Dostoyevsky, Manzini sought to achieve what she discerned in Virginia Woolf's writings: a "sense of superior geometry and architecture" in which to conglobate "the precious experience of the fragment."[11] Like Lily, the painter in Virginia Woolf's *To the Lighthouse*, Manzini "felt . . . how life, from being made up of little separate incidents which one lived one by one, became curled and whole like a wave which bore one up with it and threw one down with it, there, with a dash on the beach."[12] In Florence, Manzini's name was soon established among the elitist, avant-garde group known as Solaria, which helped to mold her in the *prosa d'arte* (artistic prose) tradition; her early stories appeared in the journal *Solaria* and subsequently in its successor, *Letteratura*. The language of her first novel, *Tempo innamorato*, was a poetics of objects by which she sought to penetrate reality and reach the center of truth of her characters.

Two collections of short stories, *Incontro col falco* (Encounter with the hawk, 1929) and *Boscovivo* (Animated woodland, 1932), together with her later collections, *Animali sacri e profani* (Sacred and profane animals, 1953) and *Arca di Noè* (Noah's ark, 1960), show Manzini's skill as an observer and imaginative painter of animals, which are present in all her works. Her explorations of the mystery, poetry, and innocence of animals may perhaps be linked with her definition of "reality" as "continuity between life and death . . . mystery." She observed, "reality is children [in whom] there is something mysterious and not cataloged."[13] Symbols of the movements of the soul, animals are seen by Manzini as sacred and indispensable to the life of human beings.

Settling in Rome in 1933, Manzini continued to write about life and death, opposing the vitality and lovingness of her characters, who are symbolic of life, to the impossibility of realizing their loves, which end in death or solitude.[14] Although her works were received with interest and respect, no literary prizes came her way until 1945, the year in which she became editor of the international literary journal *Prosa*.

Lettera all'editore (Letter to the publisher, 1945; awarded the Costume Prize) reveals her interest in the structural aspects of fiction. The novel is both literary fiction and narrative fiction, because it constructs its own plot even as the author-narrator explores the function of the novel. It is Manzini's "double adventure, personal and intellectual" (13), as she searches, like Pirandello, for a freer exchange between writer and characters. Beginning her work-in-progress with a letter to her publisher, she expounds on the difficulty of distancing herself from her narration and on her need to bring historical time into a "dazzling, sharp, totally present time" (5). While telling the publisher her own story of how she left Tuscany for Rome (using the historical past tense), she interrupts the narration to insert some event in the life of one of her characters, implicating herself in the episode: "I was intending to investigate what was going on inside him, in his tumultuous world, at a moment that is so exciting for him" (123). Manzini uses both imperfect and present verb tenses, showing that she is actively grappling with the problems of the novel's composition. At the same time, she carries on her epistolary dialogue with the publisher: "too much haste, you see, has made for sacrifice of the protagonists" (121). Early in the novel, Manzini says her "characters are interpretable according to those passions that give rise to their unlimited hankering to be wholly revealed, [and that give] meaning to their spiritual substance" (41); but toward the end of the work (and as she grows older and the events in her own life move forward), she says, "my idea of the novel has changed. . . . I can no longer recognize myself in what I used to be" (259). The narration will now be concluded "in rapid foreshortenings" and a "restless movement" that completely changes its tempo (261). Viewed as an examination of conscience, *Lettera all'editore* documents both Manzini's and all of Italy's general literary crisis during the years of fascism and the war. Her novel represents the climax of her own efforts to ascertain "the narratability of the world."[5]

Two works of unequal importance followed *Lettera all'editore*: the collection of short stories *Ho visto il tuo cuore* (I saw your heart) and the short novel *Il valtzer del diavolo* (The devil's waltz), both of which appeared in 1947. The latter, considered a key Manzinian text, is an inner diary of Dostoyevskian stamp, in which the protagonist-narrator, Silvia, goes through a process of self-identification and discovery by carrying her introspection to the extreme. In a long confession, Silvia analyzes her feelings of compassion not only for a series of lovers but also for a black beetle that unexpectedly finds its way into her bedroom and then onto the slippery slopes of her soul. Manzini uses a specifically feminine style in Silvia's monologues: she expresses herself through objects, with feminine impulsiveness, intuition, and reaction. The black beetle is crawling on her body during her sleep: "I quickly turned on the lamp, I saw [an insect] on my naked arm, crawling toward my elbow. I screamed" (18). At its next appearance, she maintains: "I swear it was looking at me. I felt it looking at me. The invisible look of a repulsive black beetle on me. . . . And it was asking pity of me. . . . Repugnant, filthy . . . it aroused my pity. . . . Something stirred within me. . . . And that something was the presumed better part of me" (24). Silvia gradually realizes that false pity had moved her to give comfort to others. Compassion, she discovers, is nothing but a driving, devilish force in a woman's life: "save me from my pity," she cries out, "save me from this horrendous pity" (26).

From the late 1940s onward, Manzini studied in her works the effects on character of a lonely childhood, chronic disease, early death, existential anguish, and the artistic mission. Together her novels may be seen as a single, autobiographical work in which the narrating "I" functions not only as a filter and mediator between the author and the other characters but as a critical discussant with the reader as well.[16]

The relationship between the soul and the body is treated in the collection of short stories *Cara prigione* (Dear prison, 1958), while the secrets of the soul buried in the "dear prison" of a chronically ill male (Manzini herself)[17] are the subject of her Viareggio Prize-winning novel, *La Sparviera* (The Sparrow Hawk, 1956). Hovering over Giovanni Sermoni like a bird of prey is a sparrow hawk—metonymy for the persistent, convulsive chest cough that has plagued him since his early childhood. Giovanni's illness heightens his sensitivity and intensifies his spirituality; but the carnivorous bird, representing an irrational force, incessantly gnaws at him and tyrannically conditions his existence. Finally the sparrow hawk leads Giovanni "on a leash" to an early death (190). The symbolism of the clutching, clawing bird is enriched by Manzini's equating it with Giovanni's ungraspable love for a creative young girl, Stella, who dies tragically, even before the hero himself, making his own death more desirable. Stella and Giovanni represent for Manzini the most complete embodiment of the underlying oneness of love and death, Eros and Thanatos. Giovanni's last act of gripping the sparrow hawk, pressing it against his chest, and possessing it as he dies is described by Manzini in specifically masculine language. She treats it as the enactment of a physical and spiritual passion. The senses of hearing, smell, and touch are aroused, together with expectation of repose after exertion and strain: "the panting sparrow hawk . . . [emitted] an odor of soggy leaves, of underbrush after the rain, of overturned soil." Giovanni sees "a gelid world, violently offered and dominated by the sparrow hawk [that promises him] an immense calm . . . provided they reach it together, united as one body" (191–92). Giovanni finally ejaculates his soul from his cough-racked body.

Active memory of the dead is one of Manzini's narrative constants. Her last two works are devoted in subject and sentiment to her dead parents, with whom she enters into mystical communion as she paints their story-portraits and forces the reader to penetrate the secret regions of their souls. In both the novel-memoir *Ritratto in piedi* (Standing portrait, 1971; awarded the Campiello Prize) and the biographical novella *Sulla soglia*, dedicated respectively to her father and mother, Manzini engages in parahuman dialogues that are far more than personal recollections. They are forms of urgent reminiscence that allow her to relive almost mythical years and events and that exorcise her parents' death. In sequences of appearing and disappearing images, she fuses life and death, as well as the real and the surreal, in her paternal and maternal figures, and then she grafts their identities onto herself.

The different personalities of Manzini's parents clashed within her psyche. "I belong to too many things, to too many contrasting sentiments," she writes in *Ritratto in piedi*. "I'm in shreds. And yet I'm a crossbreed of [many different kinds of] strength. . . . It's amazing to see how, at a certain level of suffering, so many feelings can blend."[18] Her tearful mother wooed, enticed, and blackmailed her daughter; her strong-willed father held her in thrall by his nobility and his sorrow. She was the terrain for their clashes, their "perpetual meeting place" (57), the dividing membrane through which they moved timidly, cautiously, courteously, and reservedly. She was "consumed with pity and love for her [mother]," but she knew that her father was "in the right" (166). It may be said that Manzini rejected her own cultural self-image by returning to unconscious bonds with both her mother and her father.

"In my own way, I am a casual explorer," she writes, "who happens to find herself beyond the orbit, envisioning a different plenitude, now dark, now dazzling" (*Ritratto in piedi*, 91). Neither distance nor recollection exists in what she refers to sometimes as the "implacable all-present" and other times as "the immobile present." Her time parameter is the absolute present tense, in which past and future crystallize in what seems to be spur-of-the-moment narration.[19] She explains, for example, her difficulty in overcoming her emotions each time she evokes her father in her mind. She embodies these emotions in an animal—a horse that refuses to cross Florence's Ponte Santa Trinità, because some specter prevents it from advancing. The horse, aware of something lying beyond limited human perception, is a specular image of the author, who finds herself at an impasse in her writing. To advance, she must first overcome the remorse and shame that have risen in her because she neglected her father and delayed paying him homage. Once the placatory ritual has been performed, Manzini is ready to meditate and recall. She evokes her father from "frantumate lontananze" [shattered distances] (80)—that is, from the frayed dimension of memory where she digs to reach her father's "center of truth."

Endowing her word-portrait with a dreamlike quality, she relates how her father divested himself of his possessions, committed himself totally to anarchism, and left the family for a life of rebellion and privation as an antifascist conspirator. First he was forced into compulsory residence in Porto Ercole, and he then went into voluntary exile in a mountain village near Pistoia. His wife eventually agreed to legal separation from the man she loved, realizing she could no longer be part of Giuseppe Manzini's radical lifestyle. But with his daughter the anarchist entered into an "extraordinary alliance" (27), more binding than if they had shared a common roof. Yet the father and the daughter mutually hurt each other, he by remaining outside the family, she by neglecting and sometimes misunderstanding him in his lonely exile. The father-daughter crisis is surmounted in the penultimate chapter of the novel-memoir, as Manzini pays him supreme tribute with the standing portrait that expresses her debt of gratitude. Then, in the final chapter, which has been seen as "one of the most authentic epilogues of which our [Italian] contemporary narrative can boast," and which "contains some of Gianna Manzini's most beautiful pages,"[20] the author describes her father's final agony as a flagellation, identifying him with Christ as archetype.[21]

Manzini's depiction of her mother is more ambiguous. Weak and defenseless, Leonilda Mazzoncini relies on her daughter, who attempts to lessen her mother's misery in the perennial quarrels with the relatives with whom she is forced to live. But the reader shares moments when Gianna Manzini hates the thin-skinned woman who was incapable of defending her husband against her family's snide attacks. Only late in life did Manzini attempt to understand her own responsibility vis-à-vis her mother, to whom she dedicated the profound work *Sulla soglia*, written one year before the author died and symbolically prefiguring Manzini's own death. In *Sulla soglia*, her mother becomes the mediator for acceding to the hereafter. By evoking her mother both abstractly and concretely, Manzini attaches herself once again to her family and prepares to join them in the beyond.

Lending its title to the collection of four of Manzini's most emblematic and abstract tales describing death in all its aggressiveness, *Sulla soglia* touches on the mystery of eternity. The imaginary, fragmented dialogue with the author's living/dead mother is full of recollections and meditations on death, memory, and art. "What else is art to me," the daughter asks, "if not an instrument for finding life behind life" (13).

Her dialogue with her mother takes place on the "threshold" between life and death, as the author-narrator searches for signals among intersecting railroad tracks that represent the paths of life taken by those who have journeyed before her. She is about to board the strange departing train that travels "only in one direction" (79), when her attention is caught by a sheet of paper caught up by the wind, inviting a reading but indecipherable because the letters on it are only fragments of a decomposed alphabet, symbolic of the world of silence. The sheet of paper disappears behind the narrator, while a swarm of white butterflies fills the air before her eyes, submerging her in a milky mist that she says, "took away my sight but without preventing me from advancing" (72)—the first of a series of white and gray misty tonalities that permeate the work and evoke a "flight to limbo, which is the obliteration of oneself" (88). Traditional narrative underpinnings—space, objective chronology, the figure of the author, the narrative point of view, and the characters' linear biography—are decomposed and diffused, multiple and complex.[22]

Her dead mother, bathed in an iridescent light, invites the narrator into the "narrow prison" (93)—the bewitched train compartment where the latter feels extraneous because words and recollections, so necessary in life, here seem to serve no purpose. "In words," she explains, "I had always found a basis for existence" (79). But her words disturb the other passengers, the dead—a musician, an actor, a horse breeder, and a little girl wearing white boots, all without luggage. Manzini describes the drooping eyelids of the passengers with unusual similes: "heavy and undulant like shutters" (79) or "thick as melon rinds" (130).

The narrator recalls her mother's relationship with her father, the man who described the whiteness of his wife's skin as "an alabaster lamp with a light inside" (90)—an image that is almost a refrain, reappearing in the passage in which her mother "resuscitates" an injured sparrow by unbuttoning her blouse and nestling the bird between her white breasts. A long series of images in white and gray, depicting blouse, breasts, and bird, offers one of the best examples of poetic style in the tradition of art for art's sake (95–97).

Dialoguing with her mother, the daughter hopes to reconstruct a maternal imago in which she will find her own personality reflected, but her words are constantly challenged by the other passengers' ironic interjections or moralizing observations. She then extends her dialogue to her fellow travelers, focusing her conversation on her art and on the possibilities for creative work to survive beyond the limit of time. She tries to link those who are "already on the threshold of peace" (125) with life, and thus to achieve a synthesis of word and silence.[23] She insists she must "go back" (79) to find those letters of the alphabet whose rearrangement is a symbol of her search for a linguistic mode capable of expressing a final truth for herself, about to die, and for her already dead mother.[24]

After a long series of "resurrections" through recollections, and innumerable "assassinations"—"Oh, one doesn't die only once" (134)—the narrator finally awakens from her necrological dream. The ray of sunlight shining into her room represents life, mobility, and creativity, as opposed to the immobility of death and the absence of art. Somewhat like Nietzsche's concept of eternal recurrence, Manzini's belief is that through her art—the word—the impress of eternity may be stamped on our lives. "An effect of opposition is sufficient to make words shine," she writes, "like a jewel in a ray of sunlight, and to extract from them a sort of productive risk" (90)—the productive risk being the studied combination of style and content required to obtain the effects of Manzini's uncommon contrapuntal art.

Gianna Manzini always kept her imagination active and her language creative. Her works are filled with surprising analogies. In her search for the internal rhythms of language and for linguistic shades that resemble "visual fragmentation" and "descriptive impressionism," she refuses categorically the even, uniform textures of "fully-sewn garments" (*Sulla soglia*, 129). She seeks to depict not the thing or the person but the effect, to achieve a Mallarmean "pure notion"—that is, the uncontaminated meaning of the signified. She is an exception to Julia Kristeva's claim that women writers stylistically fail to carry out the systematic dissection of language and lack a concern for musical forms in composition.[25] She is a wholly original writer, even though her mature work is readily comparable with that of Jean Giraudoux and with that of Virginia Woolf, from whom she learned a "lesson in endurance" and a way to lift the veils of "fermenting shadows."[26]

FOUR

LALLA ROMANO

A Narrator of Withdrawal

The doyenne of Italy's women authors—novelist, poet, short-story writer, translator,[1] art critic, and painter Lalla Romano—was born in Demonte (Cuneo) in the Piedmont region in 1906. She studied literature and art in Turin, where she struck up friendships with anti-fascist intellectuals, such as Leone and Natalia Ginzburg (see chap. 6), Carlo Levi, and Cesare Pavese. Although in 1989 Romano declared she was "completely alien to . . . political, social, and economic questions," she does retain a firm conviction that "fascist resurgence must be countered."[2]

Unclassifiable as a writer, Romano has produced autobiographical and fictional works that lie somewhere between "literature of memory," post–World War II neorealism, and intimism (poetic expression of one's innermost feelings) with a domestic emphasis. She distances herself from all trends and sets herself apart from literary modes, sustaining that she writes "what she likes, how she likes."[3] She repeatedly crosses swords with her critics, attempting to "save" her works and defend her choices of titles, which are often accused of missing their mark. As for her characters, they are, in Eugenio Montale's words, "imprisoned souls [who] cannot stand the sun, the cold sun of critical analysis."[4]

Romano made her literary debut in 1941 with a volume of poetry entitled *Fiore* (Flower), and she subsequently published two more collections of verses, *L'autunno* (Autumn, 1955) and *Giovane è il tempo* (Time is young, 1974). Her poetry revolves around the themes of love, beauty, sorrow, death, and the flow of time, which she transmutes into sounds, colors, and metaphors, influenced as she was by Greek and Latin lyric poets.

In 1947 she moved permanently to Milan, where, despite her success as a painter, she gave up art to write full-time. Although she had at first shunned the novel as a literary form, she adopted the genre after translating Flaubert's *Trois contes*. That work led to her discovery that prose and poetry are equally rigorous and demand of the author the same miraculous economy of style.

Romano gave up a twenty-five-year-long teaching career in 1959, to devote herself to reading and introspective writing. She concentrated particularly on the works of Dante and the French thinker Joseph Joubert, the posthumous works of Nietzsche, and Ludwig Wittgenstein's "thought." The Austrian philosopher's aphoristic prose, as well as his teaching that the world consists of "things" (simples) that are configured to "atomic facts," may have influenced Romano's oeuvre. She describes "little things" in her "search for mystery in the obvious,"[5] linking herself to a setting or a personage through her own intimate feelings.

Cultured but, by her own admission, not an intellectual,[6] Romano tries—but fails—to escape the threat posed by introspection: seeing only the "I" and forgetting the external world. She defends the "excessively autobiographic nature of [her] works,"[7] proclaiming her "faithfulness to life." She would like her name to appear in literature surveys as "an author who believed in authenticity."[8] She sees herself as a "modern" writer, judging Elsa Morante to be a "great writer of the nineteenth century" whose ever interruptive style wearies her.[9] She defines her own work as a progression from poetry to prose, implying either that she moves forward from the stylistic rigor of poetry into formal prose polish or that her poetic experience has left its imprint in her novels. In either case, her talent—as she herself recognizes—is not specifically narrative;[10] nor do her characters (the limited circle of those whom she loves and admires) extend themselves beyond household situations. These "personages" are seen not biographically but through descriptions of their traits: her parents in *La penombra che abbiamo at-*

traversato (The twilight we have lived through, 1964); her son in *Le parole tra noi leggere* (The words between us weightless, 1969); her grandson in *L'ospite* (The guest, 1973) and its sequel, *Inseparabile* (Inseparable, 1981); and her husband in *Nei mari estremi* (Far-off seas, 1987).

Romano is best known for her Strega Prize-winning autobiographical novel, *Le parole tra noi leggere*, which describes the complex relationship between a mother and her growing son. She is the first to do so after Annie Vivanti, who wrote at the end of the last century, and the Sibilla Aleramo of *Una donna*. Writing with light irony and in a well-tempered style, Romano reviews the hard process of raising her only child, Piero, born in 1933. Her tender affection for him is moderated by rationality and humor, yet behind all that there lies an abyss of remorse, suffering, and regret. Though some of her pages are hilarious, most are desolate and heartbreaking. This ambivalence—indulgence combined with resentment, tenderness with aversion, enthusiasm with doubt—lends drama to the mother's honest confession. Her relationship with her child, to use Natalia Ginzburg's words, is a "dark and visceral love . . . which has nothing to do with reason and judgment . . . [and which is] buried in the depths of the spirit."[11]

The mother and son in *Le parole tra noi leggere* both attract and repulse each other. Their strong wills clash continuously. They struggle to dominate each other—and therein lies the drama of their love. "The mother's disappointment and the son's autonomy," writes one critic, "posit a no-win or no-surrender situation."[12] A built-in power imbalance between them precludes love and complete faith as long as the mother seeks to prolong her domination over the son. As a child, the boy is powerless; as a young adult, he is in a position of inferiority vis-à-vis his mother, to whom he still owes obedience and respect. He behaves toward her with "coolness, annoyance, and even distracted courtesy."[13] He fights to dissolve the symbiotic union with her, but until his humorously described anticonformist wedding celebration at the age of twenty-nine, he remains subject to parental control.

Watching her son change from a happy, carefree, and imaginative child into a somber, preoccupied adolescent, the mother feels she has failed. She details her attempts to communicate with him: "I know that asking questions is the mistaken approach," Romano writes, "but I keep asking. He is seated in front of me, engrossed in a book. . . . I try to begin a conversation. . . . Without raising his head he responds: 'I don't know' " (20). Blinded by her love and gripped by devilish compassion, the mother clings to any pretext by which she can convince herself that Piero is merely "different" and "unique." She pardons and even justifies his quirks, encourages his bizarreness. His laziness, for her, is rejection of conformity; his disorderliness and lack of personal cleanliness are affirmations of independence and geniality; his bad manners and unsociableness are forms of extreme honesty and superiority. How does the son react to her doting? He withdraws. In the end, he flings accusations against her, spewing forth all his faults and failures and blaming them on her "irresponsibility." Thus charged, the mother confesses her defeat, yet she continues analyzing her blind love that elicits such ferocity.

A stylistic innovation in *Le parole tra noi leggere* is the extensive use of "documents"—letters, her son's poems and school compositions, descriptions of his arts and crafts, his dreams, his rare dialogues with her—which not only reveal the son's personality but also detach events from the narrator's emotions. Some have seen the "documents" as useful narrating tools that provide logical and chronological links to the mother's comments;[14] others, however, consider that they weigh the tale down and limit it to a family chronicle.[15] Documented material may be succinct and crisp, as in the son's past remark "I do not like God, He reminds me of Mussolini," evaluated in the present by his mother: "Even now logic rules his agnosticism and dictates his quick, sharp statements" (20–21). A longer dialogue "document" shows how Romano uses the technique not only to reveal her son's and her own traits but also to dispense with the necessities of word changes for indirect discourse and to slip easily from the past tense to the narrative "now":

> He is saying now that he has read somewhere about the characteristics of the asocial type and they are (correction: they were) his: anorexia, pyromania. . . . —Pyromania?—he reminds me of that time when he started a fire in the kitchen. . . . My forgetfulness is due . . . to my fear that he has a criminal streak in him. I knew his passion for fire, strolling around the city he always hoped to see a fire. . . . I know that the (aesthetic) passion for fire is not a symptom of pyromania: pyromania is caused by solitude. (88–89)

With this "document," the reader not only gains a broader understanding of the asocial son and the fearful, forgetful mother but also is drawn into the author's special way of mixing reconstructions of the past with her probings in the present.

Romano's stated intention in writing *Le parole tra noi leggere* was "to reconstruct and to be able to read [her son] (as in 'to read a book') as a hermetic and emblematic character" (vi). Her apparent desire was to make him a symbol of freedom, of rebellion against society's conditioning, and of the struggle to allow free play to "fancy." Stylistically, however, it is written by a mother more than by a writer. While some have seen the work as an illuminated experience of maternal love endowed with a metaphoric, universal value,[16] others have judged it more negatively, deploring its lack of compactness and expressivity.

Worthy of note in Lalla Romano's literary production, despite its bad reception at the time of publication, is the book that she has declared contains the essence of her literary tastes: *Le metamorfosi* (Metamorphoses, 1951).[17] The work, a collection of short prose passages, reflects the author's interest in ethnology, psychoanalysis, and the use of dream in classical and modern literature and in the visual arts. Each chapter of Romano's book is a dream narrated by a different "I"—herself, members of her family, her friends—faithfully transcribed in a free flow of imagery. Each dream is sufficient unto itself as a story, but Romano groups them thematically into "The Voyage," "The Devil," "Nothingness," "Man and Woman," "The Mother," "Youth," and so on. The overriding theme is the metamorphosis to which humans, animals, and objects are subject in a universe of sickness, decadence, and death. Romano considered the work a "book of poetry." Had it been presented as such at the time, she maintains, it might have gained the public's approval. But as it was, the book baffled its readers, who thought they were reading prose but were faced instead with short, lapidary narrations that are in essence "poems not in verse."[18] Romano also feels that the book scandalized the public because it appeared during the era of Resistance narrative. The judgment on *Le metamorfosi* by Salvatore Quasimodo, winner of the Nobel Prize for literature in 1959, is indicative of the climate of the time: "We are fighting against this literature of the absurd."[19]

Similarly, Romano's first novel, *Maria* (1953), did not meet with success. Critics saw in it a personalized, neorealistic tale about a peasant servant in the household of a Piedmontese *padrona*. Romano, the narrating "I," relates the minutiae of daily domestic life in both the peasant's and the *padrona*'s family. She places the two women on equal footing by describing the "meeting," "communication," and "osmosis" between their two different worlds. She stresses Maria's discretion and resignation, but she also shows how feminine solidarity grows between servant and mistress through feelings and intuition. When the servant leaves the bourgeois household to return permanently to her family in the country, Romano's generally light, discursive, and colloquial style changes: accumulations of such words as "darkness," "confusion," "frenetic," "shadow," "resignation," "silence," and so on, convey the saddening effects of Maria's departure. Although the work lies halfway between family chronicle and diary, it is also an attempt by Romano to capture, like her ideal model, Flaubert, the essence of *un coeur simple* (a simple heart). Guided by respect for the servant's world, where "only the essential counts, just as in the language of poetry," she bathes Maria in a "special atmosphere, almost an invisible order in the disorder of the world."[20] In her preface to the edition of the work that appeared twenty years after its initial publication, the author wrote: "I had found in Maria a style of life I admired. . . . My admiration was not so much moral as . . . aesthetic and literary, which means that for me Maria was already a personage even before it entered my mind to create her with words."[21] Eugenio Montale explained in his review of the book that its meaning is "understood when the reader becomes aware that Maria is not the central person in the work, whose value lies in the almost mystical relationship [that links] a 'master and servant.' "[22]

In the novel *Tetto Murato* (1957; the title is the name of a locality in Piedmont), four persons—two progressive, middle-class couples—coalesce against a backdrop of World War II and the Resistance. The novel illustrates Cesare Pavese's phrase that "war is [a kind of] peace,"[23] meaning that in wartime daily routine and norms are suspended, new models are established, and each person gives the best or the worst of himself or herself. In *Tetto Murato*, the new norm is set by Ada, the wife of an intellectual whose role in the partisan struggle has left him ill and disabled. Ada and her husband form a deep friendship with the second couple under abnormal circumstances: all four are evacuees in a hostile environment; all four at times share a single bed. The two couples play out a complex game of reciprocal affinities and attractions, and here Romano displays her gift for introspection and analysis. Calamity is avoided only because Ada channels the tension and drama into what has been called a "mystical happiness in friendship."[24] In *Tetto Murato*, Romano achieves a good balance between invention and her memories of Piedmont. Her descriptions of Italy's northern landscapes under blankets of snow are noteworthy because they convey not only the silence and death of a wartime situation but also a sense of waiting and expectation on the part of both her characters and nature. More universal in its connotations than her other books, she judges it the one best suited to film, but it would require a director like Ingmar Bergman to avoid the scabrousness inherent in the story.[25]

L'uomo che parlava solo (The man who talked to himself, 1961) is a tale written as the monologue confession of a male narrating "I," not unlike Dostoyevsky's *A Gentle Creature*. Romano invents the character of a mature married man with a poetic soul—an "involuntary Don Giovanni"[26]—who examines his conscience and comes to the conclusion that something is causing him to lose two diametrically opposed women: his conventional wife and his anticonformist mistress. Summing himself up, he concludes that he is "too happy [a man] for a wife, too melancholy for a young girl."[27] Through the circumscribed experience of his "double existentialist defeat,"[28] Romano tackles the problem of the relationship between existing and being, but excessive psychologizing renders the pages of the work heavy. It is clear that tales of pure invention are not Romano's forte.[29]

In writing *L'uomo che parlava solo*, Romano struggled with the possibility of using the third person but discovered that it was "impossible" and "repugnant" to her. She feels at ease only when she uses the first person.[30] From 1964, her works would be exclusively autobiographical—the genre more suited to her literary temperament. "I think that relating one's own life 'like a novel,'" she stated in 1979, "is possible for the person who has lived his/her life like a novel, not life as it is lived, but the image, the feeling of it that is recorded—at the moment itself, and then in time—as the consciousness of it grows."[31]

Parts of her own life, related "like a novel" in their intimate and private dimension, are contained in the autobiographical work *La penombra che abbiamo attraversato* (The twilight we have lived through). Of Proustian derivation (the title is a fragment of a sentence from *Le temps retrouvé* [*Past Recaptured*]), the work is a portrait of Lalla Romano as she searches for the essence of her family and of a period of her life—her magic childhood of the early twentieth century. But the "penombra," as Anna Banti pointed out, "is not twilight at all but rather the diffuse, dull, lifeless, cheerless light of dreams."[32]

Romano's native town, Ponte Stura, and her parents live again in the non-time of the narrator's mind; the present loses meaning for her because the past is forever alive in her emotional consciousness.[33] She moves in measured rhythms through shadows and ghosts, describing them in blocks of memory and sensation. In Ponte Stura, Piazza Nuova, the town's square, emerges "still pretty much the same, empty. . . . Now it's named after a partisan; but history, 'what happened after,' doesn't exist for me at Ponte. Ponte is immobile for me. . . . Was it immobile even then? Perhaps for this reason, because things don't remain immobile without losing life, Ponte Stura continues to die slowly. But I take heart, I think of that immutability that is its 'true' existence: mine."[34] Romano reveals that her relationship with history is both existential and poetic. "What happened after" cannot change her remembrances of the square. Its existence is in her memories. Her personal and poetic vision of places in Ponte Stura give those places permanence, despite the changes wrought by history.

Anna Banti judged *La penombra che abbiamo attraversato* to be an "unusual work" of poetic import, "nobly balanced between objectivity and a lyrical inner echo."[35] Others see it as "literature of memory" with sentimental overcoloring and indigestible nostalgia, which sorely try the reader's patience.[36] Inevitably, a contrast with Gianna Manzini imposes itself. Manzini also went in search of her dead parents, but she did so with artistry and originality, creating a successful union between art, death, and life. Romano's fidelity to the facts of her past existence and to the minutiae of daily life limit the scope of her novels, which mark time within the span of a single person's life. The reader never gets the feeling that Romano belongs to life generally. She tells stories of herself in domesticity, not in historicity. Although she excels in self-revelation, she seems unable to develop her works into social sagas like Natalia Ginzburg's *Lessico famigliare* or Fausta Cialente's *Le quattro ragazze Wieselberger*.

Romano's choice has been for scanty, "authentic" subjects, modeled on Piedmontese life and culture, and mostly filtered through her family's experiences. In her attempt to overcome her "Piedmontese dimension," she has experimented with new materials, such as dreams, "documents," and, more recently, family album photographs—which

she considers images and therefore "text" that can be read and interpreted like fiction—for her "photographic novels":[37] *Lettura di un'im-
magine* (Reading of an image, 1975) and *Romanzo di figure* (Novel of
pictures, 1986), subsequently combined into one volume; and *La treccia
di Tatiana* (Tatiana's braid, 1986). But whether through words or
through photographs, she inexorably describes people and aspects of
provincial life, recalling sensations and emotions that marked her childhood.

Together, *Una giovinezza inventata* (An invented youth, 1979)—a
novel of formation describing her upbringing in a middle-class environment in Turin in the 1920s—and *Nei mari estremi* (Far-off seas,
1987)—recollections of her husband and his slow, painful death—form
an introspective diary-novel of Romano's adult life. She readily acknowl-
edges that they are marred by excessive "autobiographism." *Una giovinezza inventata* tells of her *éducation sentimentale* during the years she
lived in a women's dormitory managed by nuns—the same boarding
institute frequented by another Piedmontese woman writer, the poet,
novelist, and journalist Amalia Guglielminetti (1885–194?). Although
Romano's personal disclosures lack any analysis of the position of young
women in marriage and society, the novel in a way may be seen as en-
capsulating the Italian Everywoman's youth. *Nei mari estremi* tells of her
husband, who was as grateful for his life as for his death. During the
long period of his terminal illness, he was situated "più in là" [further
beyond]—that is, in rarefied spheres of profound silence, which the
author calls "the far-off seas."[38]

Un sogno del Nord (A northern dream, 1989)[39] is a collection of occasional pieces—"moments" or "paragraphs"—about faraway cities,
places of the memory, encounters and shadows of persons of Romano's
past. The only thing that comes out of this book, by her own admission,
is exactly what she did not propose to write: a portrait of herself.[40]

Romano's recent work, *Le lune di Hvar* (Moons over Hvar, 1991), is
a collection of plotless pieces all reduced to the fixity of a color, a sensation, a photograph, or the changeableness of a moon in the sky. The
"story," told in flashes, revolves around the four summers she spent in
Dalmatia in the company of a young journalist, photographer, and
friend, Antonio Rio. The simple jottings, which are memory in its pure
state, constitute what the author has called "an impersonal adventure,
almost a monologue of solitude."[41] Although she succeeds in describ-

ing colors and the mystery of objects, she knows that *Le lune di Hvar*—neither a novel, nor a travelogue, nor autobiographical jottings, yet perhaps all these together—is "a book without a future." The slim volume defies classification: some pages are without text, some bear only a single word. "I detest saying too much," she explains; "but what remains is rigorously real: I mean limpid, not logical. Words must be few [and must lie] between space and silence; only this way can they live."[42]

Julia Kristeva practically dismisses women novelists from the literary scene because of the narrowness of their themes, the main theme being the reinvention of family histories through which they construct a reassuring identity for themselves.[43] Withdrawal into the seclusion of her home, into personal and family history, is the hallmark of Lalla Romano's writings. Her narrating "I" refers to her father, her mother, her uncle, her son, as though they had no reality apart from her sense of them. Their lives do not go on elsewhere, nor is their consciousness available to us. Romano claims that by writing about aspects of her own life, she is describing "la vita in se stessa" [life in itself], and that by writing "always in the same way" and avoiding "representation of external conflicts," her books retain a "certain immobility" that renders them always up-to-date and topical.[44] Withdrawal also characterizes her son in *Le parole tra noi leggere*, as well as the man who talked to himself and the two women who distance themselves from him both physically and emotionally. They embody the socially detached author, who sets herself outside the group, seemingly unwilling to endow her past or her present with any sociopolitical meaning. She is politically disengaged, despite a short commitment to the Italian Communist Party in 1976, when she admitted to being "bored to death" during Milan Communal Council sessions and to reading a book under the table.[45] History does not interest Lalla Romano. Her autobiographical moments are related "without heroic episodes" because, in her own words, "non amo la Storia" [I don't like History].[46] Neither does she show concern for women's participation in societal structures. Her characters have no lucid, pragmatic view of the world; the women are unconcerned that their destiny is being determined by external historical and social factors. Universal themes, potentially of great interest to her readers, are lacking in her oeuvre.

But Romano does feel the urgency of building new values and new relationships between humans and reality, of demythicizing those relationships that were typical of a long period of Italian history. She has protested against current abuses of freedom of conscience—more important now, in times of peace, than during the Resistance. "I think I should write about these things," she has stated,[47] thereby recognizing that humanity cannot abstract itself from the political dimension of life and that each individual bears a social responsibility. But no book of political or moral involvement has yet appeared.

More than one critic feels "uncomfortable" reading Romano's work, finding that a "cultural veil" seems to hang between the reader and the material contained in her books.[48] "The truth of the matter," Romano has declared, "is that my books are easy for simple people; difficult for the learned."[49] But if a reader is neither wholly "simple" nor wholly "learned," he or she remains perplexed in the face of the author's excessive "autobiographism." Nevertheless, despite their overall flatness and lacunas, Lalla Romano's works have found their way into Mondadori publishers' prestigious Meridiani *opera omnia* series, and they accordingly merit consideration.

FIVE

ELSA MORANTE

Absent Fathers, Missing Mothers, and Family Myths

L oath to reveal details of her own life, Elsa Morante (1912–85) did admit that she was born poor in Rome; that there were "two fathers" in her life, both Sicilian, but she preferred to remain silent about both; and that her northern Italian mother was "the chastest of women."[1] The dearth of biographical details about Morante's life and her reticence to reveal private experiences have been seen as the very guarantee of their universality and poetic quality.[2] The author affirmed that her entire self could be found in her books—"sono tutta intera nei miei libri."[3] Her diary, published posthumously in 1989, further discloses the inner workings of her mind and reveals her feelings toward her "father, not the natural one, but the legitimate one."[4]

Additional known facts of Morante's life and thought include a growing-up process that, like that of her characters, was both traumatic and fascinating. Having left her home in the slums of Rome when she was in her late teens, she found temporary shelter in her rich godmother's sumptuous villa. The experience filled her with both scorn and attraction for luxury and opulence; it imbued her with sensitivity to contrasts in social classes; and it fired her imagination with scintillating images that found later expression in her romantic style. Together with the children of noble families, she created a theater complete with masks and costumes, to which she harnessed her own mimetic talent. Through the theater she could substitute lies and illusions for the grayness of real life. Just as Bertolt Brecht had evolved for theater audiences what he called "the alienation effect" to destroy the illusion of reality, Morante would later move her readers away from the realists' and neorealists' world to achieve what she called "poetic truth." In her short story "Il gioco segreto" (The secret game, 1937), for example, in a gloomy, walled-in garden described as a kind of jail, there appears the figure of a "marchesa mother, a sad marionette," who tries to prevent her adolescent children from fleeing this "unamiable reality." Their sole means of escape is by playing a "secret game" of mental theater.[5] The myopic protagonist of *Aracoeli* (1982; *Aracoeli*, 1984) plays optical tricks on himself with his eyeglasses, removing them whenever he needs to shut out his sordid surroundings and reduce the world to a "shapeless sham."[6]

Morante was an anticonformist. She showed a spirit of anarchy and was inclined to historical pessimism. A utopian "anarchy that excludes any form of power or violence" was her declared political ideal, and she considered any form of financial, ideological, military, or familial domination to be "the most gloomy, hideous, and shameful thing on earth."[7] Her sympathy invariably went to those who had an essentially anarchic concept of society, and in this respect she is similar to Gianna Manzini (see chap. 3).

To Morante's eyes, her century was the theater of an unending contest between the forces of self-preservation and self-aggrandizement, on the one hand, and those of human solidarity, compassion, and love for one's neighbors, on the other. Some aspects of the contest are developed in her novel *La Storia* (1974; *History: A Novel*, 1977), which unfolds in wartime and postwar Italy. The oppressive atmosphere of the 1940s and the modern existential condition are perhaps what she intended to symbolize by the "Knights of the Woeful Countenance," devoid of all moral grandeur, who appear in her novel *Menzogna e sortilegio* (1948; *House of Liars*, 1951). They can offer the heroine, Elisa (Elsa herself), no vision of a better world.

Morante yearned for what she called the "magnificent extravagance" of an all-embracing brotherhood transcending family bonds and traditional patriarchal structures, which she contested.[8] She envisaged a universe of *felici tutti* (all happy people) as opposed to the world she knew, populated by the *Felici Pochi* (happy few) and *Infelici Molti* (unhappy many), abbreviated in her works as F.P. and I.M. Her Dostoyevskian concept of *felici tutti* is a reaffirmation of the concept of *agape*—a constant, unselfish concern for others, an affection, tenderness, and compassion for all others at all times, the assumption of continuing responsibility for others, and the loving of everyone and everything. It is an ethic of equalization, a fitting foundation for a stable society of dignified individuals who freely engage in reciprocal exchanges of benefits and requitals. Morante felt that precisely this lack of freedom in the world of historical reality precluded a world of universal love. Thus, she created a vision, in her best-known book of poems, of *Il mondo salvato dai ragazzini* (The world saved by little children, 1968).

Mainly self-educated, Morante preferred the writings of Homer, Cervantes, Stendhal, Melville, Chekhov, and Verga, because of the "extraordinary increase of vitality" they produced in her.[9] She also read Manzoni, Dante, Rimbaud, Kafka, and Freud.[10] She began her career at an early age, publishing the semiautobiographical fable "Qualcuno bussa alla porta" (Someone is knocking at the door) in a children's magazine,[11] and she continued to produce short stories, poetry, and novels up to the decade before her mental impairment and death. One of the hallmarks of her poetry, in which she ponders human destiny, is the figure of the contemporary "Oedipus," the man/woman who learns an appalling truth (*conoscenza*) and as a result falls into madness (*follia*).[12]

Menzogna e sortilegio, Morante's first novel, was awarded the Viareggio Prize in 1948, and *L'isola di Arturo* (1957; *Arturo's Island*, 1988) received the coveted Strega Prize in 1966. Her marriage to Alberto Moravia in 1941 ended twenty-one years later in de facto separation. She attempted suicide in 1983, after a two-year struggle with hydrocephalus (an excess of fluid in the cranium resulting in mental deterioration), and she died two years later in a Rome nursing home.

Like her literary contemporary Anna Maria Ortese,[13] Morante wrote in the style of "magic realism," defined by a contemporary writer as "nothing vague or romantic . . . : the brutal facts are all there, but at any moment they may be shaken up kaleidoscopically and produce a wholly new impression or pattern."[14] Both Morante and Ortese observe the true-to-life but translate it into an atmosphere of enchantment and bewitchment. Lucidly, but with the detachment of dreams, they interpret reality lyrically, endowing it with a magic hue. In *L'isola di Arturo*, for example, the island (Procida, in the Bay of Naples) becomes a pirate ship whose captain, clinging to the mainmast, is none other than the young hero perched in the branches of a tall tree; his dead mother is his "oriental queen," his "siren,"[15] whose voice has the quality of "the beautiful golden canary of fables" (136); and the island's transparent sea offers him "the most splendid of gifts: a sea urchin of a beautiful purple color" (204). In *Aracoeli* an orange grove in the midst of a flat, funereal landscape in Andalusia in southern Spain oscillates under the blazing sun like a "Japanese lantern spectacle" (129).

Repressed desires and memories exert their influence on Morante's characters, whose unresolved complexes account for their adult personality disorders. The author's strongly analytic—or rather psychoanalytic—treatment of her subjects brings them to a time beyond time. She delves into the enigmas of the collective unconscious and of individual destiny. Through storytelling and dream narration, she brings unconscious content into consciousness, often using the form of dialogue between the ego and a fantasy figure. Contemporary criticism, which increasingly uses analytic psychology to interpret Morante's works, has illustrated her use of the technique of "active imagination"—a process of deliberate participation in fantasy at a moment when the ego feels it has reached an impasse.

Morante's main characters are in essence a single, autobiographical reciting "I" that Morante conceives of as herself and as Morante interpreting herself. Wholly embodied in both her male and female characters, she earned the epithet "ragazza/ragazzo" (girl/boy). She cherished an "incurable desire to be a boy" and confessed her sense of "incompleteness," with which she grappled by impersonating herself in Arturo.[16] "Arturo," she affirmed, "sono io" [Arturo is myself].[17] The boy's profile is indeed "double-contoured,"[18] and the epigraph of the novel is "If in him I see myself, I am content"—a verse from the *Canzoniere* of Morante's friend Umberto Saba.[19]

Morante is not only Arturo. She is Emanuele, the male protagonist of *Aracoeli*. She is "L'uomo dagli occhiali" (The man with the eyeglasses, 1936); Andrea Campese, who is in love with his mother in "Lo scialle andaluso" (The Andalusian shawl, 1951); and Davide Segre of *La Storia*, who, like the author herself, drowns his torments in alcohol, discerns a brother in Christ of Nazareth, and gives no importance to the color or the gender of his fellow humans.

Morante is also her feminine characters: the little adopted girl, Lucia, in "Qualcuno bussa alla porta," as well as the omniscient and ubiquitous narrator/heroine Elisa of *Menzogna e sortilegio*. She is Aracoeli, whose nymphomania and physical degeneration reflect her own eroticism and her obsessions with deterioration and death. She is partly Nunziatella, with whom Arturo is caught up in an oedipal drama. Just as Arturo has to flee his home, so did Morante, because she was entangled in an oedipal drama with her legitimate father.[20] She is partly Ida Ramundo of *La Storia*, the daughter of a northern mother and a southern father—an anarchist with a passion for wine. Ida Ramundo loved her father, "forgot all fear at [his] side. To her, he seemed a kind of warm baby-carriage . . . more impregnable than a tank. . . . [I]n bad weather he would protect her from the rain, holding her close, under his mantle."[21] After her father's death and her rape by a German soldier, Ida's raving dreams found her "running here and there, completely naked . . . walking with her father, who shelters her beneath his cloak; but then the cloak flies off, as if on its own, without her father any more" (102).

An emblematic figure in Morante's poetry is the ageless, sexless adolescent (the *ragazzo*). He is endowed with both masculine and feminine traits—"l'ape e la rosa" [the drone and the rose]—and possessed of dual characteristics "in miraculous equilibrium."[22] He is the embodiment of the Jungian archetypal "wonder child" whose conscious triumphs over his unconscious.[23] Every passing *ragazzo* is, for Morante, "una morgana"—interpreted by some (if *morgana* is translated as "mirage") to connote the futility of seeking the unattainable.[24] But the concept may also be taken as a syncretistic identification of male and female: King Arthur's ambiguous relationship with his enchantress sister, Morgan le Fay (*la Fata Morgana* in Italian). The ambiguity of Morante's conceptions permits the reader to grasp her dialectical notion of truth and lie.[25] Her interchangeable heroes/heroines make up, in Jungian language, the "paradoxical image," often described as hermaphroditic, not unlike the androgynous type prophesied by Sibilla Aleramo (see chap. 2).[26]

The Italian title of Morante's first published novel, *Menzogna e sortilegio* (translated as *House of Liars*), means falsehood and sorcery. The heroine's parents indeed know "no happiness outside of falsehood,"[27] and the practice of sorcery and necromancy is traditional in the family. This long, bewitching novel, which lends itself to innumerable interpretations, relates the efforts of Elisa, now a young adult and the only survivor of a hideous family saga, to reconstruct the catastrophic history of her insane and now defunct relatives. Through memory, imaginative effort, and probings into the motivations for their marriages, liaisons, and intrigues, Elisa narrates, in fablelike style, their ugly scramble to climb the social ladder. The "house of liars" is a metaphor for the place where Elisa searches for the false idols of her past but finds "backstage" only a heap of "limp figures that resemble cast-off costumes . . . at the end of a theatrical show" (26).

The solitary, socially imprisoned Elisa, little loved by her father and even less by her mother, is what today would be called the "growing-up grotesque" archetype: an "old child," an "ill-grown youth" with the eyes of a "wild boy," timid, awkward, with a tendency to overdramatize and love too intensely (Morante's own traits). Elisa, whose pabulum consists of fairy tales and legends, relates myths of wealth and caste privilege in her small, unnamed, backward town of the South. She tells the story of a romantic, fanciful love affair between her humble mother, Anna, and a Sicilian nobleman, Eduardo, a first cousin. Elisa's "absent" father, whose drunkenness and madness prevented him from creating a "traditional" family, is himself "without a real family, because he was without a real father; and without a social collocation, because he was neither peasant nor gentleman" (393). Elisa yearns for union with her beautiful "missing" mother, the object of her love. But that love is constantly rejected and constantly renewed, as Eduardo, the dominating presence in Anna's life, thwarts and shunts aside the love-thirsty child.

Her mother is Elisa's first and most serious unhappy love. Maternal indifference gives her an early taste of the bitter agony of the "unaccepted lover." Elisa's only possibility, then, is to give herself up to readings and fantasies, to accept the creative power of the lie and the liberating effects of fiction. When, finally, she begins to write, the very process of narration sets her free from her own desire for her mother.[28] Through writing about the dissolution of her family, up to the tragic epilogues of their madness and death, Elisa finally escapes her self-made prison of ghosts and traumas of childhood.

The forsaken Elisa finds her male counterpart in Morante's best-known novel, *L'isola di Arturo*—Arturo being the author's namesake for Morante's favorite poet, Rimbaud. Arturo, whose mother died at his birth but remains a holy presence in his life, narrates the drama of his childhood, which unfolds in "a kind of mythical theater" (233). He worships his father, whose long absences take on the aspect of legendary heroic exploits in the eyes of his son. Just when the paternal myth is about to be shattered by the truth that his father is an unhappy homosexual at the mercy of his criminal delinquent lover, Arturo shifts his adoration to his new stepmother, Nunziatella, whom he at first hated, but onto whom he transfers his memories of his dead mother. Ultimately, Arturo abandons forever both his childhood illusions and the island where he had once known happiness and lost it, a location that represents, for Elsa Morante, absolute time and space.

A flavor of Morante's style in this novel may be gained from the way she narrates one of Arturo's dreams, which occurs at a point in the story when he still adores his hero-father, but when his hatred for Nunziatella is beginning to give way to love. In his dream, his "bad, wicked" stepmother "trickily" slips into his room at night, "pretending to be a boy like me, dressed in a shirt that hung flat over her chest as though underneath she did not have a woman's form." But Arturo "guesses" that she is a woman. He goes toward her with a knife (which must be seen as a phallic symbol), because, he says, "I didn't want women with me, in my room." Opening Nunziatella's shirt, he uncovers her "white, round breast. . . . She let out a scream"—a scream that Arturo confusedly remembers having heard on the first night that Nunziatella spent with his father in their home (155).

Morante uses this dream narration to establish the direction in which she intends to guide events: Arturo already loves his stepmother unconsciously; his superego, however, rejects this attachment. But Morante also narrates the dream in all of its theatricality: Nunziatella uses "artifice" to enter Arturo's room; she is "disguised" in male costume; he seizes the knife to punish her for her "impersonation"; she "shams" masculinity but he "gives her the lie" by revealing her breasts. Once the "show" is over, Arturo will transfer to Nunziatella the femininity of his own mother. His love will then be played out on the conscious level until he realizes that his island can no longer be the stage for his adolescent dramas.

Central to Morante's works are variations of the father-mother-child triangles of desire. Morante's boys/girls or children/adults are caught up in Oedipus/Electra complexes that are never carnally resolved but are always fully developed in their literary aspects. Innocent yet mature children, or childlike adults, all seem to bear a tragic collective destiny. (The author's poetry is an attempt on her part to help them escape that destiny and regain their mystical lost happiness.)[29] Arturo's "ideal" love for his father is supplanted by a "real" love for his stepmother, who arouses him sexually; his alternating repulsion and attraction for her prepare the theme of incest. But the forbidden act not only is not consummated; its very concept is contested by Morante as another myth to be dispelled.[30] She creates the personage of a young widow who snatches Arturo from his grotesque family and initiates him into the normalcy of licit lovemaking.

Dissolute, damaged, or incomplete families are the root cause of the children's alienation in Morante's short stories and novels.[31] Sometimes she tells of obsessive parental loves, as, for example, in the story "La nonna" (The grandmother, 1937). The protagonist here is a jealous, witchlike mother who lures her son's tiny children to a lugubrious death to punish her son for getting married and leaving her. But Morante's dominant theme is how a lack of parental love can lead to children's despair and destruction. The author lashes out against parents in society's legitimized father-mother-child triangular relationships and seeks to exclude the father and paternal authority. Both in her early story "Il ladro dei lumi" (The oil-lamp thief, 1935) and in *Menzogna e sortilegio*, young daughters contest paternal authority by using derogatory nicknames when they refer to their fathers. The heroine of "Il ladro di lumi" goes so far as to question her father's right to strike her, thinking, "why should he? I'm small but pretty, I have two long braids, and I know how to read."[32] Morante thus touches on the idea that latent rebellion against paternal authority is crucial to personal identity.

The fathers in Morante's stories are conspicuously absent and show little involvement with their children when they are present. "For me," says Emanuele in *Aracoeli*, "*paternity* meant *absence*." He feels only "rancor and dislike" for his father, whose choice of a military career leaves Emanuele floundering for an identity (183). Arturo's father is a perennial wanderer. Giuseppe, in *La Storia*, is denied all identity as Ida Ramundo's illegitimate child of rape; nor will he ever know his father, the drunken German soldier who is killed three days later.

Mothers scarcely fare better. If they are not totally missing, they bear the responsibility for transmitting to their children an absurd and alienating culture. Morante chastises mothers through her characters' words: an entire chapter of *L'isola di Arturo* consists of ironic but intentionally designed curses "contro le madri (e le femine in genere)" [against mothers (and women in general)] (142–48), who, instead of being creators of life and real love, can wreak havoc in the lives of their children.[33] Although Morante condemns the possessive, destructive love of Lucia's adoptive father in the short story "Qualcuno bussa alla porta," she does not spare the illegitimate child's negligent mother, who abandoned the child on a doorstep and then fled. In "Lo scialle andaluso," the child, Andrea Campese, loves his mother, who sacrifices him to her other loves—dancing and the theater. Each time she leaves the house, Andrea feels like an abandoned kitten; he grows up hating both his mother and the theater so much that he decides to enter the seminary. When his mother's age and loss of talent force her to give up her career, Andrea returns to their home with the illusion that she now desires to be close to him. Although she wraps her Andalusian shawl around him as a sign of reunion, Andrea realizes that his mother sought his return from the seminary for selfish motives only.

The novel *Aracoeli* tells of a mother who first is wholly united with her young son, Emanuele, in an almost animal-like relationship, but who then rejects him and ultimately becomes a slave to nymphomania. Emanuele is a child who never grows up, refuses an autonomous life, is afraid of the outside world, and loses his own identity in a pathological maternal mimesis that continues even after his mother's death. Only in adulthood does he understand the "maternal crimes" committed against him. He laments: "It would have been better if you had aborted me or strangled me with your own hands as soon as I was born instead of nourishing and raising me with your treacherous love, like a little animal being raised for the slaughterhouse. . . . The enchanted potion that you worked into my flesh night and day was nothing but your false, excessive love, to which I became addicted, as to an incurable vice" (100).

Animal imagery and the identification of children with small animals, frequent in Morante's writings, abound in *Aracoeli*. Over and over Emanuele says, "I am an animal," and, "I don't know what kind of animal I am." He describes himself as "an animal, sniffing for the odors of its own den" (9). Winding through a *regressus ad uterum* during his search for his mother, he cries out: "Aracoeli . . . mamita, help me. As mother cats do with their ill-born kittens, swallow me up again. Receive my deformity in your merciful abyss" (109). Only after waging a desperate war against his mother does he exorcise her presence in his life and thus gain release.

The name of Emanuele's Andalusian mother is Aracoeli Muñoz Muñoz, and the novel is a reconstruction of fragmentary events in Emanuele's life, as reflected in the memory of his parents. The zigzagging course of the narration takes the reader to a small town in southern Spain, El Almendral, which Morante affirmed she had imagined and fully described even before she knew it actually existed—another confirmation of the presence of collective unconscious images in her dreams and visions. Setting out in single-minded search of his mother, Emanuele undertakes a double journey: the physical trip to the village where Aracoeli was born, and a voyage into memory. His trip culminates at El Almendral, where there are a few houses and a bastard dog. Everyone in the village bears the name Muñoz Muñoz, which is at the same time ironical and perhaps suggestive of Morante's contest of the traditional family structure. Returning to Rome, he seeks out his father, now a poverty-stricken old drunk, who still loves Aracoeli and lives in a squalid apartment close to the Verano Cemetery to be near her. Emanuele suddenly bursts into tears of love for the decrepit old man. When his father dies, he sheds no tears, because, like Elsa Morante, he belongs to that category of "certain individuals more inclined to weep out of love than over death" (328). The disoriented Emanuele, who originally loved his mother exclusively but then came to hate her, now discovers, too late, that he loves his father. He is destined, like his creator, to "live without love" (327–28).

Morante's traumatic love stories are sentimental, originating in fables and romances. She narrates them in an allegorical, fablelike style, shunning the graphic eroticism of her sometime husband, Moravia. But, though explicit sexuality is absent from her works,[34] it is all-important in the dreams she narrates in her *Diario*, where the expressive language of her libido is specifically feminine. In one erotic dream, she is on her way to a mysterious room in a garden, where a naked lover awaits her. She is hampered in her advance by heaviness in her legs, accompanying the menstrual flow: "A liquid, soft, warm weight between my legs, everything weighs down heavily on me" (6). Before her marriage to

Moravia, she wrote in her diary that she felt "humiliated and alone," her wounded sexual identity covered with "blood and tears": "Last night before falling asleep I wept with rage because I wanted to make love and instead A. [Alberto Moravia] stopped by, bringing V. with him. Ever unsatisfied sexual stirring; but besides, even when we are together [words expunged by author]—I don't find my pleasure—My desire and need, and especially my insatiable longing for [words expunged by author] for the time being is satisfied only in my dreams. I want other dreams, another life" (19). She is crushed by the feeling that she remains a useless object in Moravia's life: "He is famous and rich. . . . He will be going to Paris to celebrate his recent success, and I?" (34, 35).

Morante hungered for maternity, repeatedly seeking complicity and identification with her mother, who frequently appears in her dreams as a holy figure who even walks on the sea (27). Through her mother, she is linked to archetypal concepts of femininity and maternity. In one of her dreams, she expresses remorse for not having loved her mother strongly enough: "For so many years I had you near me and didn't look for you! I was looking for Alberto [Moravia]! but what is he? an arid, selfish miser! And you were here, you were here! Oh God!" (56). She awakens, sweating, and experiencing a sharp pain in her left side (read "heart"), realizing how selfish Moravia is and how selfless her mother.

Yet, in another dream, even her mother refuses to give her daughter one of her many pink flowering plants (angiosperms, in botany, having seeds in a closed ovary) in exchange for Elsa's own fleshy-leaved plant, which does not bear flowers. "There you are," thinks Elsa, "in the whole world there isn't a single being disposed to make even the slightest sacrifice for me. . . . I was deeply pained by this lack of love" (11)—a lack of maternal love that finds such frequent resonance in her writings.

The two syllables "ma-ma"—"voices of [his] own flesh"—sound sweet and natural to the ears of Emanuele in *Aracoeli* (184). But his relationship to his mother turns sour, and he realizes that it is his lonely father whom he loves. Elisa in *Menzogna e sortilegio* is denied her defective mother's love and attempts to destroy her by condemning her in her narration. But she finds that she is writing stanzas of love for the hated woman, now dead.

Both Morante and her characters heal the traumas of love, rejection, and solitude through recall of childhood events and through retrospective narration, filling in the gaps, as Freud suggests, "according to the behests of the imagination." They use writing as an instrument of therapy. By giving free rein to the imagination, they gain cathartic relief from the disillusionment that besets them. Arturo narrates the crumbling myths of his childhood as an initiation into adulthood. Emanuele attempts to heal his psychic hurt by narrating a double journey—to El Almendral and into memory—in a final attempt to cure himself of his mother. Elisa writes her family story to exorcise myths, escape the lie, and recompose the destroyed harmony of her reason and imagination. Elsa Morante herself, in her personal "double journey" of a suicide attempt, recognized, "If I can get back to my writing, I'll be saved."[35]

SIX
NATALIA GINZBURG

The Ill-Tempered Family

N ovelist, short-story writer, essayist, and dramatist Natalia Ginzburg (1916–91) came of age under fascism. Subsequently, she survived the horrors of World War II as well as exposure to the double political risks of her Jewish heritage and her family's clandestine resistance. Up to her death in October 1991, she was a rare model of the committed Italian woman intellectual, serving as a parliamentarian of the Independent Left. She succeeded in producing a rich and varied oeuvre even while actively taking part in her nation's recent history. Although a melancholy person, deeply aware of the tragedy and absurdity of the human condition, she saw (perhaps through her Jewish heritage) the humorous and comic aspects of life, and she understood, even in her blackest moments, that "people in books" should be "funny and at the same time sad."[1] All her works are essentially pessimistic, yet some of them are shot through with real humor and display her ability to laugh at life's more absurd vicissitudes. She wields irony skillfully, as, for example, when she allows a shallow husband to interpret as a clear sign of marital incompatibility his wife's preference for tea when he likes cocoa. By documenting people's failings with a humorous eye, she helps to make the human plight just that much more tolerable.

Ginzburg always took clear and stubborn positions in public debates, championing especially the interests of the family. She did not claim that the institution of the family is happy or unhappy; indeed, she focused relentlessly on all the negative aspects of traditional family life and their destructive effect on the personality. But in the final analysis she considered it was better that the family exist, despite all its defects. Her main frame of reference is domestic life, whose foundations she saw crumbling under the absence of love, communication, and parental guidance. She deplores the unthinking stagnation so typical of Italian middle-class families in which "children don't need their parents. The less they have to do with them the better off they are."[2] Her critical biography *La famiglia Manzoni* (1983; *The Manzoni Family*, 1987) is not about "the great writer" Alessandro Manzoni (1785–1873), who is already dead when the book begins, but about his surviving family, which has fallen into disgrace, and about his children, who are irreversibly damaged by the immoral decisions of the man as a father.

The difficulties in establishing and maintaining human relationships, the lack of meaningful rapport between generations, the fate of the family, and the well-being of children are at the core of Ginzburg's concerns. Her fine sense of history, combined with her deep feeling for human injustice and suffering, guides her as she moves painstakingly through the past, recording whatever it exhibits by way of similarity to contemporary reality. In keeping with her attentiveness to the burning topics of the day and in a departure from literary themes, she prefaced and translated, for example, an account of a twelve-year-old Cambodian child's dramatic escape from the horrors in her country to begin a new life with adoptive parents in France.[3] Elsewhere, in her polemical work *Serena Cruz o la vera giustizia* (Serena Cruz, or true justice, 1990), the author defends, apropos of an explosive legal battle that divided Italy in 1989, the position of an Italian couple who illegally adopted a Philippine child.

Writing, for Ginzburg, is like living on this planet; both tasks are equally challenging, and both require great *fatica* (effort, hard work)— a word she uses repeatedly. She has always balked at being placed in the category of "women writers," most of whom, by her own admission, she dislikes. Four exceptions are her contemporary Elsa Morante, the early Lombard feminist and satirical writer Marchesa Colombi, the Virginia Woolf of *To the Lighthouse*, and Ivy Compton-Burnett, whose novels, like Ginzburg's own, reflect underlying social change. Originally, Ginzburg sought to write like a man[4]—with supreme detachment and cool reserve. Part of her objection to women writers, she stated in an interview by Oriana Fallaci,[5] is their inability to disengage from personal feelings—to write with aloofness and irony, which she qualifies as the masculine dimensions of literary art. Her own combination of instinctive feminine expression and dry masculine style produces a curiously neuter result. An androgynous quality shows through in "Casa al mare" (House at the shore, 1937), recounted in the first person singular, though the "I" is a man. In other works of a more autobiographic nature, she succeeds in so depersonalizing herself that despite her use of the narrating "I," her audience feels her distance and detachment. Ginzburg may sometimes puzzle the reader of her more didactic essays with the ambiguity of such phrases as "le persone di un sesso diverso dal nostro" [persons of a different sex from ours].

Despite her literary mannishness, Ginzburg remains a distinguished *woman* writer of moving fiction in the twentieth-century Italian tradition of *male di vivere* (the scourge of living)—that state of grim awareness of the human condition to which authors of the pre– and post–World War II era gave realistic expression. She uses a dry prose style, but she still writes very much like a woman, expressing her perception not only of historical transience but also of the difficulties that society places in the way of an orderly ethical maturation. She is cautiously aware that the dangers of Mussolini's fascist era and of long years of emotional and intellectual apathy could repeat themselves; but her main preoccupation, in all of her works, is the disintegration of home life, triggered by a lack of love and communication and by the need for authoritative parental guidance. In her portraits of women and their fragile families, she invariably underscores the dispiritedness, the sense of fatalism, and the hopelessness that bind and separate individuals. With her feminine eye, she focuses on disgruntled young people living in the uncomfortable bosom of their deteriorating families and incapable of creating adult sexual relationships. She discovers in the minds of her characters a sense of failure, loneliness, and disorientation—feelings that she exteriorizes in flat, functional words and sentences. Her simple writing style, as she digs below the surface of drab and dreary life to expose her characters' motives, has frequently been likened to that of Chekhov (for the Italian edition of whose *Selected Letters* she wrote an introduction prior to her death). Like Chekhov's, Ginzburg's characters engage in endless prattle and mindless chatter about the same little problems of daily life. Both authors show a keen sense of the social scene, the incongruities of life, and people's inability to change the folly, laziness, and ineptitude of those around them.

Fascism inflicted on the Italian young a corrupting inertia, twisted their idealism, and nourished their private obsessions. The war that followed disrupted and dispersed families, whose confused survivors regrouped, at its conclusion, to continue living out what seemed to be the same absurd daily conventions. Their talk was endless and futile; their gestures automatic and minimalist. Ginzburg creates an anatomy of this ritual "reality" inside a living room, around a dining table, within a circle of family and friends. Discussions and unsatisfactory relationships are played out within these domestic walls, which rear up to surround the characters' mounting discontent. Against a backdrop of emptiness and loneliness, Ginzburg records everyday family conversations and events, gradually building up tension over insignificant facts until they converge in an explosive climax. She gives so much attention to the minutiae of daily life to demonstrate that they can upset the social equilibrium, throw a household into disorder, and determine the behavior and fate of her characters.

Ginzburg's stylistic gift rests on what has been called by one of her translators "cumulative characterization"[6]—a method that, by dispensing almost entirely with description, gives body to solid, memorable personages by the gradual accumulation of small actions, oblique glances, and other people's opinions: "My mother . . . hardly ever goes down to the town. Aunt Ottavia says to her, 'Why don't we go to the town sometimes?' And my mother says. 'What for?' "[7] "Other people's opinions" form the basis of a narrative device frequently used by Ginzburg. Plots are developed and characterizations are provided through the eyes and the words of another person in the story. The sister of a self-centered, feckless playboy sees that her brother "has never neglected for one day to pamper his curls in front of the mirror and smile at his reflection," and she informs the reader that his future wife is short and fat with tortoiseshell glasses; has hard, round eyes, a shiny nose, a moustache, and black hair streaked with gray, crimped, and untidy; and "intended to marry . . . come what may."[8]

In Ginzburg's works, marriages crumble, or one partner seeks escape in death; ill-matched couples evade responsibility through subterfuge and infidelity; children use the excuse of the "generation gap" to escape discipline and the duties of living at home. The gallery of well-drawn but hardly melodramatic characters through which Ginzburg's readers move is derived from middle-class society: frustrated figures that she arranges in colorless narrative frames. With a woman's patience, she brings out the drabness of life's events, using the simplest of words and discarding unnecessary padding until only the essence of futility remains. "The books I write have no particular purpose," she declared in a 1973 interview; "If I had to explain why I write them, I wouldn't know what to say. . . . When I write novels I invent things and have no particular aim in mind."[9] She delves into the memories, losses, and burdens of her characters' pasts. The frustrations of human connections move her, however, to consider more stringent and absolute questions of truth and falsehood, of eternity and time. But she does so in the simplest of languages: "I have to express myself clearly and explain everything," she declared in the same interview.[10]

Pertinaciously and purposely, Ginzburg attempts to salvage some fragments of her protagonists' lives from the maw of time. Her approach to the "literature of memory," so fundamental to her oeuvre, was improved and sharpened by her reading and rereading of Proust, whose *Du côté de chez Swann* she translated into Italian in 1941–42. Like Proust she is a "confessional" writer who excels in describing the unfolding of minute inner vicissitudes of feeling and recollection; and with Proust she shares a realization of the validity of human character and personality.

Ginzburg's characters subconsciously recognize the futility of their actions, but they are too weak to cope with life's peripeteia. The recurrent pattern of the stories plots her characters' failure to grapple successfully with the meaning of existence and to regulate their own destinies. Trapped in passive surrender, even in active self-debasement, they evoke many of Dostoyevsky's useless characters, locked into a narrow and ambiguous world. Is the root cause of their disordered personality to be found in the words of Dostoyevsky's "no good, perverse, selfish, and lazy" Underground Man? "If I had had a family when I was a child, I'd have turned out quite different from what I am today."[11]

In her essays—published in *Le piccole virtù* (1962; *Little Virtues*, 1986), *Mai devi domandarmi* (1970; *Never Must You Ask Me*, 1973), and

Vita immaginaria (Imaginary life, 1974)—Ginzburg reveals her unhappiness with the contemporary world of changing human relationships. She evokes nostalgically an age of the past (her youth) characterized by pride, euphoria, self-assurance, and bright ideals now abandoned in this "upside-down world." But she also expresses the cautious hope that future generations will communicate and integrate new ideals. She urges her readers to disdain the irritating insipidness of family and social life that characterizes so many Italian households. In her theatrical works— published in *Ti ho sposato per allegria e altre commedie* (I married you for fun and other plays, 1967) and *Paese di mare e altre commedie* (Seaside town and other plays, 1973)—she concentrates on the moods and reactions of her characters to the dramatic events in their "small" lives. With barrages of trivia and streams of mindless verbiage, she draws pictures of tense relations between a husband and wife preluding a scrapping of their marriage, while fundamental problems of communication within a household underscore the ongoing disintegration of the institution of the family.

Natalia Levi was born in Palermo of a Roman Catholic mother and a Jewish father. From the age of three she lived in Turin, in an atmosphere of agnosticism that may account for the desperate bitterness and inner malaise of her early creations, though some critics ascribe those moods to the influence of American novelists of the time. Closer overall associations (however anachronistic) might perhaps be made between Ginzburg's narrative technique and that of American minimalist writers of today.

Though the Levi family shunned religious observances, they were quick to embrace socialist principles and antifascism. All the members of the family were involved in some way in Turin's clandestine opposition to Mussolini's dictatorship; and Natalia's marriage in 1938 was to a future hero of the Italian resistance, Leone Ginzburg, a professor of Russian literature, himself of Russian origin, who died in 1944 at the hands of the German occupying forces. Although Natalia Ginzburg later contracted a second marriage to Gabriele Baldini, a professor of English literature, a musicologist, and a well-known Verdi specialist, she nonetheless kept the name of her first husband.

Making her literary debut at the age of seventeen, Ginzburg early demonstrated her concise and direct style, which consisted of short, linear sentences with practically no background description; rhythmic cataloging of facts and objects; and the creation of characters through their moods and gestures. Significantly, her first two short stories were published in 1933 and 1934 in the two Florentine reviews, *Solaria* and *Letteratura*, dedicated to the cult of style as a form of aristocratic detachment from the language of fascist ideology. Her first, "Un'assenza" (An absence, 1933), is a perfectly constructed short narrative revolving around one of her recurrent themes: the laxity and inadequacy of the male and his bungling of marital situations.[12] The theme of the second, "I bambini" (The children, 1934), is that of parental neglect. In Ginzburg's third short story, "Casa al mare" (The house at the shore, 1937), the protagonists are a superficial, unfaithful wife and her weak, resigned husband. They are strangers to each other in their own home, destined to repeat mechanically their futile programs—his to compose their differences, hers to compound them—until the inevitable separation takes place.

These first three stories were published during a decade of teeming political and cultural life in Turin, where the Einaudi publishing house, founded in 1933, grouped around it a circle of gifted writers, of whom Cesare Pavese and Carlo Levi are perhaps the best known outside of Italy. Within the group, the name of Natalia Ginzburg was now becoming known. Her literary production continued with the publication of the short story "Mio marito" (My husband, 1941), in which the recurrent theme of solitude even in married life reappears. The shadow looming over the marriage of a country doctor to the lackluster narrator of the story (his wife) is his passion for a young farm girl who dies giving birth to his stillborn child. As a consequence, the doctor commits suicide, leaving his wife pitifully alone. She concludes her story with the words "there was no place in the world where I wanted to go."[13]

"Mio marito" and Ginzburg's first short novel, *La strada che va in città* (1942; *The Road to the City*, 1990), unfold in a rugged, rural setting that accentuates the bleakness and absurdity of life. Ginzburg had striven to make every sentence of *La strada che va in città* resound like a whiplash or a slap in the face, and she did not fail. The road leading from the country to the city, which supposedly offers an escape from the mental and physical aridity of rural life, is fraught with frustrations and hopelessness. In the end, the protagonists are left surrounded by broken dreams.

The most dramatic of Ginzburg's short novels, *E' stato così* (1947; *The Dry Heart*, 1990), is a masterpiece of reverse-winding suspense. It begins with the wife's "I shot him between the eyes," frequently repeated throughout the story. In a small compass, *The Dry Heart* relates, in a brisk, shorn style, the confession of a woman who kills first her husband and then herself. She describes in her long monologue the pitch to which she had been driven, as she explains the situation that led her to shoot her unfaithful husband between the eyes. The novel is the confession of a woman irremediably scarred by her experience of married life.

Another of Ginzburg's bitter tales is "La madre" (The mother, 1948), a short story fraught with fatalistic implications. At the center of the action is a young widow caught between her two small children and her elderly parents—an anomalous family group, the members of which have nothing in common with each other. Ginzburg uses short, stark sentences to describe the lonely and regulated life of the young woman: her morning marketing, her daily bicycling to and from work, and the evenings she spends mysteriously away from home. The pendulum that governs her life stops abruptly, however, when her lover, the only person able to color the grayness of her existence, suddenly deserts her. Her sense of loss and of double defeat in failing to provide a sense of cohesion to the family unit lead to the widow's suicide.

Ginzburg's stories up to and including "La madre," despite the author's careful chiseling of detail, remain curiously abstract works—as timeless and placeless as Samuel Beckett's, for instance. But abstraction, placelessness, and timelessness are supplanted by specificity in Ginzburg's first full-length novel and her contribution to the "literature of the Resistance," *Tutti i nostri ieri* (1952; *All Our Yesterdays*, 1985).

Tutti i nostri ieri tells the story of two families living through the bitter moments of the antifascist struggle and Italy's war of liberation. The novel's narrative movement takes the reader from a northern industrial town in Piedmont to a village in southern Italy—the two settings that point up the difference between heroic freedom fighters and the complacent bourgeoisie. All the children in the novel are victims in some way of free-floating discontent or of depression. Their unthinking passivity and lack of any sense of obligation beyond the basic necessities of existence make them incapable of maintaining human relationships either within family ties or in sexual passion.[14] They live in the domain of general unhappiness that Ginzburg describes also in her late novella

Borghesia (1977; translated in *Family*, 1988). Those characters who survive the war's destruction resume the tasks of life's daily routine, groping in uncertainty because there were so many "things they didn't know how to do."[5] Yet Ginzburg expresses a faint hope that they will learn, that the desire to broaden their horizon will stir within them, and that they will strive to set new directions in creating meaningful lives of their own. Perhaps the harsh experiences of all their yesterdays may presage a less uncertain future for generations to come. The novel, however, remains pessimistic, even though Ginzburg's view of history is not so apocalyptic as that of Elsa Morante in her *La Storia*.

After *Tutti i nostri ieri*, Ginzburg's production of narrative prose alternated with that of the essays and plays mentioned earlier in this chapter. Two novellas, *Sagittario* and *Valentino*, both written in 1957 (translated in *Valentino and Sagittarius*, 1987), were followed by *Le voci della sera* (1961; *Voices in the Evening*, 1989). *Sagittario* focuses on an insensitive, possessive mother whose lack of practicality and blind pursuit of futility lead her into the hands of a swindler. *Valentino* illustrates the difference between an illusion and a reality; the illusion is the ambition of Valentino's father for, and the obstinate faith of Valentino's wife in, Valentino, who is an irresponsible character. Valentino's spinelessness, which leads to torment and tragedy, constitutes the reality. *Le voci della sera* treats the theme of the death of love and the gradual extinction of an entire family against a twilight background of monotonous talk. This short novel has benefited from a close analysis by Italo Calvino, who aptly describes it as a story about the characters' vain attempt to bury their inner thoughts and seek self-identification through words and gestures alone. Instead they find themselves clamped in a relentless vise of absurdity and pain.[16]

Interruptions and intrusions into the flow of life, conveyed by the futile insistency of "voices in the evening," find resonance in Ginzburg's epistolary novels, which she conceives as portraits of the decomposition of a united family existence. Two bleak works, *Caro Michele* (1973; *Dear Michael*, 1975; also translated as *No Way*, 1974) and *La città e la casa* (1984; *The City and the House*, 1986), revolve around the themes of emigration, political extremism, drugs, homosexuality, and pseudodomesticity. The letters exchanged by family members, whose relationships have grown stagnant, are the only proof of some minimal togetherness and the only suggestion that a new lease on life is possible for Ginzburg's lonely, separated, death-seeking characters. Both epistolary novels end on a note stressing the importance of memory. "There is nothing . . . at present that can compare with the moments and places we experienced in the course of our lives," writes Ginzburg in *Dear Michael*;[17] and in *The City and the House*, a portrait, "funny and at the same time sad," is affectionately evoked from the past: "Your long thinning hair. Your glasses. Your long nose. Your long, bony legs. Your big hands. They were always cold, even when the weather was hot. That's how I remember you."[18]

Though in these works families disperse and disintegrate, a contrastingly compact unit is defined in the work that crowned Ginzburg's success as a writer. The coveted Strega Prize was awarded in 1963 to her widely read *Lessico famigliare* (*Family Sayings*, 1984), an essentially autobiographical work that the author prefers us to read as a novel. Neither an autobiographical novel nor a historical chronicle of the 1930s, *Lessico famigliare* is a combination of personal and historical events firmly soldered with Ginzburg's irony and humor. The work is inspired mainly by the author's memories, as well as by her efforts to recapture the atmosphere of the past, despite a certain agelessness that lingers in her family portraits. Her "I" is "the portrait of a voice," as Marguerite Yourcenar says, "like every story written in the first person."[19]

Lessico famigliare has been seen as an antifascist chronicle as recorded through the eyes of a young girl. In this respect, it may be suggested, Ginzburg succeeds where Lalla Romano fails. Romano remains shut within her private family life, only rarely turning her attention to public events. Ginzburg writes not only of herself and her domestic situations but also of how her family was affected by and tried to alter external events. She perspicaciously observes, for example, the evolution of language and literature during and after World War II. Because of the devastating effects of fascist censorship, real novelists and poets fell silent. But in the initial outburst of postwar enthusiasm, every writer, she writes tongue in cheek, suddenly became both a poet and a politician. The language of poetry became confused with the language of politics; words became equivocal, reality ambiguous. The complexity and obscurity of the "language" of the postwar world was such, however, that real writers, overcome by a sense of defeat, were once again forced to fall silent. "And the period that followed," writes Ginzburg, "was like a hangover, a period of nausea, languor, and tedium; and everyone felt . . .

deceived and betrayed. . . . And so each [writer] set out once again, alone and discontent, on his own path."[20] Analyses like this of the problems of Italy's literati make *Lessico famigliare* a highly useful tool in gaining insights into the cultural climate of postwar Italy.

Recording her family's lifestyle in Turin between the two world wars, Ginzburg draws word-portraits of some important political, social, literary, and academic figures from the Levis' circle of intellectual, antifascist friends. Their home had become a refuge for escapees from fascism and a meeting place for conspirators, including Natalia's future husband, Leone Ginzburg. The author meticulously conveys her family's growing sense of oppression as the fascist racial campaign intensified and Jewish families left or prepared to leave Italy.

Particularly noteworthy is the sensitivity the author brings to linguistic matters and lexical meanings (hence the word *lessico*, "lexicon," in the Italian title). The traits and qualities of her family members are recognizable by their vocal gestures and cadenzas, the musical stops and starts of the workings of their minds, their protestations and exclamations, the metaphysical leaps in the content of their uttered phrases. The word games, pet phrases, and all the esoteric references that characterize years of living together constitute a private language that binds the family indissolubly together and allows the five brothers and sisters, in later years, to live again in that former world: "one of those words or phrases sufficed for us to recognize each other . . . in the darkness of a cave, out of a million people. Those phrases are our Latin, the vocabulary of our past days, they are like the hieroglyphics of the ancient Egyptians or of the Assyro-Babylonians, they bear witness to a living nucleus that no longer exists but survives in its texts, saved from the fury of floods, the corrosion of time. Those phrases are the foundation of our family unity, which will survive as long as we are alive" (28).

The book's larger import is that Ginzburg, by describing her own close-knit family, implicitly praises the qualities of her parents, who instilled in their offspring the strictest ethical code, a physical and moral discipline, and an active vitality—in short, a hunger and love for life and knowledge. The Levis gave their children the affection and guidance that helped Natalia and her siblings grow into successful players on the Italian scene. The ever-present image of their mother, who loved Verlaine's poetry and music (especially *Lohengrin*), is that of an engaging, invariably cheerful presence in the home. If she was warm and energetic as a mother, as a wife she was an outwardly docile, submissive household manager for her difficult, scholarly husband. The multifaceted Professor Levi—a lover of England, Zola's novels, the Rockefeller Foundation, and the Valle d'Aosta's mountains and guides—was a gruff presence in the home, with his quirks and bursts of anger. But Natalia knows that his unwavering love for his family and his alertness to his children's need for guidance kept him awake at night to *almanaccare* (one of Ginzburg's pet verbs, meaning "muse upon" or "puzzle over" something). The author poignantly captures that unmistakable parental force that integrated the Levi household, so different from the families in *Tutti i nostri ieri*.

The strong, centered family with clear moral and intellectual values constituted a dignified, dramatic, and poetic world for Natalia Ginzburg. But Italy's families and children changed so drastically in the decades following World War II that by 1977 she was, according to one critic, bitterly "tearing to pieces her original idea of the family with the same savage and tribal glee as she had consecrated it."[21] Two novellas published in one volume in 1977, *Famiglia* and *Borghesia* (*Family*, 1988) reflect Ginzburg's awareness of shifts in society, altering relationships among generations, and changing Italian attitudes toward love, legitimacy, cohabitation, and sexuality. The two works confirm her preference for themes and situations that are elegiac, if not totally pessimistic. *Famiglia* focuses on an unhappy middle-aged male architect, shackled by the conventions of his upbringing, who urgently seeks a new lease on life. Undeservedly entangled in situations incompatible with his age and temperament, he may represent Ginzburg's own discomfort in the contemporary world. Similarly, the root cause of the woman protagonist's unhappiness and uneasiness in *Borghesia* is her inability to communicate with those around her.[22]

Shortly before her death in 1991, Ginzburg expounded on the difficulties facing the novelist:

> Whoever writes novels must be equipped with the present, the past, and the future, [and] must be able to believe in these three dimensions. Regarding the present, we see disorder, continuous change, precariousness. As for the past, it is filled with vice and guilt and is so heavy that we refrain from passing the load on to the new generation. As far as the future is concerned, it's best to say nothing. . . . So [to ask] in which style and in what sort of language one should write,

whether one should use the first or the third person . . . becomes irrelevant.[23]

But the ethical thread that runs through Ginzburg's entire oeuvre— that of rebellious stoicism in the face of life's events and cautious optimism that the individual can survive emotionally—still has and always will have value. Despite her deep personal bitterness at the very end of her life, compounded by political disappointment at the collapse of the utopian ideal of communism and the dissolution of the Italian Communist Party,[24] what she intimated in *Lessico famigliare* nevertheless applies: the outlook is dim; one is tempted to give in; but one must survive, sustain one's vital spirits, and find one's raison d'être in an idiosyncratic society.

SEVEN

ROSETTA LOY

Flesh and Blood Are Dust

A refined and sensitive author of "literature of memory," Rosetta Loy was born in Rome in 1931 of a Piedmontese father and a Roman mother. Of the well-to-do upper middle class, the family enjoyed the luxury of an apartment in Rome and a country home in Piedmont, with the result that Loy often sets her novels in those places, although the scope of her vision is universal. The review to which her name is attached is the prestigious *Paragone Letteratura*, to which she regularly contributes essays and short stories. The mother of four sons, Loy presently lives on the outskirts of Rome in a country setting on Via Flaminia, where she devotes herself to writing, but always with a sense of guilt for not dedicating enough time to others, especially her children. Catholic and conservative in her upbringing, Loy believes in the strength of the family unit. Her works describe the affection and sentiments that bind the members of a household and convey a sense of continuity. But she recognizes that her deep faith in the family, while offering a sense of protection, is at the same time a weakness in the face of the overwhelming social and industrial change that has been working to destroy the basic social unit in Italy.

The sounds and sights of the Italian North impress Loy most deeply and find a prominent place in her writings. She thought out a narration set in the Piedmontese massif of Monferrato, for example, by perusing a compendium of nineteenth-century events, keeping photographs of her paternal grandmother before her eyes, and skimming a dictionary of Montferrat dialect in search of words she had heard in her childhood and whose sonority fascinated her.[1]

Loy's first novel, *La bicicletta* (The bicycle, 1974), set in Rome and Piedmont and revolving around a tight-knit bourgeois family, won the Viareggio Prize for that year. Her second novel, *La porta dell'acqua* (The door of water, 1976), narrates a child's unconscious love for her governess. *L'estate di Letuqué* (Summer in Le Touquet, 1982) is a non-autobiographical story of a romance that failed. Her fourth novel, *Le strade di polvere* (Dusty roads, 1987; *Dust Roads of Monferrato*, 1991), although not a faithful reconstruction of her family, relates the gradual transformation of a paternalistic household in the region of Piedmont and won both the Viareggio and the Campiello Prizes in 1988.

The voices of Loy's characters sometimes sound like the choruses of Athenian drama, coming from a timeless afar. Her human dramas unfold against a background of muffled lamentation and primitive ritual, which serve to emphasize the cyclical nature of time and history. "Time," she writes in *La bicicletta*, "is crowded, stifled, locked in glass-covered photographs of young people turned old and of old people turned to dust."[2]

Dust is a hallmark of her works. It runs like a leitmotiv through her nonfiction, novels, and short stories, even appearing somewhat startlingly in one tale set against a watery background of rainy London's fountains and the wet banks of the Thames.[3] The author constantly suggests to her readers that just as all flesh must die, so all things, now dust, she must make live again. Through those clouds of dust that blur and dim our memories, Loy intends to show her love for life and her capacity to restore it to its previous effective state.[4] She seems to be answering, "I shall know," to William Cullen Bryant's "How shall I know thee in the sphere which keeps / The disembodied spirits of the dead, / When all of thee that time could wither sleeps / And perishes among the dust we tread?"[5]

La bicicletta is written in the rhythmic poetics of "literature of memory." Loy composes her sentences using an unusual punctuation (which is retained here in my English translations). The title of the novel symbolizes a generation of children, all of which rode bicycles: boys tie their fishing poles to them to go fishing in the Po; girls playing in the garden "pedal around the purple petunias, the gravel grinds under the bicycle wheels" (62); and the slow pace of the times is set by the father's bicycle "in the afternoons opaque with heat . . . propped against the cherry tree" (154). Swarms of bicycles fill the rice fields of the Po valley. The bicycle sets the pace in the first part of the novel, when Piedmontese tenant farmers save money under their straw mattresses, dreaming of moving to a town served by electric lighting (80, 85).

The tempo of the novel increases as the bicycle gives way to the motorcycle, the automobile, the truck, and the tractor. The new generation is different, and it is indifferent to the past. Children "don't leave time to listen and to become aware of changes, to adapt to the new era with its plastic garden-chairs, multicolored asters that substitute for the lilac petunias of the past. These children so different, strangers, indifferent, trample on relics . . . forget their toys on the lawn. Nobody rides a bicycle anymore" (154). The new generation shocks its traditional mothers by the behavior, for example, of young callers in the home: they drop in unexpectedly, use up the limited water supply, and stay uninvited to dinner. "There was a time," writes Loy, "when callers came bearing boxes of glazed marrons and sat in the Chinese parlor with their feet crossed, right hand resting on left knee, hat placed under the chair" (78). The novel's settings, from the sleepy time of bicycles, to the faster, more casual new generation, tell us that Rosetta Loy is not happy about the opening of prospects of a postwar industrial revolution in the plains and gently rolling hills of her beloved Piedmont.

Stock figures of "father," "mother," "boys," and "girls" appear in the first chapter of the book. Only gradually, as the story develops, do the children and their friends acquire names, while the "old aunts" and the servants hover vaguely in the background. This upper-middle-class family goes about the business of living in their Rome city apartment and their Piedmont country home. The family members are faceless but emerge clearly in their dominant personality traits: the physically and morally strong father; the worrying mother, who would like to tie pillows behind the heads of her roller-skating children "so that they don't break them" (12); the typical children with their typical quarrels and escapades and their adolescent love affairs, described lightly, humorously, and with compassion, but all boiling down to "riding pillion on a white papier-mâché horse" (87).

Every aspect of decrepitude is evoked in Loy's description of the "old aunts" in their long, dark dresses, kneeling piously in the family pew. All the infirmities of old age are captured in her use of color imagery combined with evocations of the weakening senses: the old aunts' smiles are of ivory grown yellow, like the keyboard of their piano; their eyes, once brown, now gaze "cold and straw-colored" (26). When the old aunts appear in the walkway, the children "disappear like darts"—in contrast to the oldsters' "slow steps and sudden memory lapses [and] faded lips that emit a breath that smells of decay" (102). In the end, the pathetic aunts are locked out of the external world because "dates and names escape their minds . . . they quarrel in loud voices because they are deaf" (138).

The war, too, is faceless. Mussolini and Hitler are there—far away—but the German soldiers are fearful and real: "at night the girls hide their heads under the sheets, once the lights go out a terrifying silence shakes the house" (9). The reader is made to feel the effects of war through tangible details of everyday objects, each with its sound, color, or texture. The appearance of the father in the domestic setting, preceded, in an effective image, by the turning of a key in the lock of the front door, indirectly communicates the war's realities: "The father is in the big dark entranceway with his bunch of keys hanging from a steel chain; these are not times for gold chains, gold to the fatherland" (7). These are times when a walnut or a tiny pear are coveted food items. The feeling of hunger is effectively conveyed by concrete, tangible images that locate hunger in unexpected parts of the body—nostrils, bones, and hands—each with its vivid characterization and specific detail. At school, there is "hunger in the red nostrils of the lay sisters who have colds, hunger in a cat's bones, hunger in hands . . . that rifle in a lunch bag" (8). But, despite all, war, hunger, and cold are nothing but a "mad desire to live" (9)—Loy's philosophy of life.

The reality of the war permeates everyday life. The burial of a German soldier is interwoven with the mundane rhythm of cooking and washing up. Shovelfuls of earth fall on the soldier's grave outdoors, while in the family's kitchen, plates slip into the dishwater, sounding like "stones in a landslide," and "the pastina swells in the boiling soup" (7). Loy evokes changes of seasons martially: "Spring launched an attack on garden vegetable patches and the German's grave" (12); summer "invades Americans English Southafricans soaking their khaki shirts in sweat" (17).

The boys bury the bodies of dead German soldiers strewn over the fields of Campo di Carne (near Rome), where army tanks "like prehistoric animals are slowly dying" (20). One of the boys, Giovanni, who spent the summer burying German soldiers, signs up "to go out and kill more" as a volunteer in the Army of National Liberation, which distresses his mother, whose "hazel-brown eyes become clouded with anguish" as she thinks of "that boy gone off to fight the Germans with a little holy medal around his neck and a sandwich, still a child who needed a shave only every other day" (21–22).

The family is gathered at the dining table on the rainy night when Giovanni is expected to return from his mission: "the father tapped with his finger among the crumbs"; "the rain dripped onto the brother's empty place" (23). Finally Giovanni—the prodigal son—appears. The mother "scoops spoonfuls of mashed potatoes from her own plate to her son's," while the servant, serving the meal in white gloves, listens to how Giovanni was assigned to cleaning latrines (23).

In the family conversation, "sentences interweave passing from one to the other together with the breadsticks the red wine and the salt." Food and mouth mix with political views and fears of postwar communism: "Giovanni eats his thick pastina in broth and the hollow of the spoon is coated with grease. . . . An impeccable [servant] gets ready to hear for the thousandth time a speech about Stalin, the red demon of the new 1950s." The mother and father discuss the deportations of kulaks, while "Maddalena rolls little balls of bread with her fingers . . . and her teeth, where pieces of almond nougat are stuck, chew slowly, with loathsome effort" (97).

Loy frequently focuses on the mouth, teeth, and food, picking up visual and aural details, transcribing their tastes, odors, and consistency with a sensuality that one critic sees as an erotic dimension of her pages:[6] "into the bread, white and compact, the teeth sink up to the gums" (27), writes Loy, or, "the crouton hisses under the metal of her teeth" (7). Her description of a freshly baked cheese soufflé (110), in its evocation of tastes, texture, and smells, is worthy of a Doris Lessing. Her "culinary" prose is like the eye of a camera, forever moving, focusing—in a single, often unpunctuated sentence—on combinations of unexpected elements: "The overcooked potatoes fall apart in the pan and white bubbles burst in the frying egg, the cat jumps down from the armchair. 'Have you seen the new well outside?' " (85).

The broad sweep of the camera moves the reader's eyes from heights to depths, from ground to sky, from inside the house to outside. Loy's unusual narrative technique shifts attention quickly from commonplace objects to artistic images of the vegetable, animal, and human domains. She creates unexpected juxtapositions of recollections of war with tranquil settings: "The dahlias bend under the jet of water and the seesaw balances itself in the midst of buzzing wasps, Giovanni is reading a book about the Nuremberg trials" (62). She captures poetically and artistically the immobility of shadows and shade, combining it with the mobility of humans and animals: "Dark furniture and grim portraits from which emerge the pale noses of the ancestors, in the garden the cat jumps down silently from the top of the wall" (49).

Each chapter of *La bicicletta* bears the name of a flower, plant, shrub, or tree that is evoked in the chapter but that is in contrast with the tragic content of each section. Even flowers evoke the horrors of war, illness and death, abortions and miscarriages. The postwar wedding ceremony of one of the children (Speranza) takes place in a musty church "without disturbing the dead solitude of the Romanesque columns or the stony odor of tombs" (126). Loy hauntingly describes the vanity of the dreams of those who were married in this church in the past: "It would be useless," she writes, "to try to find the imprint or a lasting stamp to mark the stone of life like the images carved into the pavements of basilicas" (127). The description of Speranza's opulent wedding reception at Rome's Grand Hotel is almost a caricature of this middle-class usage. Loy envelops the lushness of the affair in a heavy atmosphere and ends it with a grim conversation among some of the guests about the horror and tragedy of Dachau (129).

The era of motorcycles and automobiles has come. The pace of the novel quickens: postwar Italy is rich; its shops are filled with luxury items; hotels and hairdressing salons are astir; tuxedoed waiters bustle in restaurants; jewels flash at the opera. The small pleasures of the past have given way to double portions of shrimp cocktail (158–59). Nobler ideals are lost: "There was a time when Giovanni wanted to join Wiesenthal to help search out Nazi criminals, instead he wound up buying ice cream for his girlfriend or . . . taking her out dancing [and buying her] glasses of whiskey on the rocks" (142). Now the family's lifestyle has changed; there is no more loud, free laughter, no more quarreling in the family. Despite Italy's "economic miracle," "sadness sets its slanting rays with the afternoon sun," and "silent voids in which lizards flash gray" exist because family traditions and continuity have been swept away (137). Old homes are being remodeled to make room for "present and future husbands, children on the way" (137). As new bathroom fixtures are being installed, Loy reminisces sadly about the old-fashioned bath in "nonna's" [grandma's] day, when a washtub was set out in the sun to warm in the midst of the perfume of tomatoes and pear trees, and the water in the tub reflected the sky (137). Now, birds, ants, lizards, blades of grass, trees, wind, and clouds "come and go as tongues of cold" (115).

The era of bicycles has passed, but the family's silver forks, handed down from one generation to the next, remain. Now, however, the old farmstead is overgrown, the house is crumbling, ants have deserted the terrain, and the last old tenant farmer, who refused to budge from the land, has been carted off to the cemetery. There is desertion, desolation, and death. The father had left the farmstead to his son Michele, who goes there only to hunt from time to time. But even the hares are disappearing, and all traces of the past are being erased "in an expanding crepuscule that effaces every shadow" (154–55). At the very end of the novel, the children of the family recall the past. In their recollections, they bring alive the figure of the mother, who in turn evokes her own past; thus the novel, after having moved forward from the time of the bicycle to the time of the jet set, moves back again in time. Loy pedals backward to restore life and love to the family after all is turned to dust. She makes things of the past live in the present, even though the present time is not theirs. To the fatality and inexorability of "dust onto dust" she opposes her desire to bring sunshine into the buried past—and she succeeds.

Less acclaimed than her two prizewinning novels in the "literature of memory" tradition are Loy's second and third works. The title of *La porta dell'acqua* comes from Federico García Lorca's "Ni la mano más pequeña / quiebra la puerta del agua" [Nor can the smallest hand / breach the door of water], which serves as the novel's epigraph. The narrating "I" is a girl of about seven years of age, imprisoned in a rigid, sumptuous family cage. She performs all the rituals and devotional formulas required for a good Catholic education, but she is rewarded with only loneliness and a lack of understanding. Because her mother, who suffers from hyperanxiety, is usually absent, the child focuses her attention on the cook, the servant, the chauffeur, and especially the young German governess. *La porta dell'acqua* narrates the child's unconscious, exclusive passion for the patient but obstinate governess, whose professionalism causes the girl to experience her first disappointment in love. The book nicely balances the author's discreet criticism of upper-class society and her delving into the psyche of a forsaken child.

The narrating "I" of *L'estate de Letuqué*, Loy's third novel, is a young woman who relates the failure of an intense love affair. She tells how she was welcomed with open arms, then used, and finally rejected first by her lover, a fascinating Milanese intellectual, and then by his friends. The events unwind rapidly against a backdrop of political events in the post-Kennedy era, from the Soviet invasion of Prague to the demonstrations of young revolutionaries in the streets of Milan. The narrator's brief but deeply felt love affair brings little joy and much melancholy wrapped in Milan's subtle mist, which artistically smudges the characters, their gestures, and their recollections. Although the novel reveals Loy's sensitivity to masculine physicality, its dominant theme is love and the irreconcilable desires of men and women.[7]

Like parts of *La bicicletta*, *Le strade di polvere*, which won two literary prizes, is set in Piedmont, the Alpine buffer state, historically so important both to France and to Austria. Immutable Montferrat, the massif situated east of Turin and the scene of innumerable battles, is the real protagonist of the novel, with its winter snows that blot out all signs of roads, and its summer heat that raises white clouds of dust over parched earth. A fresco in Montferrat's Romanesque Vezzolano Abbey depicts three Dead Men and three Living Men, symbolizing the vanity and brevity of human life—dust to dust beneath the sod—which is the theme underlying Loy's novel. Her style in this work—albeit Italian and in the feminine—has been compared to that of Gabriel García Márquez in *One Hundred Years of Solitude*.[8]

Although the author harks back to the court of the Gonzagas of Mantua—because one of the family's most important strongholds was the easternmost town of the massif, Casale Monferrato—the historical time of the novel is not the Mantua Renaissance so well described by Maria Bellonci (1902–86) in her historical novels, such as *Segreti dei*

Gonzaga (1947) and *Tu vipera gentile* (1972). Rather, Loy depicts the Casale Monferrato area under French invasion and during the wars of independence against Austria (1859–70), which led to the unification of Italy as a kingdom under the house of Savoy.

Le strade di polvere is a "memory fabulation": a lived experience substituted by an imaginary adventure that the author believes in and narrates in concrete language. (Elsa Morante's *Menzogna e sortilegio* is another example of a "memory fabulation.") The events of *Le strade di polvere* are narrated in the tone of a romantic fable, against a magical Piedmontese landscape of gray skies and fog, and against a backdrop of patriarchal homes where the mysterious presences of founding fathers stalk at night.

The novel is the saga of three generations of the patriarchal family called the Gran Mastens, industrious landowning farmers of long standing, whose members have lived from birth to death in their big village home by Montferrat's Tanaro River. For about a century, the family has faced life's joys and tragedies with equanimity, in a home that smells of freshly baked bread and quince apples, of earth and honesty. Strongly attached to the land—to its rows of vineyards, orchards, and fields of corn and clover—the family respects the customs and superstitions of the villagers. In slow tempo, secret, tragic loves run their course, seemingly undisturbed by the momentous events taking place in Montferrat. The slow, rhythmic beat of the novel is its distinguishing characteristic. The narration takes place in what one critic has called "presentified" (not Proustian) time,[9] moving in dust-laden, arid regions, having neither duration nor density, and intermingled in the author's mind with recollections of her childhood. In the background are other personages who supply choral elements, adding their own faces, feelings, and dramas to those of the Gran Mastens. Ritually, they play out events in artistic patterns evocative of Greek tragedy: calm, followed by passion and crisis, then a return to calm. These grand choral effects lend both epic fullness and static tragedy to the work.

Even though the existence of the Gran Mastens seems sheltered, the book is about war—many wars. On Montferrat's battle plains, armies clash in the distant background. Men go to the battlefield, where their hopes and fears lie with them in the dust. The great facts of history lurk: the Crimean War; the 1859 war, which saw the establishment of Victor Emanuel II's headquarters in Montferrat; the sea battles on the Adriatic;

the Austrian advance stopped by Napoleon III's armies; the defeat of the hated Austrian commander, Josef Radetzky; and so on. Meanwhile, rural life in the little Montferrat village changes gradually: the male members of the family go to the city to study; the last daughter marries and goes off to live elsewhere; in the house remain only the old folk on their way to a dusty death. It is the end of an era.

The word *dust* is repeated constantly in all its substantive and adjectival forms as the novel draws to a close. In the last chapter it appears no less than four times in a single paragraph, in which the author skillfully guides the reader's eye upward from the dusty ground in a movement that ends splendidly in a symbolic dusty sun that rises as it sets: "Their feet sink into the thick dust as fine as powder. A dust that is on the hedges, on the scrubby grass along the roadside, in the hems of skirts. . . . A sunset that also seems to be of dust, dust and gold, rises from the earth toward the sky."[10]

In muted brown, white, and gray tones, Loy describes the vicissitudes of three generations of the close-knit, patriarchal farming family in a romantic, fablelike style. The physical and emotional hardships endured by the Gran Mastens are, however, real and cruel: worn-out clothing that scarcely protects from the cold, widespread contagious conjunctivitis and cholera, and natural catastrophes. But all the descriptions are toned down and softened by folklike superstitions that allow mysterious forces to make their comforting presence known. In the end, the reader is left in the twilight of an era, together with the old folk, who are "closed in an impassible circle of silence" filled only by the creaking and squeaking of the old home's timbers (240).

While the protagonist of *Le strade di polvere* is Monferrato, that of Loy's short-story collection *All'insaputa della notte* (Without the night knowing, 1984), is *la voglia d'amore* (longing for love)—a desire that in each story is led astray, unheeded, or unconsummated, because of fear, choice, circumstance, or force majeure. Unhappiness is the destiny of Loy's desirous and desirable, but fragile, heroes and heroines of the years between wars. Either they unwittingly render themselves inaccessible and unattainable, or they are forcefully separated from the object of their desire by sociocultural differences, scheming calculation, vileness, treachery, or death. Their loves are cruel and ill fated, illusory and disappointing. The protagonists are poised between desire and renunciation, and after playing muffled games of seduction and rejection, they end up as sorrowful, humiliated, or defeated combatants. "Happiness," writes Loy, "emits a tinny sound, thin in tone, atonic, without dreams and without reflections, it burns its wings thinking to create light."[11] Scenes of the daily life of the wealthy middle class are described through series of subtle images, phonograms, sensations, and recollections of sensations. Thus, the characters remain enigmatic and inscrutable, and they seem to be motivated by incomprehensible and unexplainable impulses. Their overriding feelings of bitterness and melancholy dimly presage events that culminate in the German offensive of 1 September 1939 and the outbreak of World War II—"the night" of the title, which knows nothing of the lives it hides. The end of the summer of 1939, over which destruction and death loom, coincides with painful adieus at the end of summer loves, troop-trains hurtling through the night, and a rampage of persecution against the Jews. At the same time, all the stories are thick with eroticism, even though they narrate the defeat of erotic desire. The tension of sexual desires is exasperated by waiting, extinguished by feelings of emptiness and failure, snuffed out by uncertainties.[12] The compact and intact bodies of smooth-skinned, suntanned young people seem almost immobile in their congealed sexuality. Loy's always beautiful feminine characters poise under the gaze of males who see them as beautiful because they are rich and refined.[13] The desire that fills the hearts and bodies of Loy's characters in *All'insaputa della notte*, however, is like a snake clinching its victim but never ejaculating its venom.

While the language and style of Lalla Romano and Natalia Ginzburg are simple and uncomplicated, Rosetta Loy's are complex and intricate. Her technique is distinguished by the visualization of sensations of color, sound, perfume, and desire. She transforms a sensation into a story; she evokes a historic period or a geographic place with a simple object or a gesture; a bicycle returns the reader to the past. She uses all the resources of poetry—comparison, analogy, metaphor, metonymy, and so on—in her conception of language as an animated universe informed by attractions and repulsions. Her unexpected word groupings evoke Victor Hugo's "Tout cherche tout, sans but, sans trêve, sans repos" [All seeks all, aimlessly, unceasingly, relentlessly]. Her works are sui generis; she belongs to no particular school or literary movement; her existential manner goes beyond the limits of temporal categories.

Though some of her detractors may accuse her of "traditionalism,"[14] there are other critics who consider her works masterpieces.

Lalla Romano considers Loy to be "intelligent, capable, and a bit snobbish,"[15] perhaps because her characters belong to the wealthy upper middle class, or perhaps because she remains aloof from the passions, ideas, and ideals of Italy's postwar period. Nonetheless, the reader is attracted to Loy's simple plots, her naturally witty style, and her subtle portrayals of characters. She succeeds in convincing her readers that, yes, all things return to dust, but artistic beauty, if well fashioned, does not. The intensity of Rosetta Loy's prose, her learned and erudite weaving of history, poetry, and human truths, and her gift for visualizing sensations guarantee that her name will remain on the list of outstanding Italian women authors of the twentieth century.

EIGHT
DACIA MARAINI

The Designing Woman

Dacia Maraini is undoubtedly Italy's strongest defender of all feminist causes. A prolific writer of prose, poetry, and drama and an outspoken bisexual, she is an author who both disturbs, because of her critical stand against the established order, and shocks, because she writes so freely about sex. Lately, however, her writing seems to have taken a new turn. After a second look at the feminist movement and resignation to the fact that trying to bring theater to the unprepared masses is futile, she looks to the historical past for literary inspiration. Her latest, Campiello Prize-winning novel, *La lunga vita di Marianna Ucrìa* (The long life of Marianna Ucrìa, 1990; translated as *The Silent Duchess*, 1992), unlike her previous, bitter, feminist works, is neither polemical nor scandalous. It is a poetic work to which she dedicated five years of effort, and it is so sober in its theme and so elaborate in style that some critics refer to it as her "first novel." Others have compared it to Giuseppe Tomasi di Lampedusa's *Il gattopardo* for its spirit and intensity of characterization. Her latest play, *Veronica, meretrice e scrittora* (Veronica, prostitute and poet, 1992), is based on the life of the sixteenth-century Venetian courtesan Veronica Franco, whose sexual activity became the substance of her poetry.

In focusing on the condition of women in Italy, Maraini has put maximum emphasis on sex and its deviations. She has placed full confidence in her own body and its desires: her communicative prose, splattered with signs of female imagery, depicts the female body as a receptacle of pulsations as well as a vessel of knowledge that can upset the established order.[1] Her novel *Lettere a Marina* (Letters to Marina, 1981), on the theme of lesbianism, defends any form of sexuality, including love between women, but only when this love is not imposed by fashion or ideology.[2]

Maraini's works deal invariably with the woman's endless struggle for liberation from centuries of female stereotypes and patriarchal strategy. On behalf of all women, she aims to make an impact on the male world. In all of her works, she vividly conveys images of the female as an object, "spoken" by the male, in a world that is not the woman's, because her "I" has been represented, conditioned, and distorted by the man's image of her.[3] She demonstrates this in uninhibited descriptions of sexual activity, but she places equal emphasis on the male and female bodies, transmitting a message that transcends sexual imagery per se.[4] That the fate of the male body concerns her equally as much as that of the female is demonstrated by her reaction to the electrocution of a male prisoner in the United States that was telecast in Italy: "Even the most hateful criminal has the right," Maraini wrote in a front-page newspaper article, "not to be seen in a moment when his body is being ravaged."[5]

Maraini believes that the designing woman, by not being submissive, can improve and change herself and society.[6] By diversifying her personal experiences and varying her activities, she can transform the couple's relationship.[7] Through the *inquietudine* (restlessness, uneasiness, anxiety) of her thoughts, senses, and eros, she can act forcefully on the male world and resolve crises by breaking openly with tradition.[8] Maraini's own varied activities over the years include the writing of more than two dozen books, comprising novels, short stories, poetry, and plays; journalism and documentaries for television; intense theatrical activity as both playwright and stage director; the cofounding of an experimental feminist theater; the founding of a women's cultural center in one of Rome's poor neighborhoods; campaigning for abortion rights and for the better understanding of feminism in an international context; and active participation in Telefono Rosa (Pink Telephone), an organization that succors battered women.[9]

Dacia Maraini is the daughter of the Sicilian princess and painter Topazia Alliata di Salaparuta and of Fosco Maraini, a half-English, half-Tuscan oriental scholar and ethnologist. She was born in Florence in 1936. Her father, having won a Japanese university exchange scholarship, moved his family to Japan in 1939, when Dacia was one-and-a-half years old. Because her parents were antifascists who refused to recognize Mussolini's Republic of Salò (as was then required of all Italian residents in Japan), the family was interned there in a concentration camp from 1943 to 1945.[10] Maraini recalls that when they were half-starved in the camp, her father, who understood Japanese psychology, cut off his index finger in a ritual (*yubikiri*) considered by the Japanese to be a proof of courage and honor, and thus he obtained a goat that could provide milk for his children.[11] Dacia's love and admiration for her father has marked both her life and her writings.

Returning to Italy after World War II, the family settled in Bagheria (near Palermo), in Dacia's maternal grandmother's Villa Valguarnera— the setting of *La lunga vita di Marianna Ucrìa*. Living between Bagheria and Palermo, Dacia began writing at the age of fifteen, publishing short stories in a school newspaper. After eight years of adolescence in the Sicilian environment, she fled the island to escape what she has referred to as the "schizophrenic *éducation sentimentale* of a girl in Sicily in the 1950s."[12]

Following her parents' separation in 1957, she and her father moved to Rome, where she now resides. She formed an important relationship with Pier Paolo Pasolini, with whom she traveled and made films; she founded a magazine, *Tempo di Letteratura*, with a group of young writers in Naples; and she began writing her first novel, *La vacanza*, published in 1962 (*The Holiday*, 1966).

Crudeltà all'aria aperta (Cruelty in the open air, 1966), in which she expresses her love for her father, was her first book of poetry; her most recent one is *Viaggiando con passo di volpe* (Traveling softly like a fox, 1991),[13] which she defines as a "poetic diary" of the last ten years of her life. The leitmotiv of *Viaggiando con passo di volpe* is the death of Alberto Moravia, her companion for eighteen years, but she concentrates as well on her travels, which are an expression of her "innate tendency toward nomadism."[14]

Like her contemporary, the feminist, literary critic, political writer, and social commentator Armanda Guiducci,[15] Maraini published in the 1970s confessions of various types of women to demonstrate that the abject state of females had a cultural basis in capitalism.[16] By the 1980s, however, feminists found that Marxism and socialism likewise rested on patriarchal structures—a discovery that Maraini narrates in "foul language . . . devoid of any commas"[17] in *Il treno per Helsinki* (The train for Helsinki, 1984), about a group of angry youths of the 1968 generation. The political and the personal are closely interwoven in this novel, as Maraini continued to expose the crippling myths and gender roles described in Italy's literary experiments of the 1970s.[18] But the central theme of *Il treno per Helsinki* is, according to Maraini, "male mystery": "Literature is full of books about the mystery of the woman. This, instead, is a book about the mystery of man. Armida Bianchi, the protagonist, loves Miele precisely because she can't figure him out."[19]

Although Maraini's texts have a strong feminist charge, she is an author who believes in the "variability of points of view that combine . . . to give life to the essential ingredient of the novel, which is irony."[20] She is a writer strongly given to ironies, which she utters with a dry mock. She protests the dichotomy between the sexes, the sense of weakness or inevitability that plagues the woman. The very title of her provocative collection of essays *La bionda, la bruna e l'asino* (The blond, the brunette, and the ass, 1987) is ironic because the book's epigraph— "When I speak to him, I speak to a person. When he speaks to me, he speaks to a woman"—reflects Maraini's postulation that women have always been referred to as a subclass, never as persons. The subtitle of the essay collection is *Con gli occhi di oggi sugli anni Settanta e Ottanta* (Looking at the 1970s and the 1980s with today's eyes). Reflecting on the feminism of the 1970s, Maraini writes that today the very concept makes people smile as though it were a "slightly ridiculous" historical exhibit in its "antiquated nakedness."[21]

The belief of young women today that equality of the sexes has been achieved is an illusion, Maraini sadly notes. Although she recognizes that good laws have been passed, she sees that they have also in some measure turned against women. The divorce law is in theory a progressive and just law, but in practice it brings solitude, misery, and abandonment to the older woman: "The same law that allows you to divorce is the one that condemns you to die alone," she says. "Man's sexuality has no limits. It lives as long as the man lives. The woman, at a certain age, becomes invisible [because of] social conditioning. . . . Passing a law won't change this."[22]

Ironizing on the subject of justice, Maraini wrote a feminist *racconto che si ispira dal vero* (tale drawn from true life) in 1985, entitled *Isolina: La donna tagliata a pezzi* (Isolina: The woman cut up into pieces). After rummaging in the archives of a scandalous crime case that occurred in Verona in 1900, she reconstructs the story of Isolina Canuti, an indigent, nineteen-year-old girl who was made pregnant by a military officer from an aristocratic family. Although she wanted the baby, Isolina was forced by her lover and his accomplices, including a military doctor, to abort secretly in the back room of a restaurant on a kitchen table. During the operation, she died. Her body, cut into pieces and buried, was soon discovered. During the ensuing trial, Isolina was made to appear to be a prostitute (which she was not), to absolve the officer and his accomplices. But even worse, the Italian prime minister, General Luigi Pelloux, to preserve the image of the army, "hindered" justice, and Isolina's assassins remained unpunished.

Maraini's sparse style in this thick, hard, tenaciously realistic book is as bare as the bones flung into Verona's common grave:

> Here, now reduced to bits, Isolina's broken bones were probably thrown: a fragment of tibia, a chip of her spinal column, a digital bone, a clip of cranium.
>
> There is something senseless about venting one's fury against the body of a young pregnant woman. Eliminating a life from life isn't easy. There always remains something irreducible, indestructible, that refuses to be destroyed. The Nazis, who couldn't completely eliminate the cadavers of the Jews, knew this well. . . . The bones remain, even though reduced to bits, to testify to the existence of a body that was once alive . . . [and that] continues to give signs of its existence silently but firmly, as if to say: it took nine months to give me a shape; it took years and years to make an adult out of me.[23]

Cinematographic montage, cutting and splicing, is Maraini's writing technique in *Isolina*. She saw the work as a ready-made film composed of newspaper clippings that gave the flavor of the era and that she set into quotation marks because the court proceedings had been destroyed. Although the portrait of Isolina is that of a double victim—a woman and a proletarian—the real protagonists have been seen as those who cling to convention even at the cost of human life. It is less a feminist work than an expression of Maraini's bitterness and irony on the subject of justice.

With only one notable exception, Dacia Maraini's protagonists are either young girls with no identity or rancorous, dissatisfied, lower-middle-class housewives. They tell their stories of social oppression and moral aggression. Maraini's confessional novel *Memorie di una ladra* (1972; *Memoirs of a Female Thief*, 1974)[24] and her *Donna in guerra* (1975; *Woman at War*, 1984, 1989)[25] illustrate how women's lives are structured by external, patriarchal demands. The male desire for the woman to act the fragile female has become so much part of her make-up that she represses a natural need for autonomy and independence and thus supports the very structures that oppress her.[26]

Memorie di una ladra is the result of Maraini's extensive research in the late 1960s on the deplorable conditions in women's prisons, where reeducation was aimed at producing model housewives. The novel also helped to dispel the myth that women can fulfill themselves outside the workplace. The female thief rails against the cowards who have betrayed her both in sex and in burglaries, landing her in jail.[27]

In *Donna in guerra*, an extreme expression of the plight of women in Italy in the early 1970s, Vanna, an elementary schoolteacher in Rome's suburbs, becomes increasingly aware of her subservience to her husband, Giacinto, a mechanic. Here Maraini characterizes the dichotomy between the sexes by using vocabulary and images linked to homemaking. She reproduces the societal ideal of the dutiful wife through detailed lists of domestic chores, which assume ritualistic connotations by their frequency and their rhythm.[28] Suna, Maraini's spokeswoman, asks one of the men in her underground leftist group:

—What does your mother do?
—Nothing, she stays at home.
—Do you have a maid?
—No.
—And so how can you say she doesn't do anything?
—Well, she stays at home, she does housework.
—That is she prepares lunch, she makes your bed, she washes your clothes, she irons your shirt, she does the marketing for you, she cooks, she washes the dishes. . . . Do you have any brothers or sisters?
—Six, two are still small.
—And who takes care of them?
—My mother.[29]

The sexual attitudes of the characters likewise underscore the male/female dichotomy: "You're in love with your duty," Suna tells Vanna.

"You don't get along sexually." "Not well," replies Vanna. "Giacinto says that sex counts very little when two persons love one another." "He says that," Suna retorts, "because it's convenient for him. . . . And what do you think?" "Nothing," the dutiful wife replies. "What Giacinto does I make mine. I have never ever thought of contradicting him. I believe he's better than me, that he's right, that what he says is good for both of us" (90).

Maraini deconstructs the traditional logic of lovemaking ("the female acts like a woman and stays at the bottom, the male acts like a man and gets on top" [257]) and redefines it: "Love is something you share, with kindness, with tenderness, without overbearing actions, and both people have to be happy" (258). She analyzes dependency, belonging, and exploitation—those structures that have traditionally defined love and consistently destroyed it. An excess of eroticism and pornography in Maraini's works is aimed, in part, at revealing an intimate, secret, female world that collapses the myths of conventional love, sacredness of the family, and the relationship between man and woman based on possession.[30] It also establishes a linguistic relationship between the writer and her narrative. "The modern writer," Maraini has affirmed, "needs to be outside of morals and at the same time inside language: he/she needs to deal with the general by using the irreducible, find the amorality of his/her existence through the generality of language."[31]

Maraini's first novel, *La vacanza*, tells of a fourteen-year-old girl, Anna, living in a convent boarding school. Anna feels that during her summer vacation she must "learn about life" before returning to the pious existence of the convent. But the impact of the "adult world," in which she is treated as an object of men's sexual desires, benumbs her. She mutely contemplates the curious antics of men: one youth strips her in a beach cabin; she meets an admitted homosexual; and a third man seduces her at his flat. Anna's "holiday" unfolds in 1944, as Italy awaits the outcome of the war without caring much which side wins. She lives in an atmosphere of small people struggling to survive bombings, fear, and the collapse of myths about Mussolini's invincibility in a doomed world (that of the Salò republic). An air of corruption circulates through the novel, but Anna is passive, and she returns to the nuns fundamentally untouched. She narrates in the first person, but the reader never knows her thoughts, probably because she herself does not know them, does not "think" them. This contradiction, Moravia notes in his preface to the 1962 edition, is what gives dynamism to the character of Anna, a very modern character in her complete alienation and marginal sensations.

L'età del malessere (1963; *The Age of Malaise*, 1963; also translated as *The Age of Discontent*, 1963), Maraini's second neorealistic novel, which she herself adapted as a screenplay, won her the Formentor Prize and international notoriety. Like *La vacanza*, it is an introspective narration modeled on the Moravian short story. It tells of the painful transformation of a seventeen-year-old sex object, Enrica, who lives in a poor section of Rome, has no desire to study, and is completely abandoned to her own devices. Her absentminded father spends his time building birdcages; her missing mother, who wears herself out in some dull job, is always tired. Enrica is never able to see herself as she really is; she is but a reflection of her rejecting mother.[32] She lives unconsciously, without emotions, experiencing only brief sensations of heat, cold, and boredom, and finding odd moments of pleasure when she makes love to Cesare, an eternal student from a good family. Cesare uses Enrica when he feels like making love or just to interrupt the routine of his studies. She accepts Carlo, a fellow student, and Guido, a mature lawyer, with the same indifference. Friendship with an eccentric countess is merely a temporary escape. After this period of senselessness, she convinces herself to start a new life—on her own. Aware of her worth as a woman, she now rebels against the degradation of her routine existence.

Two of Maraini's most successful novels center on handicapped women, symbols of the female condition, of the historical silence of women, of their cancellation from the world scene, and of their utter solitude within the family nucleus. Maria, the heroine of *A memoria* (By heart, 1967), is an autistic nymphomaniac who plays out a death wish. Her autism (absorption in fantasy as escape from reality) comes to an end after she fails in her search for the real values of human existence. Maria is inert in practical matters but active in scandalous, antisocial behavior. Evocative of Dostoyevsky's Lisaveta in *Crime and Punishment*, she roams the streets searching for erotic adventures with men of all kinds and classes, mostly young, which has been seen as perhaps an unconscious affirmation of Maraini's own sexuality.[33] For her social responses, Maria communicates through "exterior monologues" (the technique of *le regard* in the *nouveau roman*).[34] She moves her focus startlingly from the observation of particulars to transcendental truths, as she aims her monologues against middle-class values; against crass, prosaic individuals guided only by material concerns; against society's Babbitts and philistines. In the end, Maria plans the abulia that will lead to her own death, through the willful, systematic undermining of her health. Closed up in her apartment with only a few surrounding objects and no human contact, she lives out her last days in the eternal present and finally attains the absolute.[35]

Just as Maria's abulia may be taken as a symbol of the woman's solitude within the family, the deaf-mute heroine of *La lunga vita di Marianna Ucrìa* also is an outcast in her own home, where little consideration is granted her. Marianna, too, lives in an eternal present and attains the absolute without, however, seeking her own death. Rather, she develops her condition of nonbeing into a reservoir of strength. Initially inert as far as social matters go, she becomes more and more positive in her antisocial behavior, after the death of her unloved husband.

The story of Marianna Ucrìa's physical impairment is a poetic metaphor of the female condition. Her existence is sealed in the mysterious and disturbing silence of her mind. "In fact, the novel may be read as a metaphor of silence, of female mutilation," Maraini has stated. "Marianna's muteness is an expression of her desperation."[36]

The unusual story is set in Sicily in the late seventeenth and early eighteenth centuries—an age of darkness and an age of light, an age of misery and an age of splendor. Maraini imaginatively described both the oppression and the sumptuousness of the era. She excels in reconstructing libraries, feasts, balls, and carriages, as well as in recreating an intoxicating atmosphere of jasmine, wigs, tricornes, and snuffboxes. To capture the colors and forms of the period and to trace changes in style, set first by the somber court of Madrid and then by the more lustrous court of France, Maraini studied the history of fashion in depth.

The opening sentence of the novel introduces the reader, through a film technique, to two members of the aristocratic Ucrìa family framed in a mirror: "There they are—a father and a daughter: he blond, handsome, smiling; she ungainly, freckled, frightened. He elegant and untidy, his stockings hanging loosely, his wig askew; she tied into a dark reddish-purple corset that emphasizes her waxen complexion." That Marianna is deaf-mute is conveyed immediately: "The child follows her father in the mirror as he leans over, pulls his white stockings up over his calves. His mouth is moving but the sound of his words does not reach her; it dissolves before it reaches her ears. . . . They seem to be close, but they are a thousand miles apart. The child watches her father's lips, which are now moving faster. She knows what he is telling her, even though she does not hear him."[37] Maraini focuses specifically on all the body parts connected with the heroine's deaf-muteness: her father's mouth, her ears, her eyes that watch her father's lips, and so on. Silence takes shape through physical description.

As the father and daughter drive to their appointment, Marianna's reliance on her two hyperdeveloped senses—sight and smell—for her "knowledge of the whole world" is minutely developed by the author. The extraordinary personification of Marianna's alert and refined sense of smell (8) is an amazing intuition on Dacia Maraini's part of the recent discovery that the gene that builds the brain's cerebral cortex is almost identical to the one that coordinates the construction of the olfactory system.[38]

Marianna's imprisoned thoughts dwell on her love for her father, who is dozing in a corner of the carriage: "Signor father opened his eyes for a second and then fell asleep again. And if she were to give him a kiss? That cool cheek with the marks of an impatient razor makes her feel like kissing him. But she refrains because she knows he doesn't like mawkishness. And then, why awaken him when he is enjoying his sleep; why bring him back into another day of 'camurrìe' [annoyances, nuisances], as he says; he even wrote this on a sheet of paper in his beautiful, round, well-shaped handwriting" (8). The striking peculiarity of the novel is that dialogues are not spoken but written by the characters and that the heroine's every thought and sensation are transcribed as interior monologues.

Like her sister, Marianna is destined to marry and enrich the family with new heirs—or else to take the veil. But whereas Marianna's sister grew up in ignorance, she, being *mutola* (deaf-mute), was able to discover life through books. Maraini explains that "women [in eighteenth-century aristocratic Palermo], although enjoying the freedom to go out alone in their carriages or to have a cicisbeo, were condemned to ignorance. Marianna is an exception: since she has to express herself in writing, she has access to libraries and books; she becomes both a sharp observer of herself and a scholar. She knows Greek, Latin, French. . . ."[39]

To communicate with the world around her, Marianna, after having painfully learned how to decipher the written page, had to learn to write. She put her feelings and ideas into written words, changing her world of silence into a font of life and vitality. Whereas those around her are slaves of their words and prisoners of their noises, Marianna grows in self-awareness. She cherishes the silver writing case her father gave her, containing the tools with which to "speak." Maraini recognizes that in the figure of Marianna there is something of the "censured part" of her own self—that is, the part of her life spent in Sicily in the 1950s— which involved her love for her father: "I, too, was in love with my father. Not with his protection . . . but with his absence. . . . To him I owe my curiosity, my courage to be different, my autonomy. The desire to know and to read."[40]

Some of the finest pages in the novel are devoted to Marianna's arousing to the wonders of the Word as Logos—a divine gift to humans. Mediated through the heroine's sensitive spirit, the Word eventually integrates the deaf-mute Marianna with the rest of the world and introduces her to passion, sensuality, and even some picaresque adventures. She has been taught to bend her feelings to the demand of convention and reasons of family, but she never gives up her struggle to escape her prison of loneliness. She achieves mental freedom by cleverly molding silence into strength. Through the world of books, Marianna Ucrìa becomes cultured, reflective, and powerful. She is even able to capture the secret thoughts of others. She becomes *whole*.

Marianna is married against her will at the age of thirteen to a rich and much older uncle, whom she must respectfully call "signor marito zio." She must endure his rude, stupid selfishness as well as his sexual intercourse, like so many women not only in Italy's South but everywhere and continually. Her culture helps her blot out the horror of those moments:

> Marianna recalls their hasty couplings in the dark, he armed and implacable, she far removed, petrified. They must have been droll to look at, stupid, as only those can be who repeat without a glimmer of discernment a duty that they don't understand and for which they are not cut out.
>
> And still they have five live children and three who died before birth, which makes eight; eight times they met under the sheets without kissing and without caressing each other. An assault, a coercion, a pressing of cold knees against her legs, a rapid and angry explosion.
>
> Sometimes, closing her eyes to her duty, she distracted herself by

thinking of the mating of Zeus and Io, of Zeus and Leda, as described by Pausanias or by Plutarch. The divine body chooses an earthly simulacrum: a fox, a swan, an eagle, a bull. Then, after long ambush in the oak groves, a sudden apparition. There is no time for a single word. The animal curves its claws, spikes the nape of the woman's neck with its beak. . . . A flutter of wings, panting breath on her neck, teeth cutting into her shoulder, and it's all over. The lover goes off, leaving you sore and humiliated." (125)

The destination of the Ucrìa carriage in the novel's opening episode is the vicarage of Palermo, where Marianna is to witness a hanging. Why? Because her father knows that her deaf-muteness was caused by sexual attack when she was still a small child. He hopes that another shock—the witnessing of the hanging—will cure her. Marianna, for her part, had repressed the rape incident in her mind: "One day, without any reason, she had become deaf and dumb. Silence took hold of her like a sickness and perhaps like a vocation. No longer to hear the jolly voice of signor father had seemed very sad to her. But then she grew used to it. Now she feels a sense of joy looking at him speaking without grasping the words, almost a malicious satisfaction" (16–17). Later in the novel, when Marianna is delirious from high fever and the physician is bleeding her, she opens her eyes to look up at the bearded man. Her repressed recollections reconstruct the rape, and she suddenly realizes that her father was an accomplice in that violence: "But who is this man pressing against her and who has a strange, unpleasant odor? Someone who had disguised himself as someone else. Her signor marito? Her signor padre? *He* would be capable of disguising himself as a joke. At that moment, an idea strikes her from head to foot, like an arrow: for the first time in her life she understands with total clarity that it is he, her father, who is responsible for her mutilation. . . . It was he who had cut out her tongue, and it was he who had filled her ears with molten lead so that she could not hear any sound and would revolve perpetually around herself in the realms of silence and fear" (192–93).

Now, in the vicarage of Palermo, the scene of the horrible, bungled hanging takes place before the frightened Marianna's eyes. But the miracle does not occur: "Signor father . . . bent over his daughter . . . touches her as though he were expecting a miracle. He seizes her chin, he looks threateningly and supplicatingly into her eyes. 'You must speak,' his lips say. 'You must open that damned, dumb fishmouth of yours!' The child tries to part her lips but cannot utter a word. Her body shakes uncontrollably. . . . " (22).

The language of the first part of the novel reflects the obscurantism, rigidity, and religious oppression in seventeenth-century Sicily. But in the second part, which unfolds in the eighteenth century, Marianna breathes more freely, because her husband has died, and because, on the sociopolitical scene, Palermo is increasing its contacts with the French and the English. Palermitans in the eighteenth century were reading Voltaire and Rousseau, and a spirit of rethinking of institutions prevailed. The change of style in the novel reflects the change of atmosphere, from plodding heaviness to heady lightness.

Now forty-five, Marianna has finally discovered sensual passion. Freeing herself from a life of constricting and conditioning roles, shedding all reserve and countering any hypocrisy, she accepts her own desires and consciously chooses to enjoy a voluptuous affair with the young Saro. In two crucial scenes of typically female experience, she gives mute expression to her love for her son, Signoretto, and gives herself easily and joyfully to Saro, as though she were discovering body language. "There is a parallelism between word and body," Maraini has explained.

> One might say that separating the word from the body is a female experience because the word, as an institution, does not belong to us historically. For this reason, women have become accustomed to expressing themselves with their body; they have always used the weapons of seduction, glances, smiles. In Marianna's case, however, it's as though the word and the body went off together. . . . Precisely because she is not like other women, she doesn't even know how to use the language of the body. Her sexual relations with her husband are endured as violations, her pregnancies as encumbrances. Then her fourth son . . . invents . . . a physical language and allows her to reconcile herself with her body. And finally her lover, with whom she discovers tenderness and love.[41]

But Marianna realizes that her relationship with Saro can never be a total love. Breaking openly with tradition, she flees Sicily, leaving her lover and her grown children forever. Her decision is similar to that of Sibilla Aleramo's designing mother in *Una donna*. The choice of both women is not ideological but rather involves a more mature relationship with themselves. Through well-crafted images, Maraini portrays the deaf-mute Marianna, "half fox, half siren," now at last free to design her own destiny. As a woman, she is determined to make an impact on the male world, with the "tail [of her past] tucked up under her skirts" (256).

"I write because I am tracking down an image, my nose to the ground, like a dog sniffing out truffles," Maraini has stated,[42] and her prose style does have canine force. But she has always known how to save her characters and situations from being swallowed up and disappearing under the effects of dubious taste. In her early novels, she urgently transmitted a message of protest against patriarchal stereotyping of women by using first-person narration, slang, and vulgar dialogue, in tune with her conviction that "when you write, you have to take into account how people talk, use a language that comes close to their way of speaking and that is understandable to them."[43] Today, she uses a limpid, rational, and sober, "neoilluministic" prose style. She devoted particular care, in *La lunga vita di Marianna Ucrìa*, to what she calls the "cantabile e ballabile" [singable and danceable] quality of her writing: "Poetry is a mathematical object just as music is mathematics. . . . I have tried to make these little mathematical operations danceable through language."[44]

NINE

MATILDE SERAO
ORIANA FALLACI
CAMILLA CEDERNA

Three Women Journalists

Matilde Serao (1856–1927) was Italy's first woman journalist and the prototype of the versatile contemporary woman journalist. Sometimes, for a single newspaper edition, Serao would write the political editorial, the literary column, and the society page, all under various pseudonyms. Today, Miriam Mafai, Lina Sotis, Giuliana Del Bufalo, Sandra Bonsanti, and others share Serao's many-sidedness and move at a rapid, daily-newspaper pace. Like Serao, they are more scrupulous than their male colleagues, and having two métiers—domestic and professional—their life is doubly difficult.

Camilla Cederna (b. 1921) and Oriana Fallaci (b. 1930), in the view of younger contemporaries, are representatives of a lifestyle that is no more: working for weekly publications while still having time for private life, for cultivating friendships, and even for battling between themselves (Fallaci sued Cederna for slander in 1990). Today's frenetic world of journalism is very different from that of the 1950s and the 1960s, when Cederna and Fallaci were making their debut on the scene.

Fallaci may be placed in the mainstream of Italian journalism, which includes Serao's husband, Edoardo Scarfoglio, and Curzio Malaparte. Theirs is "literary journalism," characterized by linguistic overabundance. Cederna is in the mainstream of *giornalismo di costume* (journalism of manners; social criticism and comment). Her main weapons in her fight against Italy's vices and defeats are irony and her vision of the truth. But though Cederna's and Fallaci's approach to journalism in midcentury was inevitably very different from today's, they nonetheless remain models of courage and honesty in the profession.

Matilde Serao

Matilde Serao was born in Patras, Greece, to Paolina Bonelly, a Greek citizen born in Constantinople and a descendent of the princes of Scanavy,[1] and Francesco Saverio Serao, a Neapolitan patriot and journalist who was forced into exile in 1848 because of his anti-Bourbon political ideas. After 1860, Matilde, an only child, spent her early years in Italy alone with her mother until her father could return to his homeland, after the fall of the Bourbon monarchy. Mother and daughter lived first in the countryside at Ventaroli, Serao's hometown in the province of Caserta—where the child mixed with the poor peasants of the South— and later in Naples. She grew up as a tomboy: "I didn't play with dolls, but spun tops instead; I didn't know how to walk—only run . . . gallop . . . and jump. I was neither graceful nor gentle—more like a boy. I was eight and didn't know how to read or write, I didn't want to sew and I didn't want to knit."[2] Her mother supported the family by giving English and French lessons at home; Matilde describes her as a "highly cultured, intelligent, angelic, divine woman."[3] Paolina Bonelly remained head of household throughout her entire short life, which ended in 1879 at the early age of forty-four, from tuberculosis. Francesco Serao worked only sporadically, which meant that Matilde would replace her mother as the family's breadwinner.

To her mother's distress, Matilde refused to study as a child. But later, forced to sit at her sick mother's bedside, she learned to read. For their lessons her mother used an illustrated edition of Shakespeare, which Matilde read "three times from beginning to end and love and hate sank into my childish soul."[4] She also learned French from her mother, who kept her in school long enough to complete her secondary studies. Matilde earned a teaching certificate but never taught; instead, she found employment in the state telegraph offices from 1874 to 1877.

Later she joked to her journalist friend Olga Ossiani that she dispatched forty-three thousand telegrams in one year for eighty miserable lire a month. *Il romanzo della fanciulla* (Young girl's tale, 1886)[5] contains two early stories written in a gritty style, based on her experiences at school and in her job. She was among the first to write about school and the working world based on her personal observations.

Beginning as a "populist" author, Serao made the public aware of the plight of peasants and the lower middle class, with whom she identified viscerally. Even when she later became a militant representative of Italy's naturalistic school of verism, she remained sentimental about the exploited classes and refused to contribute to publications whose materialistic and "exclusive realism is not mine. What I mean by realism is life, all of life, with its elevated poetry and its modest prose, with its generous impulses and its real misery—I mean tumultuous passion and sweet loves."[6] Her earliest sketches and novelettes were subsequently gathered under the title *Dal vero* (Living models, 1879), which offers a moving picture of the Naples of the nineteenth century. Only later did she also write repeatedly about elegant upper-class life. There, her true inspiration goes astray.

Most of Serao's life was spent in Naples, the city she loved, with whose people she identified, sharing their fatalism and deepest feelings. But the Naples that she knew and that she considered a vital city of intelligent people was devastated by cholera, unemployment, water shortages, dilapidated buildings, overcrowding, promiscuity, and administrative abuses. She railed against the government of the newly united Italy, denouncing its politicians for neglecting her city. She demanded that Naples' greenery be saved, more schools be opened, and tourism be increased. She demanded an end to the exploitation of women workers. City hall, she cried, must be swept clean of its dishonest hacks. In a series of nine reportages written when cholera broke out in 1884, Serao provides descriptions as powerful as Goya engravings. When government officials suggested razing some of Naples' worst slums, she wrote intelligently in *Il ventre di Napoli* (The belly of Naples, 1884), "It's not enough to gut the belly of Naples: practically the whole city needs to be rebuilt."[7] She explained the pointlessness of reconstructing three or four of the oldest, most fetid parts of Naples without a total remaking of the city through social and economic reforms. How right she proved to be: Naples still sees its problems unanswered today, one century later.

Figures of all social classes—nobles, the bourgeoisie, the hoi polloi—walk the pages of the ambitious novel Serao considered her masterpiece, *Il paese di cuccagna* (The land of plenty, 1891). The entire population of Naples is under the spell of their passion for the lottery—whose illusive and elusive winnings generate only more poverty, degradation, and crime. "The lottery," Serao had written in *Il ventre di Napoli*, "is Naples' alcohol" (61). Although critics consider *Il paese di cuccagna* to be awkward, its plot fragmented, and its moralizing objectionable, Serao is at her most humane as she immortalizes scenes of nineteenth-century Naples.

After leaving the telegraph offices in 1877, she dedicated herself exclusively to writing. Even though her father's métier was second nature to her, her first experiences were discouraging: "I carve out my niche by dint of shouting and pushing, with a dogged determination to succeed, but no one ever helps me," she wrote in 1878. Her father had introduced her to the many political-literary newspapers of the time: *Il Piccolo, Corriere del Mattino, Il Giornale di Napoli*, and, outside Naples, *Gazetta Letteraria Piemontese, Illustrazione Italiana*, and *Roma Capitale*. She worked indefatigably, elbowing her way through the editorial world "without paying attention to the weaknesses of my sex, and moving along on my path as though I were a young man."[8]

At the same time, she published a collection of novelettes, *Opale* (Opal, 1878), under the pseudonym Tuffolina. Serao's first novel, *Cuore infermo* (Weak heart, 1881), set in an aristocratic ambience filled with frivolous luxury, tells the story of Beatrice Revertera, a noblewoman with a heart disease that forbids her from making love. But the inevitable occurs. As a result, Beatrice must die. *Cuore infermo* not only appealed to the reading public; it earned Serao an invitation to become a permanent editor of the Rome newspaper *Capitan Fracassa* (published from 1880 to 1891). The exceptional offer to a woman—made in the year 1882, early in the reign of King Humbert I—naturally stirred envy, malign, and calumny, which did little to deter Serao. Declaring to the editor of *Corriere del Mattino* that it was impossible to work in Naples—"too much beauty, too much poetry, too much sea, too much Vesuvius, too much love"[9]—she moved to Rome with her father in 1882.

One of the most famous newspapers of the time, *Capitan Fracassa*, whose offices were located above the Morteo beer-house on Rome's famous Via del Corso, was directed by the brilliant Luigi Vassallo-Gandolin. Important collaborators included Gabriele D'Annunzio (who settled in Rome the same year Serao did); Giovanni Verga, whose *Il marito di Elena* appeared in the pages of the newspaper in 1882; and the polemical journalist Edoardo Scarfoglio, Serao's future husband. Serao was now to begin a fifteen-year period of creative activity in Rome, in harsh contact with the strictly masculine world of journalism. Nothing daunted, and with the "spirit of a gladiator [who] needs an arena,"[10] she accepted all the assignments flung at her, meeting the requirement of two thousand lines of print for three hundred lire a month, as stipulated in her contract. This brilliant young woman covered a bewildering number of areas, from literary criticism, to fashion and society, to interior decoration. She wrote about Franco-Russian relations, masked balls, city planning, and Neapolitan art. She covered a literary symposium as easily as a Darwinian conference. By way of digression, she publicly questioned the legendary wickedness and evil of Lucrezia Borgia and Catherine de Médicis, forcing her readers to rethink their judgments of these women. By dint of perseverance, she was rewarded with the honor of having her first editorial appear on the front page of *Capitan Fracassa* on 6 March 1882.

Although Serao had succeeded in making her debut in Rome's fashionable salons, her unattractive physical appearance worked against her. The upper class looked on this lumpy and bizarrely dressed independent journalist with curiosity rather than admiration. She actually enjoyed this new lifestyle, while her own intellect helped her to stand up to the ironies of her high-class public.

Serao's stories and novels had now begun to be serialized in the pages of *Capitan Fracassa*. Her name appeared also in the columns of the literary journals *Fanfulla della Domenica*, *La Domenica Letteraria*, and *Cronaca Bizantina*, as well as in the important review *Nuova Antologia*, alongside the signatures of D'Annunzio and Capuana. In the ambience of *Nuova Antologia*, she met Count Giuseppe Primoli, who would be helpful in making Serao's works known in France. Primoli judged her 1883 novel *Fantasia* (Fantasy)—whose erotic heroine has been described as a Neapolitan Madame Bovary—to be "comparable to the best French novels."[11]

Although she wrote for *Capitan Fracassa* under such varied pseudonyms as Chiquita, Angelo di Cabruna, Paolo Spada, and sometimes even Capitan Fracassa, Serao remained herself when she authored three works inspired by her Rome experiences: the novelette *La virtù di Chec-china* (Checchina's virtue, 1884), an example of southern Italian realistic writing subsequently analyzed by Natalia Ginzburg, who compared it with Tolstoy and Maupassant;[12] *La conquista di Roma* (The conquest of Rome, 1885), a novel that documents, in the style of Zola, a provincial parliamentarian's arrival in the capital (evocative of Serao῀ ῀n arrival); and *Vita e avventure di Riccardo Joanna* (Life and adventures of Riccardo Joanna, 1887). All of Serao's first impressions of the development of Rome under the reign of King Humbert I are fixed in verbal pictures that give the reader a good feeling for the Rome of a century ago and that will certainly survive the wearing effects of time.

The more Serao produced, the lazier her father became. Out of sheer indolence, he allowed his daughter to support him, to pay for his cures and his vacations.[13] Serao's last article for *Capitan Fracassa* appeared on 27 January 1885. One month later, she married Eduardo Scarfoglio, with whom she had four sons. Scarfoglio's striking personality, his excesses and his egocentricity, was probably the inspiration for many of Serao's male narrative figures. He was a megalomaniac, a warmonger, a colonialist, and a pitiless critic/desecrator of his literary contemporaries—in part maybe because he was an unsuccessful author. The couple founded the *Corriere di Roma*, which was more a vehicle for Scarfoglio's personal rancors than a solid political-literary sheet. The *Corriere di Roma* saw publication only from 1885 to 1887, after which the Scarfoglios moved to Naples at the invitation of Matteo Schilizzi, a banker from Leghorn and the owner of *Corriere di Napoli*—a newspaper dedicated to the restoration of morality to Naples. After a falling out with Schilizzi for political and personal reasons, the Scarfoglios stopped writing for the *Corriere di Napoli* (which folded a few years later) and founded their own *Il Mattino* in 1892. Notable contributors to *Il Mattino*, which rapidly gained prestige and a wide reading public, were D'Annunzio, Capuana, and the colorful journalist and poet Countess Lara (pseudonym of Evelina Cattermole, 1849–96). Scarfoglio's name appeared as owner and director of the couple's newspaper, the political tendency of which was liberal-moderate. He filled its pages with his polemical and satirical articles; she with her polemical articles plus short stories and serialized novels. Continuing to use her *Corriere di Napoli* pseudonym of Gibus (the collapsible Parisian opera, or top, hat, intended as a symbol of aristocracy and elegance), she wrote a "frivolous" and successful society column entitled "Api, mosconi e vespe" (Bees, blowflies, and wasps). She wished to set herself up as a "mediator" between the hoi polloi and the ruling classes, whose refinement she placed in view as models of social behavior. Even though the content of many of Serao's articles seemed outwardly revolutionary, actually she conveyed messages of conservatism, propriety, and respect for sacred traditions. Her reading public consisted mainly of women, with whom she could avoid questions of principle, preferring to ease them into moderation, social correctness, and conformism. It was she who had been responsible for the conservative—even reactionary—tone of the *Corriere di Roma*, but without colliding with her husband's radicalism. Two of her novels of this period, *Addio, amore!* (Farewell, love! 1890) and *Castigo* (Punishment, 1893), are the fruits of her psychological research into women's aspirations. They lack the spontaneity, however, of her former Neapolitan novels.

In 1902 Serao founded her own small but successful weekly literary review, *La Settimana*, whose contributors were Luigi Capuana, Benedetto Croce, Edmondo De Amicis, D'Annunzio, Antonio Fogazzaro, Neera, Giovanni Pascoli, and Luigi Pirandello. *La Settimana* lasted only until 27 February 1904, perhaps because it did not satisfy Serao's love for the excitement of producing a daily newspaper. The literary review lacked the fever of last-minute preparation, the daily need for an improvised article, for a passionate discussion of daily events. She preferred the disorder and composition rhythm of a daily paper, the acrid odor of the printing press running all through the night.

Serao traveled extensively—throughout Italy and to France, Egypt, and Palestine—even as she collaborated on four other periodicals and wrote endless novels and short stories. *Nel paese di Gesù* (In the land of Jesus, 1899) tells about her trip to the Holy Land—a mystical journalistic trip that confirmed her belief that traveling, like writing, unfolds elsewhere, in a carefully sought domain of moral independence. For Serao, travel meant freedom and autonomy: "To live is not necessary," she wrote to a friend in *Lettere di una viaggiatrice* (Letters of a woman traveler, 1908), "but to be free is. And traveling contains the sublime illusion of freedom."[4]

The Scarfoglio-Serao marriage provided a rock-hard foundation for a professional alliance. But his infidelities and lack of work constancy, as well as the political differences between husband and wife (he a colonialist and warmonger; she a monarchist and pacifist) kept them apart. The aftereffects of the Seredo inquiry into administrative corruption in Naples,[15] involving the director of *Il Mattino*, traumatized Matilde and worked to bring about the Seraos' personal and professional separation. The embittered Matilde, separating legally from her husband in 1904, moved in with a lawyer, Giuseppe Natale, despite her extolling of the family institution.

She now undertook, single-handedly and in total opposition to her husband's *Il Mattino*, the founding and directing of the daily political-literary morning paper *Il Giorno*, her most important journalistic endeavor. Thanks to her name and to her social columns, "Mosconi" and "Piccola Posta"—in which she answered questions concerning etiquette, wrote horoscopes, and provided advice for lovers—the paper was a success. Although she showed sympathy for socialism and strikers,[16] the paper's political line was faith in the monarchy and especially in the queens of Italy; opposition to the Left; pacifism; and antifascism. Serao signed and published in the pages of *Il Giorno* Croce's *Il Manifesto degli intellettuali* in opposition to fascism. She continued to direct her newspaper, despite raids by the fascists during the 1920s, until her death from a heart attack at her worktable in 1927. The year before, although she had softened her attacks on the government in response to pressure from her financial supporters, the Nobel Prize eluded her, probably because of the antimilitarism of her novel *Mors tua . . .* (Thy death . . . , 1926).

Serao was at the pinnacle of her fame when she founded *Il Giorno*: twenty-five thousand copies of her books had been printed in Italy, one thousand in France. Paris acclaimed her—the dream of all authors of the time. Her translator was Georges Hérelle, who had also translated into French works by D'Annunzio, Verga, and Fogazzaro.[17] It was thanks to her connection to the French Catholic and conservative writer Paul Bourget that she had been brought to French public attention. Although her outlook on life was secular, under his influence many of her works bear a religious imprint. Dedicating her 1901 novel *Suor Giovanna della Croce* (Sister Giovanna of the Cross) to Bourget, she was proclaiming, in a way, her renunciation of the fascinating world of high society in favor of a universal morality with no social barriers. Yet during the last twenty years of her life, she persisted in setting her novels—not her best—against an aristocratic background.

Serao was the most fashionable woman writer between 1905 and 1927. Benedetto Croce recognized her "penetrating intelligence" and unique capacity for describing female erotic passion, even though he preferred her naturalistic "program" novels, such as *La ballerina* (The ballet-dancer, 1899). She found translators and readers for her "sentimental" stories practically everywhere in Europe. She stirred the hearts of duchesses and maids, but she never gained the consideration of artists and critics.[18] She lived in two different worlds: one international, mundane, and mystical; the other Neapolitan and veristic. She was a conservative diehard yet cutting in her denunciations of social injustices. She was an antimilitarist yet supported the Italian occupation of Libya. She was hard and ironic as a journalist yet sentimental and maternal as a woman. She was family-bound and promarriage yet libertarian. She opposed the conventional feminist movement of the early twentieth century yet championed women's emancipation. She was the only woman to have founded her own newspaper and to have continued to publish it for twenty-three years; the only woman to engage the government in a civil battle that included denunciations of the exploitation and degradation of women in the marketplace; and the only woman—with the exception of his mistress—who did not allow herself to be circumvented by Mussolini.

Her opposition to feminism, which particularly irked Grazia Deledda, dates back to 1876, when she was only twenty: in her article entitled "Votazione femminile" (Women at the polls), which appeared in the newspaper *Il Piccolo*, she dissociated herself from those who supported the woman's right to vote. In a front-page article of *Il Giorno* (7 November 1906) entitled "Suffragettes," she argued that the condition of women in Italy was different from that in France and England, and that the Italian woman, before aspiring to the vote, should first aspire to a better and more dignified social position. When, in 1925, women did gain the franchise in local elections only, Serao protested, crossing swords with feminists in the pages of *Il Giorno*.

The stand she took against divorce easily swayed her readers: she opposed the dissolution of the sacred bond of marriage and the severing of ties between parents and child. She argued that divorce could benefit only the wives of thieves and assassins: other divorcées would simply become merchandise that men could legally buy and sell among themselves. More probably it was Serao's conservative conscience that led her to oppose divorce.[19]

Her opposition to the woman's vote and to divorce may be explained also by the fact that she had steadily before her eyes the realities of the life of Neapolitan women. The poverty and ignorance of the poor ones and the complicity of the wealthy ones with their husbands and lovers were factors, she felt, that precluded the casting of a critical and responsible vote. As far as divorce was concerned, she felt that it would always be the weak who would be victimized—that is, women and children. But Serao's opposition to equality between the sexes in educational matters cannot be defended. She maintained that higher studies lay beyond the sphere of the average female intelligence, and she proposed instead a mediocre female model in the school system, tailored to suit the needs and interests of her vast reading public.

Serao describes women as easy prey to social snobbishness, attracted by the next higher rung on the social ladder, captivated by suave, dashing males. Ladies of the upper classes hide their secret passions behind their frivolous fans as they savor multicolored sherbets and fancy pastries. The lowly women of Naples, in an often-quoted portrayal, "are thirty but look fifty, they are bent and balding, their teeth are yellow and black, they walk as though they were lame, they wear a dress for four years and an apron for six months. They don't complain; they don't cry; before they reach the age of forty, they go to die in a hospital of malignant fever, pneumonia, or some other horrible disease. And how many of them succumb to cholera!" (*Il ventre di Napoli*, 37). But even though Serao understands women so well, delves so deeply into their psychological motivations, and shares so intimately their passional conflicts, her female figures seem reduced to stereotypes stepping out of Naples' slums or glittering salons, mechanically and voicelessly.

In her journalistic articles, Serao wrote frequently about her women friends—Neera, Sibilla Aleramo, the journalist and writer Gemma Ferruggia, and Countess Lara—as well as about other contemporary Italian and French women writers. She also serialized a novel by Edith Wharton in the pages of *Il Giorno*. Upon reading Sibilla Aleramo's descriptive account of her lesbian love affair with Lina Poletti in *Il passaggio* (see chap. 2), Serao dedicated to the subject a piece of writing that goes far in exalting personal choices in life and in art, in the name of the "myth of freedom." Hers was the only voice raised in defense of Aleramo over the din of Italy's militant critics and prudes.

But it is the figure of Eleonora Duse whom Serao evokes most frequently in her articles. She met Duse, the young actress performing at the Teatro dei Fiorentini in Naples, in the autumn of 1879. So began a long friendship marked by frequent encounters and an intense correspondence lasting until Duse's death in Pittsburgh in 1924. Serao's true, secret love was for artists—including theatrical artists—and especially for Duse, whose career she followed closely, throughout Italy and even to Egypt. Duse's fragility and poor health stirred maternal feelings in Serao. At the same time, she saw the actress as a woman of scandal, a femme fatale who fascinates other women and is fascinated by them in a play of motherliness and eroticism. Duse also incarnated the freedom to transgress radically—the very freedom that Serao the journalist, mother, wife, and mistress never completely achieved. The illegitimate daughter born to Serao and Giuseppe Natale was named Eleonora in honor of her godmother, Eleonora Duse, who was planning at the time of her death to found a Teatro delle Donne (Women's Theater) with Sibilla Aleramo in Matilde Serao's house in Naples.

The novel most closely linked to Serao's experience as a journalist is *Vita e avventure di Riccardo Joanna*. It sums up perfectly the life of a struggling journalist whose entire existence is devoted to the newspaper. The work focuses realistically—but not without some passages of decadent aestheticism—on the poverty of Neapolitan slum life, observed firsthand: the unbearable living conditions of workers and artisans; the incredibly low salaries of newspaper typographers; the lack of adequate food, clothing, and shelter; and, above all, the thwarted desire for human affection.

The novel tells of a widower, Paolo, a journalist in Naples struggling to make ends meet for himself; his son, Riccardo; and his simpleminded housekeeper from the province of Campania. Paolo grubs incessantly just to pay the rent for the room in which all three live. His fatigued and woeful countenance is hauntingly described by Serao, as are the figures of the wretched, underpaid employees of the newspaper office and print shop, who work long hours in the deafening noise of the presses. Outside, malnourished street urchins are gathered, waiting for the newspapers that they will peddle through the streets of Naples. But first they must learn from the distributor, through rote repetition, what headlines to shout, since they themselves cannot read. Paolo struggles each day to meet deadlines. Because of self-neglect and malnourishment, he contracts first bronchitis and then pneumonia, which results in his early death. Even though he has worked heroically up to the last days of his life, his funeral expenses have to be paid out of alms contributed by his colleagues and the director of the newspaper. Through the latter's efforts, Paolo's penniless son, Riccardo, obtains a clerical job in a government ministry in Rome, where, however, poverty continues to stalk him. Balking at the routine clerical work and the horribly bad food that are his fare, Riccardo, "in whose veins flow printer's ink,"[20] gives up his job to become a journalist, despite the vow he had made to his dying father not to do so. In the end, he is defeated. He finds no way to escape the misery and oppression that fatally plague him and all the poor people of Naples.

Although Serao's thirty novels and more than one hundred short stories are highly readable and convey a sort of symbolic Neapolitanism, it is in her journalistic style that she excels. Her visual and creative acuity—her exceptional skill in observing detail—has been compared to a walking microscope that focuses on the tiniest aspects of people and objects. She succeeds in rendering the South's social and economic disintegration and the immobilism of the ruling classes through description of the movement of crowds, clothing, hairdos, facial expressions, gestures, feasts and fairs, patriotic demonstrations, and parliamentary sessions. She captures and reproduces events and scenes with photographic accuracy, without allowing herself time for reflection or correction.

Serao instinctively trusted in the lexicon and syntax that were closest to the language of the people. For her linguistic negligence, she was reproached by her critics and was accused, even by her husband, of not knowing how to write correct Italian. She addressed the problem of language by distinguishing the three forms it takes in Naples: a purist, literary, classroom language that "one dreams about [but that] is not real"; a dialect that is alive, clear, picturesque, ungrammatical, and nonsyntactical; and a middle level, "bourgeois" language found in newspapers, which shears the dialect of its vivacity, attempting to imitate classroom Italian, but never achieving its clarity. Serao admitted that she did not know how to write Italian well, offering two reasons: a personal one (her incomplete studies) and an environmental one (daily exposure to

Naples' three different languages). But, she concludes, even if she had learned the "shiny, clear, pure, gelid" language of the classroom, she would not use it because she believed that her living linguistic style lent warmth to her works. Her public read and enjoyed her writings in incorrect Italian. So why should these works die?[21] Critics today agree that the more Neapolitan Serao is, the more sincere and authentic is her writing, and the more universal are her works.[22]

The relationship between Matilde Serao and writing is visceral and uncritical. Her fierce will and exuberant spontaneity tend to produce an overabundance of descriptive adjectives, redundancies, and long accumulations of detail. Her faithful transcriptions link her to the school of verism, but her real strength lies in her gift for gripping narration despite a journalistic writing style. She started out as a verist but broke away from naturalism to obey only her own inspiration. She was an objective writer, with no gift for the lyrical or the autobiographical. Unlike Lalla Romano, she rarely narrated in the first person singular, because she failed to see herself as an interesting subject for her journalistic prose or novels.[23]

Whether Serao's journalism was harmful to her activity as a novelist is a moot point. During almost fifty years of journalistic activity, she impatiently put her words on paper without waiting for or expecting success. She gained immediate satisfaction from her articles and through them became a living legend in Naples. In a speech Serao made to the Genoa Press Association—published in 1906 as *Il Giornale* (The newspaper)—she proclaimed newspapers to be "the entire story of a society . . . [with] the power of all good and all evil." She declared that "the journalist is the apostle of good, the exalter . . . of peace, virtue, heroism. . . . The newspaper is the noblest form of human thought; the newspaper of the future will synthesize . . . all activities of value. The future belongs to newspapers."[24]

Oriana Fallaci

Whereas Matilde Serao is historically Italy's first woman journalist, Oriana Fallaci (b. 1930) is surely the best known, both in Italy and abroad. Whereas Serao wrote in slipshod Italian, Fallaci wields the language to perfection. Serao's journalistic vociferousness is matched by Fallaci's pugnaciousness. A long list of lawsuits, clashes with colleagues, world leaders, and keepers of the peace, and a reputation for female narcissism and a bad character have combined to create a myth of Oriana Fallaci as the prima donna of the press. By her own admission, she is a "quarrelsome . . . intolerant . . . Florentine."²⁵ She combines unorthodox reporting and interviewing techniques with a talent for writing best-selling novels, even though one of her negative critics has judged her Viareggio Prize-winning novel, *Un uomo* (1979; *A Man*, 1980), to be an "indecent mixture of Liala and of Hemingway at his worst."²⁶

Fallaci was born in Florence to Tosca Cantini, a seamstress, and Edoardo Fallaci, a cabinetmaker and political activist. She began working at the early age of fourteen, contributing to the family's sole luxury, "culture"—that is, the buying of books on an installment plan. An avid reader in her youth, especially of Russian, English, and American classical novels, she considered Nathaniel Hawthorne's *The Scarlet Letter* the premier novel. But she particularly enjoyed reading Zane Grey and Jack London, whose *The Call of the Wild* stirred her ambitions of emulating the American novelist, journalist, adventurer, and war correspondent.

Oriana was deeply attached to her father, a leader of the Tuscan Resistance movement. As a child, she ran courier missions for him during World War II. She recalls that one of her assignments was to take a basket of food containing a revolver to Carlo Levi (the author of *Christ Stopped at Eboli*, 1945), who was in hiding opposite Florence's Pitti Palace. Levi took the food but returned the gun, so Oriana was twice exposed in her risky mission. The daughter shared proudly in her father's clandestine activities for Florence's Justice and Liberty group of the national Action Party. She attended her first political rally in Piazza della Signoria at the age of fifteen and ever since has remained politically involved, always on the side of the opposition.

Having been told in her childhood that "justice, resistance to evil and oppression, a search for good, were the highest human activities,"²⁷ she expected postwar leaders to aspire to these ideals. Her expectations were not fulfilled, and she began to mistrust organized authority. "The younger generation," she declared in 1979, "feels deceived by all the dreams and hopes of the [Italian] resistance. We thought the world would change. It hasn't."²⁸ Fallaci's works trace her growing awareness that *homo homini lupus* (humans are wolves to humans) and bitterness at the discovery that politicians are "not necessarily bad" but that "power changes them."[29] When her scrupulously honest politician father died in 1988, she herself, although observing no religion, pronounced his funeral oration from the pulpit of the cemetery chapel, praising Edoardo Fallaci for his lifelong moral inflexibility, which she has inherited.[30]

Following World War II, Fallaci began her medical studies in Florence, because her journalist uncle Bruno Fallaci (Gianna Manzini's husband) had told her that the study of medicine helps one to understand human beings and write about them. (But, she would declare in 1991, to understand human beings' "beauty and ugliness, intelligence and stupidity, bestiality and humanity, courage and cowardice, war serves the writer more than anything else.")[31] To earn a living during her studies, she sought work as a reporter—unusual in an era when Italy's few women journalists were columnists rather than reporters. Although Fallaci was a liberal socialist, the director of the Christian-Democratic Florentine daily newspaper, *Il Mattino dell'Italia Centrale*, saw fit to hire her. Assigned to cover local news, her first article was a damning piece about a Florentine dance hall where mothers accompanied their daughters looking for husbands. Thus Fallaci, formed directly in her profession without the benefit of any preparatory study, began a journalistic career that ended with her reportage of the Persian Gulf War for the *Corriere della Sera* in 1991.

After covering criminal and judiciary news for *Il Mattino dell'Italia Centrale* for several years, she obtained a regular contract with the newspaper at the age of twenty, when she had already dropped out of medical school. Two years later, however, she was fired for refusing to write a satirical piece about the Italian Communist leader Palmiro Togliatti. Through her uncle's intervention, she obtained a position with the widely read magazine *Epoca*, which she subsequently left to join *Europeo*, the magazine with which her name was closely connected during the 1950s and the 1960s. Her first article for *Europeo* was about the death of a Fiesole Communist denied religious burial in sacred ground by the church authorities. The title of Fallaci's provocative article, splashed in large print, was "Anche a Fiesole Dio ha avuto bisogno degli uomini" (Even at Fiesole God needed men).[32]

In 1954, Fallaci settled in Rome, whose dolce vita she described in the pages of *Europeo*. Then she eagerly accepted transfer to the magazine's Milan office as a special envoy to cover the Hungarian revolt of 1956, Hollywood's golden era, and the war in Vietnam. She also focused on the burning issues of Italian society, producing a vast number of works, including essays and a first collection of interviews, *Gli antipatici* (1963; *Limelighters*, 1967; also translated as *The Egotists*, 1968). She then turned her attention to interviews with powerful protagonists on the world scene, documenting their most intimate thoughts and political convictions in scenarios that have made her famous. World leaders both intrigued her and filled her with indignation because "they rule our lives, command us, decide whether we live or die, in freedom or in tyranny."[33] General Giap's answer to her question: "Is it true that 45,000 of your men died at Dien Bien Phu?" makes her tremble with rage each time she recalls it: "Madame, every two minutes 300,000 persons on this planet die. What are 45,000 in one battle? In war death doesn't count."[34]

Fallaci earned the title "avenging angel" for her severe articles and incisive interviews, which have been likened to boxing matches or love scenes. She corners her subjects with sharp questions and elicits from them revealing answers. Her candor and her controversial method of questioning have been turned on such personages as Golda Meir, Haile Selassie, the shah of Iran Mohammad Reza Pahlavi, Henry Kissinger, Mu'ammar Gadhafi, and many more. She defends the aggressivity of her interviewing techniques on the grounds that she is not simply a journalist but a historian as well: "A journalist lives history in the best of ways, that is, in the moment that history takes place. He lives history, touches history with his hands, looks at it with his eyes, listens to it with his ears. . . . I am the judge. I am the one who decides. . . . If I am a painter and I do your portrait, have I or have I not the right to paint you as I want?"[35] She disdains objectivity, preferring to use the words *honest* and *correct* when describing her reportages.

Her main efforts for *Europeo*, from whose staff she resigned ostensibly to write a novel but actually because she opposed its change of directorship, are preserved in *Intervista con la storia* (1974; *Interview with History*, 1976), a collection of eighteen famous interviews in which she "bullies, baits, and charms statesmen."[36] A book about power, *Intervista con la storia* is dedicated to Fallaci's mother because, she says, "my mother doesn't understand power. . . . In her innocence, she can't understand how there can be a lord, or a lady, up there on top, who tells us what we have to do."[37] Of the eighteen personages interviewed, seven,

Fallaci asserts (but without naming them), have compromised the history of humanity.[38] No holds are barred in her interviews with contemporary world leaders; she delights in recording, with devastating openness, their tics and arrogance. She fits Milan Kundera's definition of the journalist: "not a person who asks questions, but a person who has the sacred right to ask questions, to put questions to anyone about anything."[39]

In her preface to *Intervista con la storia*, Fallaci wrote: "I do not feel myself to be, nor will I ever succeed in feeling like, a cold recorder of what I see and hear. On every professional experience I leave shreds of my heart and soul; and I participate in what I see or hear as though the matter concerned me personally and were one on which I ought to take a stand (in fact I always take one, based on a specific moral choice)."[40] Her anti-American and pro-Vietcong stance earned her an invitation to Hanoi to interview General Giap—an interview that became Henry Kissinger's *livre de chevet* (bedside book). During her stay in Hanoi, her perceptions underwent a noticeable change, as she came to understand and describe the evil on that side, too. It was not until 1988, however, that she publicly revised her thinking about the Vietnam War and took her share of responsibility with other journalists for having wrongly demonstrated that the United States was engaged in an unjust war. Her self-criticism was, however, met by attacks from both the Left and the Right.[41]

Each of Fallaci's interviews is "a portrait of myself. They are a strange mixture of my ideas, my temperament, my patience, all of these driving the questions." A case in point is her interview with Henry Kissinger (which he subsequently described as the stupidest error of his life), in which she badgered him into a thundering peroration about the role of the United States in the battle against evil (Communism) and induced him to describe himself as the lone cowboy of American foreign policy—for which he was ridiculed by press and public.[42]

Fallaci is widely read in China, where her *Lettera a un bambino mai nato* (1975; *Letter to an Unborn Child*, 1976), for example, is even used as a text in a Shanghai high school. Perhaps for this reason she alone among Western journalists was chosen by then deputy prime minister Deng Xiaoping for an interview. During 1982, her most dramatic encounters were with Mieczyslaw Rakowski, vice prime minister of Poland (*Europeo*, 8 March 1982), and General Leopoldo Galtieri during the war in the Falklands (*Europeo*, 28 June 1982). Her interview with Mu'ammar Gadhafi (serialized in *Corriere della Sera*, beginning 20 April 1986) was reconstructed from notes and recordings made seven years earlier, when she called the Libyan leader the "new Mussolini of the Mediterranean" and unabashedly made fun of his homosexuality. The encounter was described in one Italian newspaper as the first hard-core interview in the history of journalism.

Now disillusioned with journalism,[43] Fallaci's main activities are reading (García Márquez's *One Hundred Years of Solitude* has impressed her deeply) and writing novels (her recent literary models are Proust and Bukovsky).[44] For the last twenty-seven years, her main residence has been a brownstone house on Manhattan's Sixty-first Street, where she literally confined herself for five years to write her latest novel, *Insciallah* (As God wills, 1990),[45] which has met with sharply divided criticism.

Fallaci is widely read in American universities and is the first Italian woman to have received an American doctorate in letters *honoris causa* (from Columbia College in Chicago, in 1977). Her interviews with the world's political leaders have become subjects of mass communication study in American universities. Tapes of her interviews are kept in special refrigerated shelves of the Boston University Library as precious documents of spoken history.

Although many consider her to be ill bred, acerbic, contradictory, and implacable, she is a woman of honor and actually a tender, sensitive person in her complicated way. Writing, she has stated, requires irony and pity—"a smile on one's lips and tears in one's eyes."[46] For her, as for Robert Musil, irony is not an expression of superiority but rather a form of struggle.

The Greek poet and Resistance hero Alexander Panagoulis was the single, great, desperate love in the life of Oriana Fallaci. Panagoulis was condemned to death in 1968 after a bungled attempt on the life of the Greek military junta chief, Georgios Papadopoulos. Fallaci flew to Athens to interview Panagoulis when he was released from prison in 1973 in a general amnesty. The released political prisoner and his interviewer succumbed to what Fallaci calls "the most dangerous love that exists: the love that mixes ideals and moral commitments with attraction and with emotions."[47] She describes his exit from jail, in existential terms, in *Un uomo*:

> You were at the [prison] gate. . . . Before you there was a chasm so broad, so deep, so empty that merely perceiving it made you nau-

seated. . . . And this chasm was space. . . . A terrible thing, because it was like a thing that wasn't there. There was no wall to limit it, no ceiling to cover it, no door to close it out, no lock, no bars . . . nightmarish. But the worst thing was the sky. . . . It burned your pupils worse than acid. . . . You closed your eyes so as not to be blinded, you stretched out your arms so as not to fall. . . . The thought of your cell gripped you, along with an . . . irrepressible desire to go back there, to take refuge in its darkness, in its narrow and safe womb. . . .

There were shadows over there . . . coming toward you, swaying, waving, strange appurtenances that seemed at first like wings, or were they arms? . . . And then all were on top of you, friends and relatives and reporters. . . . The bewilderment that you had felt on seeing that chasm was now being translated into a precise intuition, into the awareness that freedom for you would mean another suffering, another grief.

And this was the man that I would meet the next day, at last, crashing into him like one train colliding with another.[48]

Panagoulis outgrew his ideas on the utility of violence ("the real bombs are ideas"), but like Fallaci, he scorned the "politics of the politicians." In 1976, at the age of thirty-six, after having raised a political storm by making public some secret documents of the colonels' dreaded military police, he was killed by a political assassin. Grief and rage moved Fallaci to write *Un uomo*, in which she combines autobiographical memoir, historical document, and political pamphlet. She was determined that "Panagoulis never be forgotten," claiming: "He is not defeated. I talk for him."[49] The work is dominated by a sense of immobility, because she talks directly to the dead Panagoulis in his grave.[50] But in so doing, she narrates the odyssey of a hero who fought and died alone for truth and liberty.[51] She does not hide his inconsistencies and weaknesses: he vacillates constantly between Eros and Thanatos. Her heroic fable is a minor classic and has been seen as one of the most extraordinary examples of the historical and inner biography of a man ever written by a woman.[52]

In a pun on the word *uomo*—"man"—Fallaci, who has never resigned herself to the fact that she was born female, early in life declared her determination to become at least a "uoma" (man/woman), protesting that "males have organized the world to suit themselves."[53] Her models have always been men—from her antifascist father to her journalist uncle, from Jack London to Ernest Hemingway and Norman Mailer. "I've always lived with men ... who have left a mark on my life," she declared in 1990. "I know how to write only about men."[54] In the same year, she offered an explanation for why she had become a journalist: "I owe everything to journalism. I was a poor child: to journalism I owe the fact that I am not a poor woman. I was a woman full of curiosity, desirous of seeing the world: and I did, thanks to journalism. I grew up in a society where women are oppressed, maltreated: and to journalism I owe the fact that I have been able to live like a man."[55]

Her admiration for women came late in life. It was sparked by her reading of Pearl Buck's *The Good Earth*, which stimulated her as much as her earlier reading of London's *The Call of the Wild*.[56] Up to 1974, Fallaci paid no attention to, or snubbed, feminists. Yet two of her early lesser works revolve around the female condition and contain feminist ideas ahead of their time. *Il sesso inutile: Viaggio intorno alla donna* (The useless sex: Trip around the woman, 1961; *The Useless Sex*, 1964), of little literary value by her own admission, is a survey of the status of women in the countries she had visited during a thirty-day trip around the world for *Europeo. Penelope alla guerra* (1962; *Penelope at War*, 1966), a partly autobiographical novel, she characterizes as a divertissement but affirms that it still has relevance today. It is the story of a young woman who "surrenders" her virginity only to find herself in the position of having to console the penitent male.

Fallaci always lived as a feminist, and her name came to be associated with the Italian feminist movement, which she saw as the most necessary revolution of our times. By 1978, however, she admitted her disappointment with the movement: it had become "fashionable" and therefore needed to be revised—not ideologically, but "from the inside." For Fallaci, the revolution could not be fought without men: "Feminism without men is a vengeance and nothing else; it means substituting one oppression for another, one humiliation for another. It's making harems in reverse, putting a veil on men instead of women."[57]

She split from the feminist movement also on the issue of abortion. Her novel *Lettera a un bambino mai nato*, an intimate confession of her problems of unsuccessful motherhood, became something of a cause célèbre when it was first published. It was deemed a literary success even though some accused her of "opportunism" because it was published at the height of the abortion debate in Italy.[58] Inspired by Fallaci's own three-month pregnancy, which ended after a ten-day automobile trip to carry out a magazine assignment, the work is a long monologue addressed to the protagonist's captive audience: the unborn child. Presented as a novel, it formulates all sides of the abortion issue. The protagonist judges the child's father severely, rejects indignantly his offer of money for an abortion, and champions the woman's right to decide for herself whether to give life or deny it. The novel is Fallaci's personal reflection on the purpose and value of human existence, as well as on the meaning of motherhood in contemporary society. The real theme of the work, however, is the inevitable solitude of the unmarried, liberated career woman. Fallaci waxes poetic about the mother-child relationship, but she has not a single positive word to say about the man-woman relationship, either in marriage or outside of it.[59]

Maternity was never to be Fallaci's destiny in life. Rather, she bore the imprint of war, which had been part of her childhood during the Resistance. As an adult, despite gunshot wounds received during the 1968 revolts and the massacre in Plaza Tlatelolco in Mexico City, she has chosen to spend much of her life in the midst of wars because of what she calls "perverse nostalgia." A relentless recorder of the sufferings of soldiers and civilians alike, she has targeted the atrocities perpetrated during the conflicts in Vietnam, Lebanon, Greece, Israel, and Argentina. Her reasons for covering the Persian Gulf War for *Corriere della Sera* despite her success as a novelist were not so much for the sake of journalism as for "personal egoism." Had she not gone personally to the area of conflict, she would have felt like a deserter—both of herself and of her profession.[60] To write, she needs adventure, which she defines as "searching for life where death is in command. It's also a taste for not knowing whether tomorrow you will still be alive." Each time she escapes a battle unscathed, she feels "a thousand times more alive."[61] Her activism in news reporting places her in the school of "New Journalism" that uses the resources of fiction for writing nonfictional prose. Fallaci's success lies precisely in her ability to communicate directly an investigation of war as though it were a novel.[62]

Both *Niente e così sia* (1969; *Nothing and Amen*, 1972)[63] and *Insciallah*—diaries or "journalistic novels" based, respectively, on the Vietnam and Lebanese wars—are ramifications of the New Journalism. In these works, Fallaci makes her readers privy to her personal experience that "battles stink; they have a bad, poisonous odor of gunpowder, smoke, and cadavers."[64] Her eyewitness accounts permit the reader to experience with her the sights, sounds, and smells of war from the vantage point of an observer. But what is so remarkable is that, in the midst of the worst atrocities, Fallaci does not turn cynical but rather remains incurably sentimental. Her own emotions, opinions, ideas, and commitments permeate her stories even as she communicates her characters' physical features, personalities, and frames of mind in the face of war. This private slant permits a broader perspective than a first-person account and generates as well a climate of intimacy and closeness. Fallaci uses the technique of "social autopsy"—one of the distinguishing features of journalism—which implies close attention to a subject's manners and moods as well as to symbolic details that represent entire patterns of behavior and position in the world. The result is a complete picture that provides insights into personalities and situations. Characters are rendered with unexpected clarity, their inner spirit elicited by the author's own observations. Fallaci's use of the technique permits her to satirize the obvious weaknesses of her characters, which is the hallmark of her literary portraits.[65]

War is a metaphor for our world; Vietnam and Lebanon are metaphors for our times—the universe of the Irrational, according to Fallaci. It represents utter chaos: "There was a chaos that was almost gay in this Saigon in November of 1976," she writes in *Niente e così sia*. "It seemed more like a postwar period: the markets filled with food, the jewelry shops stocked with gold, the restaurants open, and all that sunshine. . . . Dying didn't occur to you."[66] But soon the reader is brought into the killing fields; innumerable grisly incidents are described in Fallaci's rapid, terse style—"the bodies shot out in pieces. A head in one place, a foot in another" (158)—yet all seems to move slowly as death hovers everywhere. Both *Niente e così sia* and *Insciallah* are very real, very modern war stories, the latter mirroring some of the most violent images contained in the Vietnam diary: the severed head of a soldier-friend, a dead child symbolizing the endless slaughter of innocents, and so on. To those who accuse Fallaci of cherishing a taste for the macabre and the melodramatic akin to that of Curzio Malaparte,[67] she caustically retorts that persons who have seen war only at the movies while munching peanuts could scarcely imagine that war is really as she describes it.[68]

Fallaci is obsessed with the concept of death, whose "faceless smile" she brought to life in her novel, *Un uomo*: "I wanted to write a book about Death; I wanted to write a book about Life, the life of a man. But the grand protagonist of life is Death, so it turned out to be a book about Death. In any case," she concludes, "life and death are the same thing."[69] Among her purposes in writing *Insciallah* was to try to "exorcise death": one of the protagonists of the novel "is obsessed with an equation . . . in which he sees the formula of Death. So he starts looking for the formula of Life. And he finds it, one second before dying, intuiting that Death doesn't exist: it's the food of Life."[70]

All of the 103 characters in *Insciallah* remain somewhat unreal and impalpable. They are subjected to the torments of the suffocating city of Beirut, which has been seen as the single real character of the novel.[71] Fallaci transforms Beirut, the city of no escape, from a perfumed paradise of cedars into a stinking mass of blood, garbage, and stray dogs, the paradise of jackals, where everybody shoots at everybody. She provides descriptions of massacres, lootings, bombings, grenades, and kamikaze trucks that wipe out hundreds of human beings in seconds. She vividly describes Beirut's territories guarded by teenagers armed with Kalashnikov rifles; thugs incited by fanatics and criminals; corpses and rubble; the remains of the city's former luxurious life; the fear and claustrophobia that now reign. She condemns the senseless genocide in Lebanon and rejects the idea of the inevitability of war. She sees male jingoism as an ingredient of all wars (a thesis supported by the contemporary French historian Georges Duby). She gives her characters the names of rapacious birds—Condor, Hawk, Eagle—or ironic names—Sugar, Rambo, Sandokan, Passepartout—with the express purpose of degrading the "heroes" of her epic tale. No longer do these killing humans have the right to bear the names of men. Their nicknames reflect and flout the essence of their physical and psychic makeup.[72] *Insciallah* is "the truest, the most absurd, and most human book about . . . the shamefully inhuman and bestial war in Lebanon," according to one critic, who has linked it to Hemingway's *For Whom the Bell Tolls* and André Malraux's *L'espoir*.[73] "History doesn't change," writes Fallaci in *Insciallah*. "Eternal history, the eternal story of Man, who in war shows himself in all his truth, because nothing shows him *plain* as much as war."[74]

One of the novel's obsessive themes, the linguistic babel of Beirut, is the supreme metaphor of chaos. Angelo, a young intellectual in the Italian peacekeeping force, would like to put the rationality of science at the service of humankind to exorcise chaos. Angelo recalls his study of

Ludwig Boltzmann (1844–1906), who, by introducing into thermody-namics the methods of statistics, had succeeded in translating into mathematical terms the concept of entropy—that is, chaos.[75] Boltz-mann had formulated an equation (S = K ln W) that obsesses Angelo and that is repeated over thirty times in the novel as its dominant leit-motiv, expressing the eternal struggle between life and death. If Boltz-mann's equation is the formula of death, as Angelo believes, then he is determined to find the equation of life. Later, however, he learns that Boltzmann committed suicide, perhaps because he had discovered the invincibility of death or the totality of chaos.

Many critics have seen the worth of *Insciallah* consumed in Fallaci's excess of demagogic zeal, her incompetence as a psychologist, and her desperate desire to make everything about her characters clear to the reader. She endows each of them with a past, a childhood, and a chorus of relatives and friends—with banal results. So that the reader will un-derstand the babel of languages, she translates into Italian each phrase or expression in a dialect or a foreign language, from the slang of American soldiers to the Latin spouted by a snobbish cavalry colonel—translations that destroy the dramatic effect of the sentences. The book suffers from cumbersome hypotaxis (syntactic subordination by the use of conjunctions) and lists of easily predictable adjectives. One critic com-plains that each trait of each of the characters—such as the colonel's pas-sion for horses, whose deaths move him more than the death of four hundred humans—is stated, confirmed, exemplified, repeated, and il-lustrated ad nauseam.[76] Nonetheless, Fallaci's brash adventure into the domain of mathematics and philosophy has been highly praised for the irony of certain pages, for the many memorable personages and events portrayed, and for the passages in which the author reaches the heights of tragic intensity.[77]

Oriana Fallaci combines talent as a reporter and interviewer with a proven ability to write readable, best-selling novels. She has successfully demonstrated that it is possible to write accurate nonfiction even while using such literary devices as traditional dialogue and stream of con-sciousness. She relies on the techniques of the realistic novel, even though she makes use of the literary conventions of mood develop-ment, interviews, character portrayal, satire, and humor. By so doing, she changes what would have been an objective record of armed con-flicts into a fresh form of art.[78] Her style is always clear and never pompous. She paints from life, looking at everything from close range, even while narrating her stories as fables or legends. Obsessed by certain "great ideas," she brings her public face to face with overwhelming disasters, fears, tensions, adventures, and terrors. She writes about them with passion and impetuosity, but simply. She does not hide, withdraw, or disguise her presence in a world of her own construction, which she narrates in very personal, direct terms. The end result is not fictional but imaginative literature, quite different in style from cold, clipped, factual reportage.

A writer who cannot separate form from substance, Fallaci is outraged by the language of Italian daily newspapers.[79] Unlike many of her colleagues, she pays close attention to her choice of words, sentence structure, and phonetic rhythms, frequently with considerable success. Her obsession with form and linguistic musicality rendered her writing of *Un uomo*, for example, doubly difficult: her anguish in reliving the Panagoulis affair was compounded by a consuming effort on her part to find the right verbal architecture for her novel. "To write well," says Fallaci, "is . . . a torture that verges on masochism."[80]

Even though some critics find Fallaci's works to be intolerably sentimental and verbose, she has inventive capacity and the disciplined talent needed to sustain the difficult literary form of the monologue, as in her *Lettera a un bambino mai nato*. She writes in impeccable Italian, yet she is a "popular" writer. One of Italy's "cult figures," Oriana Fallaci's presence on the literary scene is hard to escape.

Camilla Cederna

A justice-thirsty journalist, noted for her irony and persiflage as well as for her ability to displease both the Left and the Right, Camilla Cederna is a sharp observer with a keen sense of humor. Although she has written no novels, her literary production reads like a twentieth-century saga of the manners, customs, and changes in the most influential segments of Italian society. After forty-five years of indefatigable description of the excesses and idiocies of her stereotyped compatriots, the triteness of their language, and their capitulations to bribes, Cederna wryly states that Italians have decidedly "lost their charm."[81] With similar terseness she describes world tragedies, Mafia crimes, and the corruption of Italy's governing institutions.

Like Oriana Fallaci, Cederna has faced several lawsuits for libel and slander. She states quite simply that she is only doing her duty as a journalist: "In the press, there must be no crimes of opinion or of indiscretion. There is only one crime: keeping silent, not denouncing injustice and abuse of power." She does not deny that her demands for government transparency are rigorous and that she is a meddlesome moralist. "There always winds in me a thread of moralizing," she admits, "even when I'm talking about a celebration."[82] But, she explains, "it's a family disease—a family that includes rigorous magistrates or committed journalists, like my brother, . . . who has always denounced ecological crimes."[83] Cederna is faithful to a single imperative: reject indifference and neutrality, and sound the alarm when others remain silent.

Her irony falls mainly on those who have played a major role in shaping Italian culture and who consider themselves above the law: a small group of arrogant, destructive Italians wielding immense power. She denounces Italy's royal family as accomplices in the fascist shame; pinpoints flights of capital and the flight from Italy of corrupt bribe-receivers who label themselves political refugees hunted by the Communists. Her controversial book *Giovanni Leone: La carriera di un presidente* (Giovanni Leone: A president's career, 1978) documents the corruption of Leone's Christian-Democratic government and its cover-up of scandals. It reveals the Christian Democrats' connection with, and/or protection of, the Mafia and the extreme Right, and it may have been influential in inducing the president to resign from office before the expiration of his term.[84] Although the work initially did not receive much publicity, because it appeared on the eve of the Aldo Moro kidnapping, in less than four months it had produced a collective frenzy among Italian readers. She had chosen the right moment to attack Italy's main symbol of corruption—the debased president and his Christian-Democratic supporters. Cederna sensed the country's mood. Giovanni Leone and his generation had perpetrated an unjust social system based on patronage, which was to give rise to the terrorism that began plaguing the nation in the 1970s. But her courageous revelations and withering denunciations barely grazed the politicians involved. In the postscript of her latest book, *Il lato forte e il lato debole* (The strong side and the weak side, 1992), she writes with a pessimism belied by subsequent events: "one thing is certain: that we will die (and even the youngest among us) with the Christian Democrats in power" (273). The volume contains one of the most devastating satirical portraits of the "dangerous Christian-Democratic politician" Giulio Andreotti, to whom she gives the papal title "Giulio VI," alluding to his number of terms in office (274–75).

The stages of Cederna's life are described with wit, irony, and detachment in her autobiographical *Il mondo di Camilla* (Camilla's world, 1980), which offers a spectrum of Italian history. She was born in Milan in 1921 into a Roman Catholic but anticlerical family. Her father, a bit of a fascist, was an industrial chemist of Valtellina (Lombardy) origin. The son of one of the founders of the Alpine Club, he was deeply concerned with the reforestation of the San Bernardo Mountain—more attracted by the mountain than by his family and his textile industry. Her mother was a graduate in French literature who imposed the learning of the French language on her children through daily readings of the works of the Russian-born French writer of famous books for children, Comtesse de Ségur.

Camilla began to read at a young age, mostly sentimental stories and fables (she especially liked the cruel ones), as well as children's versions of Shakespeare's plays. She enjoyed reading her father's collection of war books and works on African exploration. Gradually her reading repertory extended to include most of the works of Annie Vivanti, Jack London, the French novelist Henri Barbusse, and D'Annunzio. Later, she turned to Dickens, Defoe, the early Balzac, Henry James, and all the nineteenth-century English women writers.

A rowdy child, Camilla did not get good marks at school for comportment, but when she entered the *liceo* (Italian secondary school), she discovered the Greek poets—Sappho, Anacreon, Alcaeus, and Alcman. They so inspired her that she learned to read them in the original and committed whole passages to memory. Going on to the university in Milan, she studied Latin, Greek, paleography, and the history of the Risorgimento. Her graduation dissertation (written after obtaining Church dispensation to read the "obscene" epigrams of Martial and Juvenal) was on the subject of "Le prediche contro il lusso delle donne dalla filosofia popolare greco fino ai padri della Chiesa" (Preachings against female extravagance from Greek popular philosophy up to the Fathers of the Church)—a study that would color her future descriptions of Milan's society ladies. The thesis began with a description of the lasciviousness of women of antiquity and ended with an exposé of Tertullian's *De cultu feminarum*, in which he exhorts Christian women to avoid pagan fashion. Camilla's professor considered it a meritorious work but judged its tone to be journalistic rather than scholarly, giving its author an early clue to her future vocation.[85]

On completion of her university studies, Cederna tried her hand but failed at both nursing and private tutoring. She was experiencing the World War II siege of Milan when she wrote her first published article in 1943: "La moda nera" (Black fashion), in which she mocked fascist women's militaristic garb, their phallic fixations, and Mussolini's "rural housewife" mystique. The article led to her arrest the following year, when she spent two weeks in prison, suspensefully described in one of her articles, "Paura a Sondrio" (Fear in Sondrio [a town in Lombardy]).[86] Her imprisonment set off the mechanism of Cederna's sharpest journalistic weapon: outrage and indignation.

Immediately after the war, in 1945, Cederna became one of the founders of the political-cultural Milanese weekly *Europeo*. As the only woman on the editorial staff, she was required to write the society column. Although she has always deplored male domination in the world of journalism,[87] she did not resent her assignment, because it offered her a vantage point for viewing the new quirks of her contemporaries. During her eleven years of work for *Europeo*, Cederna was steadfast in writing like her male colleagues: rarely sentimental, never self-commiserating, and nonchalantly demonstrating her own bravura.

In 1958, she became editor and special Rome envoy of the magazine *L'Espresso*, contributing a weekly variety column, "La milanese" (The Milanese woman), which gained her a reputation as a chronicler of the vices and virtues of Milan's affluent upper-middle-class society. For *L'Espresso*, she created in the 1960s a social and literary column whose title has since become her hallmark: "Il lato debole" (The weak side). A collection of the best pieces from her column was published in 1977 under the title *Il lato debole: Diario italiano* (The weak side: An Italian diary). She joined the staff of the weekly *Panorama* in 1980, where she now works as an editor and featured columnist, contributing her "Il lato debole" every other week. She is currently writing a book about Trapani (in Sicily), "the premier of Mafia cities," which she has described as the spiniest in Italy's "crown of thorns."[88]

Cederna's so-called first period refers to her writings prior to her decision to focus on political repression and injustice in Italy. As she sparkled in Milan's exclusive salons, she chronicled society's rituals and extravagances, partly as an accomplice and partly as critic. She wrote in what she describes as a "continuous wave motion," oscillating between frivolity and indignation.[89] The pages of *Noi siamo le signore* (We are the ladies, 1958), *La voce dei padroni* (The voice of the bosses, 1962), *Signore e signori* (Ladies and gentlemen, 1963), *Fellini 8 1/2* (1963), and *Il lato debole: Diario italiano* contain ironic descriptions of the moments of enlightenment as well as of the chronic obtuseness of Milan's wealthy old families and its nouveaux riches. They also contain pungent portraits of such personalities as Fellini, Toscanini, the inscrutable pianist Arturo Benedetti, Michelangelo, Pope John XXIII, television host Mike Bongiorno, and singer Adriano Celentano. Cederna's description of Lyndon Johnson on his presidential campaign in the early 1960s offers a good sample of her humorous and satirical style: "Johnson is very tall, a little bit flabby, with a cunning pink-and-gray face that looks like rubber, since it can distort and return so quickly to normal when he speaks. Johnson has very long ears; his right hand is double the size of his left because of the many handshakes he gives and receives."[90]

Cederna also tackled such issues as the war in Algeria and the Greek military regime's political oppression, through firsthand observation. She traveled to Germany and China, she studied the question of the two Koreas and of the Vatican II Council, and she investigated Milan's social ills and its immigrants' problems. But her "first period" is best remembered for her elegant demystification of Italy's "Danaë society" (reference is to the princess who was visited by Zeus in the form of a shower of gold), which was developing during the country's first and only economic boom.

The Italian economic miracle, with its wild consumerism and will to waste, was sharply and critically observed in retrospect by Cederna, especially in *Nostra Italia del miracolo* (Our Italy of the miracle, 1980). The gist of this book is that Italy's economic miracle—a happy feast that closed its eyes to the country's political misery—did not work the miracle of a new and different social justice. Cederna focuses specifically on the world of women, whose frivolity during the "miracle" only masked insecurity and provided further impetus for the bourgeois neofeminism of the 1970s. The women Cederna describes in *Nostra Italia del miracolo* are, in fact, those who marched for abortion rights, opened feminist bookshops, and militated in organizations protesting violence in Italy.

In other works, Cederna depicts Italy's insolent, grotesque social climbers with "faces like hyenas and Dobermans," scrambling to reach "the top of the top." She ridicules the "dynamic, well-balanced manager" with his tics and superstitions. She records the "illuminating" conversations and the peculiarities and petty miseries of the wealthy; she mocks their sumptuous weddings, stressing that they are "running [so fast] toward social success" that they forget to say "thank you" for the expensive wedding gifts they receive—a social error those of the lower classes would never commit.[91]

Cederna's recollections of the years of her "first period"—the "distant" world described in her volume *Vicino e distante* (Near and far, 1984)—stop in the year 1968, when Italy's festive, forgetful, and startled "Danaë society" was faced with a country in revolt. By the 1970s, widespread social unrest and violence prompted Cederna to enter the ring as a battling journalist.

Having returned from an assignment in Chappaquiddick in 1969, she found her native city of Milan in the throes of violence and confusion. She participated in marches, signed appeals, and underwrote declarations during the Milanese student revolt of February and March 1969. Terrorism, which broke out in the autumn of that year (and today it is still unclear whether it was incited by the extreme Left or the extreme Right), drove her to police headquarters, tribunals, and cemeteries to seek the truth that was hidden under the lies, cover-ups, and payoffs of government officials. Democratic journalism had, in fact, been in a state of alarm since 1964, when the incipient neo-Fascist movement sought to destabilize the country and drive it to the Right. Together with other tenacious, civically involved journalists, she produced "counterinformation" designed to combat the misinformation official sources gave out for public consumption. These journalists denounced police cover-ups and the corruption of magistrates and did not hesitate to implicate the highest government officials in scandalous activities. Now Camilla Cederna communicated with her public in a generally serious manner, only sparingly interspersing humorous portraits

in her writings.[92] She published two denunciatory works against the police. The first, *Pinelli: Una finestra sulla strage* (Pinelli: A window on the
massacre, 1971), exposes the extent to which the judiciary was subjected to political pressure, and it totally rehabilitates the victim of a
state-sponsored conspiracy, the anarchist Pinelli, accused of terrorist
activity and supposed to have jumped through a window during inter-
rogation. The second, *Sparare a vista: Come la polizia del regime DC
mantiene l'ordine pubblico* (Shoot on sight: How the police of the Christian-Democratic regime maintain public order, 1975), describes police
violence and exposes the indirect role played by corrupt officials in controlling the press, in obtaining the dismissal of honest judges, and in
covering up murders. *Sparare a vista* denounces the violent social repression in the Italy of the 1970s and is one of Cederna's strongest statements
against the unpunished abuse of power.[93]

Her faith in democracy and its values unbending, she proceeded to
write the most polemical of all her politically oriented works, *Giovanni
Leone*, for which she paid damages after losing the libel suit brought
against her. By this time she had also lost friends who had traditionally
admired her and invited her to their salons. Now she was considered too
"leftist," and she was slowly gaining a reputation for subversive propa-
ganda. Cederna had accepted the risk of unpopularity by taking part in
the battles for civil and political liberties.

The opulent society that rejected Camilla Cederna are the makers
of what John Kenneth Galbraith calls the "culture of contentment."
What is most striking for American readers of Cederna's latest book, *Il
lato forte e il lato debole*, is how closely the Italian society she describes
parallels that of the United States. One critic has compared her to Bob
Woodward and Carl Bernstein,[94] the authors of *All the President's Men*,
but behind her political exposés stand figures of Italy's big business-
people. They are engaged in a war for the conquest of territory, destroying whatever lies in their path that might prevent them from controlling
the market. Denouncing them in print, she removes them from the
niches they have carved for themselves. She also deplores northern Italy's
racist attitude toward southerners. More importantly, she sees the dan-
ger of Italy becoming ever more racist as an unprecedented number of
black and Arab immigrants settle in the peninsula—immigrants from
the developing world that Mussolini once dreamed of molding into
Rome's colonial empire. The analogy with the problems of immigrants

to the United States from lands south of the border, associated with the "colonialism" of the past—and many other "strong" and "weak" analogies—will not escape the American reader of *Il lato forte e il lato debole*. Cederna's intent is to divulge empirical truths for the sake of upsetting her readers and to stimulate them to think about what lurks beneath the "culture of contentment."

With a good dose of malice and a few drops of poison, *Il lato forte e il lato debole* takes aim at the "neo-vulgarity" of the nouveaux riches, at "personalities . . . rendered invulnerable by power" (13), and at corrupt politicians as well as the "soubrettes" in their lives (49). Cederna documents the fact that Italy in the late 1980s was in a moment of regression regarding the condition of women, despite legislation in their favor. She looks with horror at the enthusiastic steps being taken to reopen houses of prostitution, cheerlessly describing the colorless clients of Italy's colorless prostitutes (24–25).

In a light, ironic, and disenchanted manner, she stoops to gather the absurdist fragments of Italy's daily life: Milanese intolerance of southern fruit and vegetable vendors, taxi drivers, and so on, whom she in turn satirizes because they foolishly attempt to "Milanize" themselves linguistically and socially. She parodies the wealthy who busy themselves with following the very latest fashions, choosing the most expensive resorts, and engaging in the absurdest and tritest conversations on the world's swankiest beaches. She spoofs another "weak side" of the Italians: their insistence on taking their own spaghetti and Tuscan olive oil on their trips abroad (84).

She makes fun of joggers in Italy's overpolluted cities, suggesting that they read Henry Thoreau's meditations on man's relationship to nature and walk, not run, in the countryside (117–18). She is unsparing in her descriptions of wealthy women who can afford to visit their plastic surgeon in his "splendid vacation island in the Pacific" (50) but who, no matter how much they spend for youth products, do not succeed in stopping the aging process and as an alternative become alcoholics (59). With real humor, she describes the farcical labeling of the rejuvenating products these women use, creating highly comical effects through her cataloging technique of an extraordinary number of substantives and adjectives manufacturers use to list the beneficent contents of, for example, a beauty cream (69).

The chichi audience at La Scala Opera House is composed of

women attired in "fireworks" and men who are either politicians or corrupt millionaires (186). Through the eyes of the chic single ladies at a Milan luncheon, she focuses on a handsome cosmopolitan: Gore Vidal. Cederna skillfully transforms the ladies' thirsty gaze into some penetrating remarks on democracy and politics in the United States:

> One of the guests asked him whether his feelings for his native land could be defined love/hate. And at this point the ironic flash in Vidal's eyes disappeared; no longer was he the worldly dandy; his tone became bitter. According to him, America was the country where the opulent majority did not want the poor minority to get rich. Result? Democracy with the rich in power. He himself felt in solidarity with the opposition minority. But another question was enough to restore all his usual verve: how come, when so many people thought that the American woman had gained power, his Myra [Breckenridge] wanted to turn this situation around? And Vidal answered with the first sentence that Myra would pronounce in the film version . . . : 'In America, to become a man I had to begin by being a woman.' " (20–21)

Cederna, like Natalia Ginzburg, is concerned about the disintegration of the family. The extreme discipline offered by nuns in Italy's cloistered Catholic schools does not guarantee better mothers: the young ladies groomed in these schools later "distinguish themselves [for their] bad conduct," forcing their husbands to "console themselves . . . with some chorus girl" (200). Separated parents—hardly recognizable as adults because of their attire and their behavior—accompany their spoiled brats to school after decking them out in expensive and elegant accoutrements (105). The split families celebrate a "completely pagan, neurotic and externalized" Christmas, whereas "mommy" might have done better by having her child's teeth straightened (191). Cederna makes fun of the hypocrisy of illegitimate "couples" who spend the torrid month of August imprisoned in an apartment in the deserted city of Milan: "he" has sent his wife and children to the beach (where he probably longs to be); "she" has declined her girlfriend's invitation to the mountains (where she would be cool and free from housekeeping chores) (47–48).

The list of subjects that stir Camilla Cederna's indignation is long: publishing houses' mania for printing the private life and love letters of such well-known authors as Calvino and Pavese "which add nothing to the reader's knowledge of the author" (178); devastatingly unequipped public hospitals where suntanned medical "professors" arrogantly make their rounds followed by twenty sheepish interns (180); the degradation of Italy's resorts, overrun by cement, discotheques, and motorcycles; some people's use of the dirty streets of her city as urinals, even without waiting until dark; the inanity of certain television shows and the ignominious use of children as objects for publicity; the South's *case del fanciullo* (homes for unwed expectant mothers), whose directors, priests, and psychologists rejoice when the unwanted babies are adopted by "good people" who pay all expenses until the child is born and then take it away from its mother (98).

In a satirical description of the pope's visit to Naples in 1990, Cederna observes that, no sooner does he leave than criminality resumes, involving such large sums of money that the value of life preached by the pope is negligible. But this chapter of *Il lato forte e il lato debole* offers the reader a surprising aspect of the maligned city of Naples: enlightened intellectuals are engrossed in the publication of the complete works of Hegel; and an architect, at his own expense, is building "Neagorà" (a meeting place of Naples, Europe, and Africa) at the foot of the symbolic thirteenth-century castle Maschio Angioino. This, for Cederna, is the real "Italian miracle," and it is possible only in Naples—"a metropolis of grandiose urban and social contradictions" (211–18).

In the postscript of *Il lato forte e il lato debole*, Cederna writes: "Today, everything makes me indignant, the process of social decomposition that plagues our country, the scornful cynicism of our political figures who have continued to plunge Italy into debt . . . [and] pay no heed to that target-shooting that Mafia crimes have become, have not the slightest concern for this Italy that has become the homeland of *bustarelle* [payola], fixed bids, easily obtained building permits, job handouts. . . . In Italy, the prime enemy of liberty is power" (271). Like Oriana Fallaci, Cederna is an enemy of power, and like Fallaci, she lashes out against the tragic commonplaces of history in an effort to demonstrate that events are not immutable, that society can change, and that the quality of life can be bettered if people's indignation is sufficiently aroused. But whereas Fallaci "lives" history in the field,

Cederna seems to stumble on it almost accidentally, as she pumps persons as high up as possible and makes them responsible for her country's political, social, and ecological degradation.

Cederna has repeatedly asserted her belief in an informative and instructive press, complaining with reason that "the language of the [Italian] newspapers is not suitable for the people because it's difficult, abstruse, complicated. When they write about politics, you can't understand a thing."[95] Although her own journalistic style is more "American" and up-to-date, she deplores misused, abused, and overused words in the Italian press—*carisma, perverso, alla grande, fatiscente*, and *caos*, for example. She satirizes the general public's parroting of neologisms and new idioms, which they either do not understand or misuse: *choccante, slalomeggiare, big*, and *vip* (VIP). The Italian language, she laments, is degenerating under the onslaught of gallicisms and anglicisms: *éclatante, peluche, buvette, apaisant, managerialità, in tilt, feeling*, and *stress* have usurped the place of perfectly good Italian words.

Writing with linguistic propriety as well as a sense of humor, Cederna is always amusing, even when serious or irreverent. She adapts politics and religion to her own brilliant manner of expression. Few journalists have her skill in finding "frivolous" adjectives capable of bringing the most gruesome drama into the limits of readability. Not even the cruelest truths exclude ridiculousness: her Leone, for example, does not come through as a historically mediocre person but only as humanly ridiculous; the horrors of the heroin traffic enthrall the Mafia city of Trapani, but "the people worship the madonna fervently here."[96] Cederna's style is clear and incisive, rapid and savory, and often chatty and colloquial. She attracts the reader's attention immediately, by opening an article with a striking quotation or a pointed comment, which she then develops smoothly, avoiding abstraction. She goes beyond mere accumulation of facts to create sensitive and artistic portraits of her contemporaries, choosing imaginative words that match her acute powers of observation, and indicating specific details that correspond to personality traits.[97] Her penetrating eye and rapacious ear snatch every detail: description of a murdered man will include even the color of his necktie; southern vegetable vendors, by way of "Milanizing" themselves, "offer their produce as though they were speaking another language: 'i *tomàti*' [*pomodori* in Italian], they say, and with a vaguely German accent: . . . 'i mè *articiòk*' [*carciofi* in Italian]" (my emphasis).[98]

Perhaps Cederna's political passion and her insistence on the negative aspects of Italian society slow down the rhythm of her scintillating descriptions. Sometimes she falls into pettiness, which repels intellectuals who accuse her of writing ephemeral sensationalism rather than books of historical interest. Nonetheless, Cederna is able to portray her country's cultural and social history vividly, humorously, and truthfully. Her work possesses both literary and journalistic qualities and serves to highlight the heartbeat of contemporary Italy.[99] One critic has gone so far as to define Camilla Cederna as "one of our major contemporary writers, in fact one of the few poets of the Italian reality we have lived through and are still living now."[100]

POSTSCRIPT

Feelings of physical, mental, and moral malaise, as expressed by Italian women writers, are apparently diminishing with the approach of the year 2000. But over the course of this century, a corpus of literature has transmitted valuable signs and images of Italian women. They fight, which is supposed to be a man's business. Their men are weak, which is a woman's blemish.

Grazia Deledda, author of over fifty works, including novels, short stories, essays, and autobiography, waged a heroic battle to realize her potential as a writer, despite the guilt feelings instilled in her by her fellow Sardinian islanders. Sibilla Aleramo's feminine mystique guided her passionate protest against the social conventions that bind a wife to her husband against her will. Gianna Manzini rejected her own psychocultural self-image by returning to her unconscious bonds with her parents, while Lalla Romano has brought us a wealth of fictionalized reminiscences sustained by ideas of normative human behavior. Elsa Morante, using a wide variety of techniques and themes, skillfully wielded writing as an instrument of psychological therapy, while Natalia Ginzburg's works reflect her metaphysical and spiritual preoccupations, even as they document the situation of Italian women in a changing society. The quiet style and visualization of sensations in Rosetta Loy's novels, so difficult to imitate and to translate, must be set in stark contrast to Dacia Maraini's aggressive subversion of male language through the figure of the female warrior. Maraini goes the farthest of all in demonstrating that society, rather than biological destiny, is responsible for the inferior status of the "second sex." The works of three Italian women journalists, which are shorn of any "female sensitivity," trace the development of Italian society from the nineteenth century to our own day. They range in style and form from Serao's sentimentalism and verism, to Cederna's pungent social irony, to Fallaci's dramatic version of the New Journalism.

It is too early, however, to attempt a "gynocritical" study of Italian women's writing as an aesthetic and political act. Although images of Italian women are evolving, the country has still not shaken off the legacy of Catholic ideology. Italy is too beset by problems of a societal and institutional nature, too divided between northern and southern mentalities, to permit a unified reassessment of the role of women in Italian culture of the twentieth century. How the ideation, theorization, and perception of gender and genre roles has affected the course of Italy's cultural history still remains to be probed.

NOTES
SELECTED
BIBLIOGRAPHY
INDEX

NOTES

1. Grazia Deledda

1. Grazia Deledda, *Il nostro padrone* (Our master), in *Romanzi e novelle*, 4 vols. (Milano: Mondadori, 1950–55), 3:156; hereafter cited in text.

2. Grazia Deledda, *Il Dio dei viventi* (The God of the living), in *Romanzi e novelle*, 3:254, 289, 317.

3. Quoted in Antonio Piromalli, "Grazia Deledda," *Letteratura Italiana. Novecento. I Contemporanei* 3 (1979): 2617.

4. Grazia Deledda, *Colombi e sparvieri* (Pigeons and hawks), in *Romanzi e novelle*, 1:184; hereafter cited in text. For an analysis of Deledda's writings in the context of Sardinia's socieconomic problems at the turn of the nineteenth century, see Antonio Piromalli, "Grazia Deledda," *Letteratura Italiana. Novecento. I Contemporanei* 3 (1979): 2624–32.

5. Grazia Deledda, *Canne al vento* (Reeds in the wind), in *Grazia Deledda. Le opere: Il vecchio della montagna, Elias Portolu, Cenere, Canne al vento* (Milano: Mondadori, 1955), 644; hereafter cited in text.

6. Grazia Deledda, *Il paese del vento* (The land of wind), in *Romanzi e novelle*, 3:825.

7. Letter dated 28 July 1891 to Stanis Manca, quoted in "Note su *Cosima*" by Antonio Baldini, in *Romanzi e novelle*, 3:1039.

8. Women's local costume in central Sardinia includes an outer corset of the type depicted on ceramics of the serpent goddess of the Mycenaean Age and geometrical ornaments of Minoan design.

9. The story appeared in Rome's weekly illustrated magazine *Paradiso dei Bambini* (Children's paradise), published by Edoardo Perino.

10. The story appeared in the literary review *Ultima Moda* (Latest fashion), published by Edoardo Perino.

11. Letter dated 2 November 1893 to Stanis Manca, quoted in "Note su *Cosima*" by Antonio Baldini, in *Romanzi e novelle*, 3:1043.

12. Grazia Deledda, *Cosima*, in *Romanzi e novelle*, 3:1015.

13. Letter dated 16 January 1892 to Epaminonda Provaglio, quoted in "Note su *Cosima*," in *Romanzi e novelle*, 3:1039.

14. Quoted in Mario Miccinesi, *Deledda*, Il Castoro 105 (Firenze: La Nuova Italia, 1975), 3.

15. Neria De Giovanni, *L'ora di Lilith: Su Grazia Deledda e la letteratura femminile del secondo Novecento* (Roma: Ellemme, 1987), 23–50. Similarly, see Patrick W. Shaw, *Willa Cather and the Art of Conflict* (Troy, New York: Whitston Publishing Company, 1992), for a discussion of Cather's homoerotic tensions as the energy source for her creativity.

16. "Note su *Cosima*," in *Romanzi e novelle*, 3:1041.

17. De Giovanni, *L'ora di Lilith*, 67.

18. Quoted in Piromalli, "Grazia Deledda," 2617.

19. Lorenzo Greco studies the theme of love between cousins in Deledda's work in "Amore fra cugini: Letteratura e contesto antropologico nella Deledda," *Il Ponte* 1–2 (1982): 109–22.

20. See Miccinesi, *Deledda*, 30.

21. Luigi Capuana, *Gli "ismi" contemporanei* (Catania: Giannotta, 1898), 153–61.

22. Miccinesi, *Deledda*, 29.

23. Miccinesi, *Deledda*, 11.

24. Grazia Deledda, *Elias Portolu*, in *Le opere: Il vecchio della montagna, Elias Portolu, Cenere, Canne al vento* (Milano: Mondadori, 1955), 246; hereafter cited in text.

25. Grazia Deledda, *L'edera*, in *Opere scelte*, edited by Eurialo De Michelis (Milano: Mondadori, 1964), 511.

26. Grazia Deledda, *Premio Nobel per la letteratura 1926* (Milano: Fabbri, 1966), 22.

2. Sibilla Aleramo

1. Sibilla Aleramo, *Il passaggio*, 3d ed., with a new preface by the author (Milano: Mondadori, 1932), 77, 90, 91; hereafter cited in text.

2. Sibilla Aleramo, *Dal mio diario: 1940–44* (Roma: Tumminelli; 1945), 55; hereafter cited in text.

3. Sibilla Aleramo, *Una donna* (reprint, Milano: Feltrinelli, 1982), 114–15; hereafter cited in text.

4. *Confessioni di scrittori (Interviste con se stessi): Quaderni della Radio XI* (Torino: Edizioni Radio Italiana, 1951), 9; hereafter cited in text.

5. Sibilla Aleramo, *Amo dunque sono* (Milano: Mondadori, 1927), 66.

6. Elda Maria Bertelli, "Sibilla Aleramo," in *Romanzieri e novellieri d'Italia nel secolo ventesimo* (Roma: Edizioni de "Le Stanze del libro," 1936), 1:173.

7. Emilio Cecchi and Leonetta Cecchi Pieraccini, "Quel Dino Campana 'selvatico e diabolico,'" *La Repubblica*, 26 May 1990, 21. Aleramo's correspondence with Campana was published under the title *Quel viaggio chiamato amore* (That journey called love) (Roma: Editori Riuniti, 1987).

8. "[Sibilla] arrivava spesso verso l'ora di cena, chiedeva magari un uovo, anche piccolo: finché, tra i borbottii di mio padre [Emilio Cecchi], mia madre [Leonetta

Cecchi Pieraccini] non la invitava a sedersi a tavola con noi" [(Sibilla) often called on us toward dinner time, asking perhaps for an egg—even a small one—until, to the grumblings of my father (Emilio Cecchi), my mother (Leonetta Cecchi Pieraccini) would invite her to sit down at table with us] (Margherita Ghilardi, "Lettere da un matrimonio," *La Repubblica*, 26 May 1990, 19).

9. Giuliana Morandini, *La voce che è in lei: Antologia della narrativa femminile italiana tra '800 e '900* (Milano: Bompiani, 1980), 21–22.

10. The first French edition was *Le passage* (Paris: Editions Bieder, 1922).

11. Sibilla Aleramo, *Lettere a Elio* (Roma: Editori Riuniti, 1989).

12. Fiora A. Bassanese, *"Una donna*: Autobiography as Exemplary Text," *Quaderni d'italianistica* 11 (1990): 43.

13. Anna Nozzoli, *Tabù e coscienza: La condizione femminile nella letteratura italiana del Novecento* (Firenze: La Nuova Italia, 1978), 39–40.

14. The early twentieth-century critic Arturo Graf objected that a more plausible solution and ending for the novel would have been to allow the heroine to escape with the child and for justice to take its course. A contemporary woman critic claims, however, that the real drama of Aleramo's novel lies in the same deepening disaffection and lack of communication between mother and son as existed between the heroine and her own mother. There is no dialogue between the mother and the child, who is not a fruit of love. The heroine identifies not with the social roles of mother and wife but rather with the male role she had enjoyed in her youth. Her escape to independence, together with the retarding force represented by her son, would therefore have constituted an implausible ending for the novel. Cf. Arturo Graf, "Sibilla Aleramo, *Una donna*," *Nuova Antologia* A. 41, no. 840 (1906), 722; and Maria Pia Pozzato in Marina Federzoni, Isabella Pezzini, and Maria Pia Pozzato, *Sibilla Aleramo*, Il Castoro 161 (Firenze: La Nuova Italia, 1980), 53.

15. Novalis, *Hymns to the Night and Other Selected Writings*, translated by Charles E. Passage (New York: Bobbs-Merrill, 1960), 7.

3. Gianna Manzini

1. Gianna Manzini, "Mirrored in a Dream," *Life and Letters*, August 1949. The collection of short stories *Arca di Noè* (Milano: Mondadori, 1960) has been translated into Dutch; of the novels, *La Sparviera* (Milano: Mondadori, 1956; hereafter cited in text) has been translated into French, Portuguese, and Czech, and *Un'altra cosa* (Milano: Mondadori, 1961; hereafter cited in text) into Serbo-Croatian.

2. *Confessioni di scrittori (Interviste con se stessi): Quaderni della Radio XI* (Torino: Edizioni Radio Italiana, 1951), 56.

3. Gianna Manzini, "Gelosia," in *Incontro col falco* (Milano: Corbaccio, 1929), 271.

4. Gianna Manzini, *Sulla soglia* (Milano: Mondadori, 1973), 95; hereafter cited in text.

5. Gianna Manzini, *Lettera all'editore* (reprint, Milano: Mondadori, 1946), 171, as translated by Giovanna Miceli-Jeffries, "Gianna Manzini's Poetics of Verbal

Visualization," in *Contemporary Women Writers in Italy*, edited by Santo L. Aricò (Amherst: University of Massachusetts Press, 1990), 92. Many of the English translations of quotations from Manzini's works throughout this chapter have been drawn from Miceli-Jeffries' essay.

6. Patricia M. Spacks, *Imagining a Self* (Cambridge: Harvard University Press, 1976), 18.

7. Gianna Manzini, *Tempo innamorato* (reprint, Milano: Mondadori, 1973), 134; hereafter cited in text.

8. Gianna Manzini, *Il valtzer del diavolo* (Milano: Mondadori, 1947), 87.

9. *Lettera all'editore*, 11; hereafter cited in text.

10. Gianna Manzini, "Parole povere," in *Album di ritratti* (Milano: Mondadori, 1964), 229.

11. Gianna Manzini, "La lezione della Woolf," in *Forte come un leone* (reprint, Milano: Mondadori, 1947), 79.

12. Virginia Woolf, *To the Lighthouse* (London: Dent, 1971), 54.

13. Interview quoted in Lia Fava Guzzetta, *Manzini*, Il Castoro 96 (Firenze: La Nuova Italia, 1974), 5.

14. Fava Guzzetta, *Manzini*, 8.

15. Fava Guzzetta, *Manzini*, 36.

16. Fava Guzzetta, *Manzini*, 13.

17. Like Elsa Morante (see chap. 5), Manzini is embodied in the male protagonists of her works, in whom she blends masculine and feminine traits. She has been seen as an exceptionally sensitive amalgamator of animus and anima—"authoritative and at the same time humble, extremely intelligent and defenseless, complex and evident, rigorous and flexible" (Giacomo Debenedetti, "La Manzini, l'anima e la danza," in *Intermezzo* [Milano: Mondadori, 1963], 130).

18. Gianna Manzini, *Ritratto in piedi* (Milano: Mondadori, 1971), 78–79; hereafter cited in text.

19. Fava Guzzetta, *Manzini*, 17.

20. Salvatore Battaglia, "Le 'frantumate lontananze' di Gianna Manzini," *Il Dramma* 6 (1971): 104–5.

21. Gino Rizzo, "L'*imago* paterna in G. Manzini," *Albero* 51 (1974): 30.

22. Fava Guzzetta, *Manzini*, 12.

23. Fava Guzzetta, *Manzini*, 123.

24. Miceli-Jeffries, "Gianna Manzini's Poetics," 102.

25. Cf. Rosalind Jones, "Julia Kristeva on Femininity: The Limits of a Semiotic Politics," *Feminist Review* 18 (1984): 63.

26. Gianna Manzini, "La lezione della Woolf," in *Forte come un leone* (Milano: Mondadori, 1947), 77, 78.

4. Lalla Romano

1. Romano has translated Flaubert's *Trois contes* (1994) and *L'éducation sentimentale* (1984); selected pages of Delacroix's *Journal* (1945); and Béatrix Beck's *Léon Morin, prêtre* (1954).

2. Lalla Romano, *Un sogno del Nord* (Torino: Einaudi, 1989), 87.

3. Lalla Romano, "Lalla Romano: In punta di penna il sapore delle cose," interview by Maria Pia Bonante, *Madre* 11 (1987): 127.

4. Eugenio Montale, "Non mettetela nell'apartheid," *L'Espresso*, 21 April 1991, 115.

5. Lalla Romano, "Ogni mio amore è un libro," interview by Simonetta Fiori, *La Repubblica*, 22–23 September 1991, 33.

6. Sandra Petrignani, "Bricciole di gloria," *Panorama*, 13 October 1991, 157.

7. Fiora Vincenti, *Lalla Romano*, Il Castoro 94 (Firenze: La Nuova Italia, 1974), 2, 5.

8. Romano, "Ogni mio amore," 33.

9. Petrignani, "Bricciole di gloria," 157.

10. Lalla Romano, *Opere*, edited by Cesare Segre, vol. 1 (Milano: Mondadori, 1991), 1067.

11. Natalia Ginzburg, *Never Must You Ask Me* (London: Joseph, 1973), 150.

12. Flavia Brizio, "Memory and Time in Lalla Romano's Novels, *La penombra che abbiamo attraversato* and *Le parole tra noi leggere*," in *Contemporary Women Writers in Italy*, edited by Santo L. Aricò (Amherst: University of Massachusetts Press, 1990), 74. Some of the English translations of quotations from Romano's works throughout this chapter have been drawn from Brizio's essay.

13. Lalla Romano, *Le parole tra noi leggere* (Torino, Einaudi, 1969), 20; hereafter cited in text.

14. Brizio, "Memory and Time," 71–73.

15. Vincenti, *Lalla Romano*, 57.

16. Paola Blelloch, *Quel mondo dei guanti e delle stoffe . . .* (Verona: Essedue Edizioni, 1987), 101.

17. See "La scrittura e l'inconscio," in *Un sogno del Nord*, 179–80.

18. Lalla Romano, "Intervista a Lalla Romano," interview by Alfredo Barberis, *Millelibri* 2, no. 8 (1988): 64.

19. Romano, "Ogni mio amore," 33.

20. Lalla Romano, *Maria* (Torino: Einaudi, 1953), 5.

21. Lalla Romano, preface to *Maria* (reprint, Torino: Einaudi, 1973), quoted in Vincenti, *Lalla Romano*, 19.

22. In Romano, *Opere*, lxxviii.

23. In Romano, *Opere*, lxxix.

24. In Romano, *Opere*, lxxix.

25. Romano, "Intervista," interview by Barberis, 70.

26. In Romano, *Opere*, lxxxi.

27. Lalla Romano, *L'uomo che parlava solo* (Torino: Einaudi, 1961), 171.

28. Vincenti, *Lalla Romano*, 35.

29. See Vincenti, *Lalla Romano*, 39.

30. In Romano, *Opere*, lxxxi.

31. Lalla Romano, " . . . Che cosa ci aspettiamo anche dal linguaggio dell'arte, se non verità, che vuol poi dire ricerca dell'autentico?" *Uomini e libri* 15, no. 76 (1979): 58.

32. Anna Banti, "Lalla Romano," *Paragone Letteratura* 178 (1964): 97.

33. Brizio, "Memory and Time," 68–69.

34. Lalla Romano, *La penombra che abbiamo attraversato* (Torino: Einaudi, 1964), 24.

35. Banti, "Lalla Romano," 96, 98.

36. Vincenti, *Lalla Romano*, 45.

37. Flavia Brizio, "The Photographic Novels of Lalla Romano" (paper presented at the ninth annual conference of the American Association for Italian Studies at the University of Lowell, Lowell, Massachusetts, 13–16 April 1989).

38. Lalla Romano, *Nei mari estremi* (Milano: Mondadori, 1987), 220.

39. Not to be confused with her essay "Un sogno del Nord," written in 1992 as the introduction to Touring Club Italiano's volume on Finland, Norway, and Sweden.

40. In Romano, *Opere*, xcix.

41. Lalla Romano, "Intervista a Lalla Romano per *Le lune di Hvar*," interview by Claudio Toscani, *Otto/Novecento* 15, no. 6 (1991): 145.

42. Romano, "Ogni mio amore," 33.

43. Cf. Carol M. Lazzaro-Weis, "From Margins to Mainstream: Some Perspectives on Women and Literature in Italy in the 1980s," in *Contemporary Women Writers in Italy*, edited by Santo Aricò (Amherst: University of Massachusetts Press, 1990), 199.

44. Romano, "Lalla Romano: In punta di penna," 126. Natalia Ginzburg, by way of contrast, shunned literary "immobility," which she defined as "ceasing to search for signs of life in the world around us" (Alan Bullock, *Natalia Ginzburg: Human Relationships in a Changing World* [New York and Oxford: Berg Publishers, 1991], 8).

45. In Romano, *Opere*, xci.

46. Lector [Claudio Marabini], "Lalla Romano parla di *Inseparabile*," *Resto del Carlino*, 5 September 1981, 8.

47. In Romano, *Opere*, lxxiv.

48. Sergio Antonielli, "Lalla Romano, *L'ospite*," *Belfagor* 29 (1974): 229.

49. Romano, "Ogni mio amore," 33.

5. Elsa Morante

1. Jean-Noël Schifano, "Barbara e divina," *L'Espresso*, 2 December 1984, 123, 127, 131. Morante's brother clarifies the question of the two fathers in Marcello Morante, *Maledetta benedetta: Elsa e sua madre* (Milano: Garzanti, 1986), 9–20.

2. Donatella Ravanello, *Scrittura e follia nei romanzi di Elsa Morante* (Venezia: Marsilio, 1980), 15.

3. Schifano, "Barbara e divina," 123.

4. Elsa Morante, *Diario 1938*, edited by Alba Andreini (Torino: Einaudi, 1989), 7; hereafter cited as *Diario*. Translations from the diary are my own.

5. Luigina Stefani, "Elsa Morante," *Belfagor* 26, no. 3 (1971): 290–91.

6. Elsa Morante, *Aracoeli* (Torino: Einaudi, 1982), 52: hereafter cited in text.

7. Elsa Morante, *Il mondo salvato dai ragazzini* (Torino: Einaudi, 1968), x. See also Morante's unfinished letter to the Red Brigades in "Pagine di diario," *Paragone Letteratura* 456 (1988): 15–16.

8. Ravanello, *Scrittura*, 42, 44, 69 n. 18, 84.

9. Elsa Morante, "Nove domande sul romanzo," *Nuovi Argomenti* 38–39 (1959): 38.

10. Morante, *Diario 1938*, xi.

11. Published serially in *I Diritti della Scuola*, 25 September 1935 to 15 August 1936.

12. Stefani, "Elsa Morante," 304.

13. See Ines Scaramucci, "Anna Maria Ortese," *Letteratura Italiana: I Contemporanei* 5 (1974): 887–901; Franca Bosco, "L'ultimo libro di Ortese: Tra sonno e veglia memorie e visioni," *Esperienze Letterarie* 14 (January–March 1989): 105–7; and Alba Amoia, *Women on the Italian Literary Scene: A Panorama* (Troy, New York: Whitston Publishing Company, 1992), 21–24.

14. John Bayley, "Off the Map," *New York Review of Books*, 12 May 1994, 23.

15. Elsa Morante, *L'isola di Arturo* (Torino: Einaudi, 1957), 73, 204; hereafter cited in text.

16. "Una lettera inedita del febbraio 1957 a Giacomo Debenedetti," *Corriere della Sera*, 26 November 1985, 3.

17. Schifano, "Barbara e divina," 133.

18. Giacomo Debenedetti, "L'isola della Morante," in *Intermezzo* (Milano: Mondadori, 1963), 110.

19. Saba, Sandro Penna, and Pier Paolo Pasolini were Morante's closest poet friends. Cf. Carlo Sgorlon, *Invito alla lettura di Elsa Morante*, 3d ed. (Milano: Mursia, 1978), 10, passim.

20. Morante, *Diario 1938*, viii, 7.

21. Elsa Morante, *History: A Novel*. Translated by William Weaver (New York: Knopf, 1977), 37; hereafter cited in text.

22. Angelo R. Pupino, "Elsa Morante," *Letteratura Italiana: I Contemporanei* 3 (1969): 735, 740.

23. Gianni Venturi, *Morante*. II Castoro 130 (Firenze: La Nuova Italia, 1977), 18.

24. Stefani, "Elsa Morante," 303.

25. Venturi, *Morante*, 52.

26. Coincidentally, Morante and Aleramo shared a common private ideal: "to travel around the world as a street singer," in Morante's words, in the conviction that only this way could contact be made with a public capable of hearing "the word of poets" (*Il mondo salvato dai ragazzini*, x).

27. Elsa Morante, *Menzogna e sortilegio*, 1st ed. in the "Struzzi" series (Torino: Einaudi, 1975), 21; hereafter cited in text. Quotations are from this edition, in my translation.

28. Valeria Finucci, "The Textualization of a Female 'I': Elsa Morante's *Menzogna e sortilegio*," *Italica* 65 (1988): 308–9, 315.

29. Stefani, "Elsa Morante," 306.

30. Ravanello, *Scrittura*, 69 n. 18.

31. Ravanello, *Scrittura*, 44, 46.
32. Elsa Morante, "Il ladro di lumi," in *Lo scialle andaluso* (Torino: Einaudi, 1963), 15.
33. For discussion of Arturo's father's narcissistic rejection of womanhood, see Luisa Guj, "Illusion and Literature in Morante's *L'isola di Arturo*," *Italica* 65 (1988): 149–50.
34. Ravanello, *Scrittura*, 85, 87 n. 23.
35. Schifano, "Barbara e divina," 127.

6. Natalia Ginzburg

1. Natala Ginzburg, quoted in Alan Bullock, *Natalia Ginzburg: Human Relationships in a Changing World* (New York and Oxford: Berg Publishers, 1991), 11.
2. Natalia Ginzburg, *Paese di mare ed altre commedie* (Milano: Garzanti, 1973), 172; hereafter cited in text.
3. Molyda Szymusiak, *Il racconto di Peuw, bambina cambogiana*, translated with a preface by Natalia Ginzburg (Torino: Einaudi, 1986).
4. Natalia Ginzburg, *Le piccole virtù* (Torino: Einaudi, 1962), 82.
5. Natalia Ginzburg, "Con molto sentimento," interview by Oriana Fallaci, in *Gli antipatici* (Milano: Rizzoli, 1963), 355.
6. Isabel Quigly, in *Contemporary Literary Criticism*, edited by Dedria Bryfonski (Detroit, Michigan: Gale Research Company, 1979), 11:230.
7. Natalia Ginzburg, *Voices in the Evening* (New York: Arcade; Little, Brown, and Company, 1989), 113; hereafter cited in text.
8. Natalia Ginzburg, *Valentino and Sagittarius* (Manchester: Carcanet, 1987), 10–11, 49; hereafter cited in text.
9. Natalia Ginzburg, "Questo mondo non mi piace," interview by Raffaello Baldini, *Panorama*, 3 May 1973, 135.
10. Ginzburg, "Questo mondo non mi piace,", 132.
11. Fyodor Dostoyevsky, *Notes from Underground*, translated with an afterword by Andrew R. MacAndrew (New York: Penguin, 1980), 170.
12. Alan Bullock devotes a long chapter to the male characters in Natalia Ginzburg's works in *Natalia Ginzburg*.
13. Natalia Ginzburg, "Mio marito," in *Cinque romanzi brevi* (Torino: Einaudi, 1964), 395.
14. For a psychoanalytic study of the two sisters in *Tutti i nostri ieri*, see Bettina L. Knapp, *Women in Twentieth-Century Literature: A Jungian View* (University Park and London: Pennsylvania State University Press, 1987), 69–85.
15. Natalia Ginzburg, *Tutti i nostri ieri* (reprint, Torino: Einaudi, 1975), 321.
16. Italo Calvino, "Natalia Ginzburg o le possibilità del romanzo borghese," *L'Europa Letteraria* 9–10 (June–August 1961): 132–38.
17. Natalia Ginzburg, *Dear Michael* (London: Owen, 1975), 161.

18. Natalia Ginzburg, *The City and the House* (Manchester: Carcanet, 1986), 219.

19. Marguerite Yourcenar, *Alexis ou le traité du vain combat* (Paris: Au Sans Pareil, 1929), xi.

20. Natalia Ginzburg, *Lessico famigliare* (Torino: Einaudi, 1963), 173; hereafter cited in text.

21. Cesare Garboli, quoted in Corrado Stajano, Salvatore Mannuzzu, and Natalia Ginzburg, "Ritratto: Natalia Ginzburg," *Leggere* 37 (1992): 27.

22. Bullock, *Natalia Ginzburg*, 224, 227.

23. Natalia Ginzburg, "Nove domande sul romanzo," interview, *Nuovi Argomenti* 38 (1991): 91–92.

24. Stajano, Mannuzzu, and Ginzburg, "Ritratto," 27; and Daniela Pasti, "La profondità di un cuore semplice," *La Repubblica*, 9 October 1991, 33.

7. Rosetta Loy

1. Cf. Mirella Serri, "Una saga in Monferrato ispirata dalla foto della nonna," *La Stampa*, 12 December 1987, 3.

2. Rosetta Loy, *La bicicletta* (Torino: Einaudi, 1974), 36; hereafter cited in text.

3. Rosetta Loy, "Gli orecchini," *Paragone Letteratura* 468 (1989): 20. This tale became the first chapter of Loy's 1992 novel, *Sogni d'inverno* (Milano: Mondadori).

4. Angela Bianchini, "Il vivere quotidiano," in *Scritture, scrittrici*, edited by Maria Rosa Cutrufelli (Milano: Longanesi, 1988), 34.

5. William Cullen Bryant, "The Future Life," stanza 1, in John Bartlett, *Familiar Quotations* (Boston: Little, Brown, and Company, 1950), 373.

6. Elena Gianini Belotti, "Letteratura femminile: Quattro campioni di erotismo," *Paragone Letteratura* 478 (1989): 96.

7. Belotti, "Letteratura femminile," 95–96.

8. Marisa Rusconi, "Nuovi percorsi tra esperienza e scrittura," in *Scritture, scrittrici*, edited by Maria Rosa Cutrufelli (Milano: Longanesi, 1988), 23.

9. Cesare Garboli, quoted in Angela Bianchini, "Il vivere quotidiano," in *Scritture, scrittrici*, edited by Maria Rosa Cutrufelli (Milano: Longanesi, 1988), 33.

10. Rosetta Loy, *Le strade di polvere* (Torino: Einaudi, 1987), 217; hereafter cited in text.

11. Rosetta Loy, *All'insaputa della notte* (Milano: Garzanti, 1984), 40; hereafter cited in text.

12. Belotti, "Letteratura femminile," 97.

13. Gabriella Lapasini, "I gesti dell'amore," in *Scritture, scrittrici*, edited by Maria Rosa Cutrufelli (Milano: Longanesi, 1988), 67.

14. Among Loy's detractors are Natalia Ginzburg, Lucio Villari, and Guglielmo Petroni. See Laura Lilli, "Premio Viareggio: La parte del leone tocca a Einaudi," *La Repubblica*, 2 July 1988, 21.

15. Lalla Romano, "Ogni mio amore è un libro," interview by Simonetta Fiori, *La Repubblica*, 22–23 September 1991, 33.

8. Dacia Maraini

1. Grazia Sumeli Weinberg, "All'ombra del padre: La poesia di Dacia Maraini in *Crudeltà all'aria aperta*," *Italica* 67 (1990): 453.
2. Paola Blelloch, *Quel mondo dei guanti e delle stoffe* . . . (Verona: Essedue Edizioni, 1987), 120.
3. Sumeli Weinberg, "All'ombra del padre," 453.
4. Anthony J. Tamburri, "Dacia Maraini's *Donna in guerra*: Victory or Defeat?" in *Contemporary Women Writers in Italy*, edited by Santo L. Aricò (Amherst: University of Massachusetts Press, 1990), 143.
5. Dacia Maraini, "Bruciare vivi davanti alla televisione," *L'Unità*, 3 February 1992, 1.
6. Robin Pickering-Iazzi, "Designing Mothers: Images of Motherhood in Aleramo, Morante, Maraini, and Fallaci," *Annali d'Italianistica* 7 (1989): 336.
7. Tamburri, "Maraini's *Donna in guerra*," 140–41.
8. Dacia Maraini, "Nove domande sul romanzo," interview, *Nuovi Argomenti* 38 (1991): 101.
9. Telefono Rosa, in the belief that solutions to the plight of women require both male and female cooperation, plans to offer "gender-blind" courses in sexuality and the rights of women. See Marina Garbesi, "Sposate alla paura: Il marito le picchia nessuna si ribella," *La Repubblica*, 7 March 1992, 7.
10. See Dacia Maraini, *La nuit de Tempaku-ryô*, interview by Ryôji Nakamura and René de Ceccatty, *Europe* 693–94 (1987): 140–54.
11. Dacia Maraini, "Con Pasolini e altri amici in una città amata e odiata," interview by Antonio Debenedetti, *Corriere della Sera*, 15 July 1984, 2.
12. Dacia Maraini, "Perché questa donna? Mi è venuta a cercare . . . ," interview by Filippo Abbiati, *Il Giorno*, 10 September 1990, 3.
13. The title of the collection was suggested to Maraini by a Japanese fable she had heard as a child in Kyoto. The fox, in Japanese tradition, is never simply an animal but rather a woman transformed into a fox by some secret spell.
14. Dacia Maraini, "Dacia Maraini: 'La mia innata tendenza al nomadismo,' " interview by Antonio Debenedetti, *Corriere della Sera*, 15 November 1991, 5.
15. Cf. Fiora A. Bassanese, "Armanda Guiducci's Disposable Women," in *Contemporary Women Writers in Italy*, edited by Santo L. Aricò (Amherst: University of Massachusetts Press), 153–69.
16. Carol Lazzaro-Weis, "From Margins to Mainstream: Some Perspectives on Women and Literature in Italy in the 1980s," in *Contemporary Women Writers in Italy*, edited by Santo L. Aricò (Amherst: University of Massachusetts Press), 202.
17. Roberto Wis, "La Dacia in fallo," *Il Giornale*, 14 April 1986, 3.

18. Carol Lazzaro-Weis, "Gender and Genre in Italian Feminist Literature in the Seventies," *Italica* 65 (1988): 304.

19. Maraini, "Con Pasolini," 2.

20. Maraini, "Nove domande," 101–2.

21. Dacia Maraini, *La bionda, la bruna e l'asino: Con gli occhi di oggi sugli anni Settanta e Ottanta* (Milano: Rizzoli, 1987), 65.

22. Dacia Maraini, "Siamo sempre state donne, mai persone," interview by Lidia Ravera, *Corriere della Sera,* 7 April 1987, 3.

23. Dacia Maraini, *Isolina: La donna tagliata in pezzi* (Milano: Mondadori, 1985), 63; hereafter cited in text.

24. For an analysis of this novel's picaresque elements, see Lazzaro-Weis, "Gender and Genre," 298–300.

25. For an analysis of this novel, see Tamburri, "Maraini's *Donna in guerra,*" 139–49; and Lazzaro-Weis, "Gender and Genre," 300–304.

26. Lazzaro-Weis, "From Margins to Mainstream," 205; and "Gender and Genre," 295.

27. Lazzaro-Weis, "Gender and Genre," 299.

28. Pickering-Iazzi, "Designing Mothers," 335.

29. Dacia Maraini, *Donna in guerra* (Torino: Einaudi, 1975), 72. This and subsequent translations are drawn from Tamburri, "Maraini's *Donna in guerra.*"

30. Sumeli Weinberg, "All'ombra del padre," 453.

31. Maraini, "Nove domande," 102.

32. Sumeli Weinberg, "All'ombra del padre," 461.

33. Dacia Maraini, *A memoria,* with an introduction by Renato Barilli (Milano: Bompiani, 1967), 10.

34. Maraini, *A memoria,* 10.

35. Maraini, *A memoria,* 15.

36. Dacia Maraini, "Il Settecento delle donne? Un secolo muto," interview by Monica Ricci Sargentini, *L'Unità,* 7 March 1990, 15. The novel was inspired by a 1724 portrait and a box of written notes that the author discovered on a return visit to Villa Valguarnera in Bagheria. The painting depicted a lady, Countess Marianna Alliata di Valguarnera (1706–50), one of Maraini's maternal ancestors, holding a sheet of inscribed laid paper. Marianna Ucrìa's name and her title of duchess in the novel are fictitious, but her physical handicap is not.

37. Dacia Maraini, *La lunga vita di Marianna Ucrìa* (Milano: Rizzoli, 1990), 7; hereafter cited in text. A stage version of the novel, in Sicilian dialect, was produced by the Teatro Stabile of Catania in January 1993. Translations from the novel are my own.

38. See Arnaldo D'Amico, "Nei segreti della mente: 'Il cervello? E' solo un naso iperevoluto,' " *La Repubblica,* 12–13 July 1992, 22.

39. Alessandra Venezia, "Il filo di Marianna," *Panorama,* 4 March 1990, 19.

40. Dacia Maraini, "Perché anch'io sono stata muta," interview by Stella Pende, *Europeo,* 21 September 1990, 35.

41. Maraini, "Il Settecento delle donne?" 15.

42. Maraini, "Nove domande," 101.
43. Dacia Maraini, "Un nuovo linguaggio per il teatro italiano," interview by Roberta Sibona, *La Repubblica*, 20 January 1983, 29.
44. Maraini, "Dacia Maraini," 5.

9. Matilde Serao, Oriana Fallaci, Camilla Cederna

1. The name is connected with the empire of Trebizond.
2. Quoted in Michele Prisco, "Matilde Serao," *Terzo Programma* 3 (1963): 59.
3. Quoted in Isabella Pezzini, "Matilde Serao," in *Carolina Invernizio, Matilde Serao, Liala*, edited by Umberto Eco, Marina Federzoni, Isabella Pezzini, and Maria Pia Pozzato, Il Castoro 145 (Firenze: La Nuova Italia, 1979), 82.
4. Wanda de Nunzio Schilardi, *Matilde Serao giornalista (con antologia di scritti rari)* (Lecce: Milella, 1986), 24.
5. A recent edition of this work (Napoli: Liguori, 1985) has been reviewed by Lucienne Kroha in "Matilde Serao: *Il romanzo della fanciulla*," *Quaderni d'italianistica* 11 (1990): 152–57.
6. Schilardi, *Serao giornalista*, 29.
7. Matilde Serao, *Il ventre di Napoli* (Milano: Treves, 1984), 31; hereafter cited in text.
8. Letter of 22 March 1878 from Serao to Gaetano Bonavenia, *Nuova Antologia* 16 (1938): 4.
9. Schilardi, *Serao giornalista*, 30.
10. Letter of February 1882 from Serao to Ulderico Mariani, quoted in Anna Banti, "La Serao a Roma (1882–84)," *Paragone Letteratura* 182 (1965): 42.
11. Undated letter from Count Giuseppe Primoli to Enrico Nencioni, quoted in Anna Banti, "La Serao a Roma," 49.
12. Natalia Ginzburg, "Scrittori della realtà," *Leggere* 37 (1992): 33–35.
13. Letter from Serao to Ulderico Mariani of 18 April 1882, quoted in Anna Banti, "La Serao a Roma," 44.
14. Matilde Serao, *Lettere di una viaggiatrice* (Napoli: Perrella, 1908), 20.
15. Cf. Schilardi, *Serao giornalista*, 99.
16. Schilardi, *Serao giornalista*, 114.
17. But see M. G. Martin Gistucci, "Lo specchio ribelle," in *Matilde Serao tra giornalismo e letteratura*, edited by Gianni Infusino (Napoli: Guida Editori, 1981), 45–60, for a portrait of Hérelle as Serao's "traduttore e traditore" [translator and traitor].
18. Pezzini, "Matilde Serao," 94.
19. For analyses of the female universe in Serao's novels, see Pezzini, "Matilde Serao"; Gianni Infusino, "Aristocrazia e popolo (le donne negli scritti di Matilde Serao)," in *Serao tra giornalismo e letteratura* (Napoli: Guida Editori, 1981), 61–72; and Schilardi, *Serao giornalista*, 59–73.
20. Matilde Serao, *Vita e avventure di Riccardo Joanna* (reprint, Milano: Garzanti, 1939), 78.
21. Matilde Serao, 1894 interview, quoted in Prisco, "Matilde Serao," 63.

22. Prisco, "Matilde Serao," 85.

23. Schilardi, *Serao giornalista*, 24.

24. Schilardi, *Serao giornalista*, 21–22.

25. Oriana Fallaci, "Mi piace l'idea di vendicare tutte le donne," interview by Giancarlo Graziosi, *Domenica del Corriere*, 12 May 1974, 83.

26. Ruggero Guarini, in Marco Fini, "Fallaci Oriana la Veterana," *Epoca*, 20 March 1988, 41.

27. See Elizabeth Peer, "The Fallaci Papers," *Newsweek*, 1 December 1980, 54.

28. "Monument to a Martyr," *Time*, 17 September 1979, 31.

29. Peer, "Fallaci Papers," 54.

30. Oriana Fallaci, "Grazie, babbo, della tua inflessibilità," *Europeo*, 18 August 1990, 63–64.

31. Oriana Fallaci, "Speciale," interview, *Europeo*, 12 April 1991, 7.

32. Marco Nozza, "Guerra e amore nel 'suo' Libano," *Il Giorno*, 7 August 1990, 3.

33. Oriana Fallaci, quoted in *Contemporary Authors*, edited by Frances C. Locher (Detroit, Michigan: Gale Research Company, 1979), 77–80:134.

34. Fallaci, "Speciale," 10.

35. Locher, *Contemporary Authors*, 77–80:134.

36. Peer, "Fallaci Papers," 53.

37. Nozza, "Guerra e amore," 3.

38. Fallaci, "Mi piace l'idea," 83.

39. Quoted in Marco Fini, "Signora grandi firme," *Epoca*, 30 June 1990, 32.

40. Oriana Fallaci, *Intervista con la storia* (Milano: Rizzoli, 1974), 5.

41. Cf. Salvatore Scarpino, "Rambo, l'ultimo amore di Oriana," *Il Giornale*, 3 March 1988, 1; and Fini, "Fallaci Oriana la Veterana," 40–45.

42. Locher, *Contemporary Authors*, 77–80:134.

43. Fallaci deplores the amount of abuse, prevarication, and gratuitous cruelty there is in journalism if it is practiced without intelligence and morality. A case in point is her interview with Lech Walesa: she admitted that she was insincere, that she did not like him, that she hesitated before publishing the interview, but that meeting deadlines favors the committing of judgmental errors.

44. There are similarities between the prison descriptions and the analysis of the relationship between prisoner and jailer in Vladimir Bukovskij's *The Wind Goes and Comes* and Fallaci's *Un uomo*. But she had already written her novel when she read Bukovskij's book.

45. A book with the same title appeared in 1924 on the subject of Italy's colonial war in Libya: Giannetto Bongiovanni, *Insciallah!* (Milano: Sonzogno).

46. Furio Colombo, "Fallaci," *La Stampa*, 8 June 1990, 15.

47. Peer, "Fallaci Papers," 53.

48. Oriana Fallaci, *A Man* (New York: Simon and Schuster, 1980), 132–33; hereafter cited in text.

49. "Monument to a Martyr," 31.

50. Luciana Marchionne Picchione, "Oriana Fallaci, *Un uomo*," *Canadian Journal of Italian Studies* 4 (1979): 327–28.

51. Oriana Fallaci, "Volevo scrivere un libro sulla Vita," interview by Davide Lajolo, *Corriere della Sera*, 15 July 1979, 8.

52. Paola Blelloch, *Quel mondo dei guanti e delle stoffe* . . . (Verona: Essedue Edizioni, 1987), 75.

53. Domenico Porzio, in *Primi piani* (Milano: Mondadori, 1976), quoted in Nozza, "Guerra e amore," 3.

54. Colombo, "Fallaci," 15.

55. Nozza, "Guerra e amore," 3.

56. Fallaci sought Buck out in Philadelphia for an interview and was incensed to learn that the *New York Times* had rejected the latter's favorable review of *Se il sole muore* (1965; *If the Sun Dies*, 1966), Fallaci's book about the American space adventure, because the editor of the newspaper's literary section was a friend of Werner von Braun, whose Nazi past Fallaci had exposed.

57. Oriana Fallaci, "Oriana Fallaci," interview by Patrizia Carrano, in *Le signore "grandi firme"* (Rimini and Firenze: Guaraldi, 1978), 97–99.

58. Adele Cambria, "Gli anni dei movimenti," in *Scritture. scrittrici*, edited by Maria Rosa Cutrufelli (Milano: Longanesi, 1988), 44.

59. Blelloch, *Quel mondo*, 73.

60. Fallaci, "Speciale," 9.

61. Umberto Cecchi, "Una notte, cercando Insciallah," *Europeo*, 18 August 1990, 60.

62. Santo L. Aricò, "Oriana Fallaci's Journalistic Novel: *Niente e così sia*," in *Contemporary Women Writers in Italy* (Amherst: University of Massachusetts Press, 1990), 181.

63. Santo L. Aricò has studied this work closely in "Oriana Fallaci's Discovery of Truth in *Niente e così sia*," *European Studies Journal* 3 (1986): 11–23; and in "Oriana Fallaci's Journalistic Novel," 171–82.

64. Claudio Altarocca, "Fallaci sola a New York col diavolo in corpo," *La Stampa*, 9 August 1991, 15.

65. Aricò, "Oriana Fallaci's Journalistic Novel," 178.

66. Oriana Fallaci, *Nothing and Amen* (New York: Doubleday, 1972), 3; hereafter cited in text.

67. Fallaci has been called the "female Curzio Malaparte" for her arch-Italianism as well. Her master for both writing and lifestyles, Malaparte predicted she would be successful outside Italy but not in it. See Laura Lilli, "Come Eco più di Eco?" *La Repubblica*, 26 July 1990, 29.

68. Altarocca, "Fallaci sola," 15.

69. Fallaci, "Volevo scrivere," 8.

70. Altarocca, "Fallaci sola," 15.

71. Anthony Hartley, "Dungeons and Dragons in the Beirut Rubble," *The European*, 19–21 October 1990, 4.

72. Claudio Gorlier, "Feuilleton Oriana," *La Stampa*, 11 August 1990, 3.

73. Giancarlo Vigorelli, "Il racconto più umano sul dramma d'un popolo," *Il Giorno*, 7 August 1990, 3.

74. Oriana Fallaci, *Insciallah* (Milano: Rizzoli, 1990), 207; hereafter cited in text.

75. For a "mathematical review" of *Insciallah* by a mathematician, see Michele Emmer, "Alibi per la matematica," *L'Unità*, 29 September 1990, 16.

76. Guido Almansi, "La montagna e il cagnolone," *Panorama*, 5 August 1990, 91.

77. Gorlier, "Feuilleton," 3; Silvia Sereni, "Una mezza critica," *Epoca*, 21 November 1990, 26.

78. Aricò, "Oriana Fallaci's Journalistic Novel," 172.

79. Fallaci, "Oriana Fallaci," 92.

80. Fallaci, "Volevo scrivere," 8.

81. Camilla Cederna, *Il lato forte e il lato debole* (Milano: Mondadori, 1992), 84; hereafter cited in text when quoted there directly. This work is a collection of pieces, most of which were published earlier in various dailies, weeklies, and monthlies (*Corriere della Sera, Gioia, Grazia, King, Panorama,* and *Quattrozampe*).

82. Giampaolo Martelli, "Il lato debole d'una radical-chic," *Il Giornale*, 19 April 1979, 3.

83. Alberto Salani and Carla Stampa, "Camilla tra i leoni," *Epoca*, 26 April 1978, 93.

84. According to experts, even though Leone was already under investigation, Cederna's book removed the last doubts of the opposition parties on the Left, who, thus provoked, had no alternative but to call for the president's resignation.

85. Maria Luisa Agnese and Rachele Enriquez, "Furia Camilla," *Panorama*, 1 December 1980, 164.

86. Cederna, *Il lato forte e il lato debole*, 204–7.

87. Adolfo Chiesa, "Tutti i nemici di Camilla," *Paese Sera*, 8 December 1980, 3.

88. Rachele Enriquez, "Viaggio con grinta e sberleffo," *Panorama*, 28 February 1983, 135.

89. Camilla Cederna, *Il mondo di Camilla* (Milano: Feltrinelli, 1980), 12.

90. Camilla Cederna, *Signore e signori* (Milano: Longanesi, 1966), 561; translation from Giovanna Bellesia, "Camilla Cederna: Portrayer of Italian Society," in *Contemporary Women Writers in Italy*, edited by Santo L. Aricò (Amherst: University of Massachusetts Press, 1990), 186.

91. Cederna, *Il lato forte e il lato debole*, 193.

92. Bellesia, "Camilla Cederna," 188.

93. Bellesia, "Camilla Cederna," 192.

94. Bellesia, "Camilla Cederna," 185.

95. Camilla Cederna, "Camilla Cederna," interview by Patrizia Carrano, in *Le signore "grandi firme"* (Rimini and Firenze: Guaraldi, 1978), 59.

96. Cederna, *Il lato forte e il lato debole*, 225.

97. Bellesia, "Camilla Cederna," 186.

98. Cederna, *Il lato forte e il lato debole*, 11.

99. Bellesia, "Camilla Cederna," 196.

100. Oreste del Buono, "La dottoressa Jekyll, presumo," *Europeo*, 31 January 1985, 95.

SELECTED
BIBLIOGRAPHY

Sibilla Aleramo

Primary Works

Novels

Una donna. Roma-Torino: Società tipografico-editrice Nazionale, 1906. Reprint, Milano: Feltrinelli, 1982. (*A Woman at Bay*. Translated by Maria H. Lansdale. New York and London: G. P. Putnam's Sons, 1908. *A Woman*. Translated by Rosalind Delmar. Los Angeles: University of California Press, 1980.)

Il passaggio. Milano: Treves, 1919. 3d ed., with a new preface by the author, Milano: Mondadori, 1932.

Amo dunque sono. Milano: Mondadori, 1927.

Il frustino. Milano: Mondadori, 1932.

Nonfiction

Andando e stando. Firenze: Bemporad, 1920.

Gioie di occasione. Milano: Mondadori, 1930.

Orsa minore. Milano: Mondadori, 1938.

Dal mio diario: 1940–44. Roma: Tumminelli, 1945.

Confessioni di scrittori (Interviste con se stessi): Quaderni della Radio XI. Torino: Edizioni Radio Italiana, 1951.

Diario di una donna: 1945–60. Milano: Feltrinelli, 1978.

La donna e il femminismo. Roma: Editori Riuniti, 1978.

Quel viaggio chiamato amore. Roma: Editori Riuniti, 1987. Contains correspondence with Dino Campana.

Lettere a Elio. Roma: Editori Riuniti, 1989. Contains correspondence with Elio Fiori.

Play

Endimione. Roma: Edizioni Stook, 1922.

Secondary Works

Bassanese, Fiora A. "*Una donna*: Autobiography as Exemplary Text." *Quaderni d'italianistica* 11 (1990): 41–60.

Bertelli, Elda Maria. "Sibilla Aleramo." In *Romanzieri e novellieri d'Italia nel secolo ventesimo*, 1:143–91. Roma: Edizioni de "Le Stanze del libro," 1936.

Ceccatty, René de. *Nuit en pays étranger*. Paris: Juillard, 1992.

Cecchi, Emilio, and Leonetta Cecchi Pieraccini. "Quel Dino Campana 'selvatico e diabolico.' " *La Repubblica*, 26 May 1990, 20–21.

Conti, Bruna, ed. *Sibilla Aleramo: La donna e il femminismo*. Roma: Editori Riuniti, 1978.

———. "Intervista impossibile con Sibilla Aleramo." *Il Ponte* 2 (1986): 145–57.

———. "Dino e Sibilla." *Paragone Letteratura* 444 (1987): 63–67.

Delli Colli, Lino. "Letteratura e società: Giovanni Cena, Ada Negri, Sibilla Aleramo." *Letteratura Italiana Contemporanea* 1 (1979): 215–30.

Federzoni, Marina, Isabella Pezzini, and Maria Pia Pozzato. *Sibilla Aleramo*. Il Castoro 161. Firenze: La Nuova Italia, 1980.

Fusella, Patrizia. "*A House in the Shadows* by Maria Messina." *Italian Americana* 2 (1993): 270–73.

Ghilardi, Margherita. "Lettere da un matrimonio." *La Repubblica*, 26 May 1990, 19.

Graf, Arturo. "Sibilla Aleramo, *Una donna*." *Nuova Antologia* A. 41, no. 840 (1906): 720–24.

Guerricchio, Rita. *Storia di Sibilla*. Pisa: Nistri-Lischi, 1974.

Jewell, Keala Jane. " 'Un furore d'autocreazione': Women and Writing in Sibilla Aleramo." *Canadian Journal of Italian Studies* 7 (1984): 148–62.

Livi, Grazia. "*Una donna*." *Paragone Letteratura* 282 (1973): 119–21.

Lombardi, Olga. "Sibilla Aleramo." *Belfagor* 5 (1986): 525–44.

Lombardi, Olga, Emilio Cecchi, and Sergio Solmi. "Sibilla Aleramo: Vita e arte-passione per 'l'apologia dello spirito femminile.' " *Letteratura Italiana. Novecento. I Contemporanei* 1 (1979): 736–64.

Mariani, Anna L. "Sibilla Aleramo. Significato di tre incontri col teatro: Il personaggio di Nora, Giacinta Pezzana, Eleonora Duse." *Teatro e Storia* 2 (1987): 67–133.

Mazzotti, Artal. "Sibilla Aleramo." *Letteratura Italiana. I Contemporanei* 1 (1977): 211–36.

Nicoletti, Giuseppe. "*Storia di Sibilla* di Rita Guerricchio." *Paragone Letteratura* 304 (1975): 119–22.

Pickering-Iazzi, Robin. "Designing Mothers: Images of Motherhood in Novels by Aleramo, Morante, Maraini, and Fallaci." *Annali d'Italianistica* 7 (1989): 325–40.

Pozzato, Maria Pia. *Sibilla Aleramo*. Il Castoro 161. Firenze: La Nuova Italia, 1980.

Quasimodo, Salvatore. *A Sibilla: Lettere d'amore di Salvatore Quasimodo 1931–36.* Milano: Rizzoli, 1983.

Zambon, Patrizia. "Aleramo, Sibilla (1876–1960)." In *Dizionario critico della letteratura italiana,* edited by Vittore Branca, 2d ed., 1:19–20. Torino: Unione Tipografica Editrice Torinese, 1986.

Camilla Cederna

Primary Works

Nonfiction

Noi siamo le signore. Milano: Longanesi, 1958.
La voce dei padroni. Milano: Longanesi, 1962.
Fellini 8 1/2. Milano: Longanesi, 1963.
Signore e signori. Milano: Longanesi, 1966.
Maria Callas. Milano: Longanesi, 1968.
Pinelli: Una finestra sulla strage. Milano: Feltrinelli, 1971.
Sparare a vista: Come la polizia del regime DC mantiene l'ordine pubblico. Milano: Feltrinelli, 1975.
Il lato debole: Diario italiano. Milano: Bompiani, 1977.
Giovanni Leone: La carriera di un presidente. Milano: Feltrinelli, 1978.
Nostra Italia del miracolo. Milano: Longanesi, 1980.
Casa nostra: Viaggi nei misteri d'Italia. Milano: Mondadori, 1983.
Vicino e distante. Milano: Mondadori, 1984.
Il meglio di. Milano: Mondadori, 1987.
Introduction to *Caro Duce.* Milano: Rizzoli, 1989.
Il lato forte e il lato debole. Milano: Mondadori, 1992.

Autobiographical Works

Il mondo di Camilla. Milano: Feltrinelli, 1980.

Interviews

"Camilla Cederna." Interview by Patrizia Carrano. In *Le signore "grandi firme,"* 45–68. Rimini and Firenze: Guaraldi, 1978.

Secondary Works

Agnese, Maria Luisa, and Rachele Enriquez. "Sulla pelle del Leone." *Panorama,* 22 August 1978, 57–59.
———. "Furia Camilla." *Panorama,* 1 December 1980, 164–67.
Aspesi, Natalia. "Mi vogliono sul rogo per poi farmi beata." *La Repubblica,* 9 February 1979, 13.

————. "Camilla nel salotto buono." *La Repubblica*, 20 May 1980, 19.

————. "Piccole storie vicine e lontane." *La Repubblica*, 12 February 1985, 20.

————. "Un bignè per la cavalla." *La Repubblica*, 10 December 1986, 30.

Bellesia, Giovanna. "Camilla Cederna: Portrayer of Italian Society." In *Contemporary Women Writers in Italy*, edited by Santo L. Aricò, 185–96. Amherst: University of Massachusetts Press, 1990.

Bianconi, Giovanni. "Un duello Marina-Camilla." *La Stampa*, 6 March 1991, 10.

Bignardi, Irene. "Cara Italia, odiate sponde." *La Repubblica*, 11 March 1983, 20–21.

————. "SuperCamilla." *La Repubblica*, 29 December 1987, 24.

Bocca, Giorgio. "Incontrando Camilla." *La Repubblica*, 17 December 1980, 18.

Chiesa, Adolfo. "Tutti i nemici di Camilla." *Paese Sera*, 8 December 1980, 3.

Conti Bertini, Lucia. "Il meglio di Camilla." *Il Ponte* 38 (1982): 415–16.

del Buono, Oreste. "La dottoressa Jekyll, presumo." *Europeo*, 31 January 1985, 95.

Emiliani, Vittorio. "Camilla Cederna." In *Perché lei*, 63–82. Bari: Laterza, 1985.

————. "Venga avanti la vera Camilla." *Europeo*, 19 October 1985, 207–9.

Enriquez, Rachele. "Viaggio con grinta e sberleffo." *Panorama*, 28 February 1981, 134–35.

Madeo, Liliana. "Duello tra le regine del giornalismo." *La Stampa*, 23 December 1990, 7.

Martelli, Gianpaolo. "Il lato debole d'una radical-chic." *Il Giornale*, 19 April 1979, 3.

Monicelli, Mino. "L'ha aiutata la frivolezza." *Millelibri* 53 (1992): 54–57.

Musumeci, Remo. "Camilla Cederna: 'E' un bidone rifilato alla gente.'" *L'Unità*, 8 October 1991, 28.

Nascimbeni, Giulio. "Camilla Cederna racconta il suo viaggio italiano." *Corriere della Sera*, 2 April 1983, 3.

Nozza, Marco. "Il 'mondo di Camillo' non è più sull'*Espresso*." *Il Giorno*, 5 March 1981, 3.

Pesenti, Roberto. "Incontri/Camilla Cederna." *Il Messaggero*, 16 April 1983, 5.

Regazzoni, Enrico. "Un presidente tra principini e troppi amici pericolosi." *La Repubblica*, 14 March 1978, 12.

Salani, Alberto, and Carla Stampa. "Camilla tra i leoni." *Epoca*, 26 April 1978, 90–94.

Grazia Deledda

Primary Works

Novels and Short Stories

Stella d'Oriente. Cagliari: Tipografia dell' "Avvenire di Sardegna," 1891.

Fior di Sardegna. Roma: Perino, 1892.

Racconti sardi. Sassari: Dessì, 1894.

Anime oneste. Milano: Cogliati, 1895.

La via del male. Torino: Speirani, 1896.

Il vecchio della montagna. Torino: Roux e Viarengo, 1900. Also published in Italian as a college text, edited by Joseph G. Fucilla (Chicago: University of Chicago Press, 1932).

Dopo il divorzio. Torino: Roux e Viarengo, 1902. Reprint, under the title *Naufraghi in porto*, Milano: Treves, 1920. (*After the Divorce: A romance*. Translated by Maria Horner Lansdale. New York: Henry Holt and Company, 1905.)

Elias Portolu. Torino: Roux e Viarengo, 1903.

Cenere. Roma: Ripamonti e Colombo, 1904. (*Ashes: A Sardinian Story*. Translated by Helen Hester Colvill. London and New York: John Lane, 1908.)

L'edera. Roma: Edizioni "Nuova Antologia," 1908.

Il nostro padrone. Milano: Treves, 1910.

Sino al confine. Milano: Treves, 1910.

Colombi e sparvieri. Milano: Treves, 1912.

Canne al vento. Milano: Treves, 1913.

Marianna Sirca. Milano: Treves, 1915. Also published in Italian as a college text, edited with introduction, notes, and vocabulary by Maro Beath Jones and Armando T. Bissiri (Boston: D. C. Heath and Company, 1940).

L'incendio nell'uliveto. Milano: Treves, 1918.

La madre. Milano: Treves, 1920. (*The Mother*. Translated by Mary G. Steegmann, with an introduction by D. H. Lawrence. London: Jonathan Cape, 1928. *The Woman and the Priest*. Translated by Mary G. Steegmann. London: Jonathan Cape, 1922.)

Il Dio dei viventi. Milano: Treves, 1922.

Romanzi e novelle. Edited by Emilio Cecchi. 5 vols. Milano: Mondadori, 1941–69.

Romanzi e novelle. 4 vols. Milano: Mondadori, 1950–55.

Grazia Deledda. Le opere: Il vecchio della montagna, Elias Portolu, Cenere, Canne al vento. Milano: Mondadori, 1955.

Opere scelte. Edited by Eurialo De Michelis. Milano: Mondadori, 1964.

Nonfiction

Premio Nobel per la letteratura 1926. Milano: Fabbri, 1966. Contains Swedish Academy discourse and unpublished letters.

Autobiographical-Fictional Works

Il paese del vento. Milano: Treves, 1931.

Cosima. Milano: Treves, 1937. (*Cosima*. Translated with an introduction by Martha King. New York: Italica, 1988.)

Secondary Works

Aste, Mario. "Grazia Deledda: *Cosima*." *Italica* 66 (1989): 49–50.

Bo, Carlo. "Ritratto di Grazia Deledda." *Nuova Antologia* 2160 (1986): 352–59.

Borgese, Giuseppe Antonio. "Grazia Deledda." In *La vita e il libro*, 2d ed., 2:95–104. Torino: Bocca, 1911.

Branca, Remo. *Bibliografia deleddiana*. Milano: L'Eroica, 1938.
————. *Il segreto di Grazia Deledda*. Cagliari: Fossataro, 1971.
Cantarella, Michele. "Grazia Deledda, 1871–1936." *Italica* 13 (1936): 105–7.
Capuana, Luigi. *Gli "ismi" contemporanei*. Catania: Gianotta, 1898.
Convegno Nazionale di Studi Deleddiani: Atti. Cagliari: Fossataro, 1974.
De Giovanni, Neria. *L'ora di Lilith: Su Grazia Deledda e la letteratura femminile del secondo Novecento*. Roma: Ellemme, 1987.
De Michelis, Eurialo. *Grazia Deledda e il decadentismo*. Firenze: La Nuova Italia, 1938.
Dolfi, Anna. *Grazia Deledda*. Milano: Mursia, 1979.
Greco, Lorenzo. "Amore fra cugini: Letteratura e contesto antropologico nella Deledda." *Il Ponte* 1–2 (1982): 109–22.
Lombardi, Olga. *Invito alla lettura di Grazia Deledda*. 2d ed. Milano: Mursia, 1983.
Miccinesi, Mario. *Deledda*. Il Castoro 105. Firenze: La Nuova Italia, 1975.
Mortara Garavelli, Bice. "La lingua di Grazia Deledda." *Strumenti Critici* 65 (1991): 145–63.
Petronio, Giuseppe. "Grazia Deledda." *Letteratura Italiana: I Contemporanei* 1 (1977): 137–58.
Piromalli, Antonio. *Grazia Deledda*. Firenze: La Nuova Italia, 1968.
————. "Grazia Deledda." *Letteratura Italiana. Novecento. I Contemporanei* 3 (1979): 2613–70.
Pirotti, Umberto. "Per *L'edera* di Grazia Deledda." *Italianistica* 20, no. 1(1991): 31–54.
Ramat, Silvio. "Due saggi su Grazia Deledda." In *Prontonovecento*, 67–192. Milano: Il Saggiatore, 1978.
Tanda, Nicola. "Grazia Deledda." *Letteratura Italiana Contemporanea* 1 (1979): 129–44.
Tecchi, Bonaventura. "I romanzi sardi della Deledda." In *Maestri e amici*, 32–43. Pescara: Tempo Nostro, 1932.
Vittorini, Domenico. "Deledda e i suoi primi contatti letterari." *Italica* 16 (1939): 123–27.

Oriana Fallaci

Primary Works

Novels

Penelope alla guerra. Milano: Rizzoli, 1962. (*Penelope at War*. London: Joseph, 1966.)
Lettera a un bambino mai nato. Milano: Rizzoli, 1975. (*Letter to an Unborn Child*. New York: Simon and Schuster, 1976.)
Un uomo. Milano: Rizzoli, 1979. (*A Man*. New York: Simon and Schuster, 1980.)
Insciallah. Milano: Rizzoli, 1990.

Nonfiction

I sette peccati di Hollywood. With a preface by Orson Welles. Milano: Longanesi, 1958.

Il sesso inutile: Viaggio intorno alla donna. Milano: Rizzoli, 1961. (*The Useless Sex*. New York: Horizon, 1964.)

Gli antipatici. Milano: Rizzoli, 1963. (*Limelighters*. London: Joseph, 1967. *The Egotists*. Chicago: H. Regnery, 1968.)

Se il sole muore. Milano: Rizzoli, 1965. (*If the Sun Dies*. New York: Atheneum House, 1966.)

Niente e così sia. Milano: Rizzoli, 1969. (*Nothing and Amen*. New York: Doubleday, 1972.)

Intervista con la storia. Milano: Rizzoli, 1974. (*Interview with History*. New York: Liveright, 1976.)

"Grazie, babbo, della tua inflessibilità." Funeral oration delivered 9 February 1988. *Europeo*, 18 August 1990, 63–64.

Interviews

"Mi piace l'idea di vendicare tutte le donne." Interview by Giancarlo Graziosi. *Domenica del Corriere*, 12 May 1974, 83.

"Orianna Fallaci." Interview by Patrizia Carrano. In *Le signore "grandi firme*," 69–102. Rimini and Firenze: Guaraldi, 1978.

"Volevo scrivere un libro sulla Vita." Interview by Davide Lajolo. *Corriere della Sera*, 15 July 1979, 8.

"Speciale." Interview. *Europeo*, 12 April 1991, 6–15.

"Ma il successo può essere fonte di grande infelicità." Interview by Paola Fallaci. *Oggi*, 23 December 1991, 24–28.

Secondary Works

Almansi, Guido. "La montagna e il cagnolone." *Panorama*, 5 August 1990, 91.

Altarocca, Claudio. "Fallaci sola a New York col diavolo in corpo." *La Stampa*, 9 August 1991, 15.

Aricò, Santo L. "Breaking the Ice: An In-Depth Look at Oriana Fallaci's Interview Techniques." *Journalism Quarterly* 63 (1986): 587–93.

———. "Oriana Fallaci's Discovery of Truth in *Niente e così sia*." *European Studies Journal* 3 (1986): 11–23.

———. "Oriana Fallaci's Journalistic Novel: *Niente e così sia*." In *Contemporary Women Writers in Italy*, 171–82. Amherst, University of Massachusetts Press, 1990.

Bocca, Giorgio. "Che rabbia, anzi, no, che invidia!" *Europeo*, 28 September 1980, 41.

Botta, Adriano. "Ma quanti bei premi per l'Oriana superstar." *Europeo*, 2 August 1991, 26.

Cambria, Adele. "Gli anni dei movimenti." In *Scritture, scrittrici*, edited by Maria Rosa Cutrufelli, 37–45. Milano: Longanesi, 1988.

Cecchi, Umberto. "Una notte, cercando Insciallah." *Europeo*, 18 August 1990, 59–62.

Cittadini, Giulio. "Uomo e donna." *Humanitas* 2 (1991): 173–4.

Colombo, Furio. "Fallaci." *La Stampa*, 8 June 1990, 15.

———. "Chi ha paura di Oriana?" *Europeo*, 18 August 1990, 23–25.

Di Renzo, Renzo. "Ire Fallaci." *L'Espresso*, 5 August 1990, 23–25.

Duby, Georges "Come imparammo ad amare le guerra." Translated by Simona Cigliana. *La Repubblica*, 2 June 1992, 34–35.

Emmer, Michele. "Alibi per la matematica." *L'Unità*, 29 September 1990, 16.

Felicetti, Fabio. "A Firenze, i bambini di 'Insciallah.'" *Corriere della Sera*, 21 December 1990, 5.

Fini, Marco. "Fallaci Oriana la Veterana." *Epoca*, 20 March 1988, 40–45.

———. "Signora grandi firme." *Epoca*, 30 June 1990, 30–35.

Gandus, Valeria. "L'Oriana furiosa." *Panorama*, 4 May 1986, 60.

———. "Calzini e cazzotti." *Panorama*, 13 January 1991, 48–49.

Gorlier, Claudio. "Feuilleton Oriana." *La Stampa*, 11 August 1990, 3.

Griffith, Thomas. "Interview, Soft or Savage." *Time*, 30 March 1990, 10–11.

Hartley, Anthony. "Dungeons and Dragons in the Beirut Rubble." *The European*, 19–21 October 1990, 4.

Lilli, Laura. "Come Eco più di Eco?" *La Repubblica*, 26 July 1990, 29.

Locher, Frances C., ed. *Contemporary Authors*. Vols. 77–80. Detroit, Michigan: Gale Research Company, 1979.

Marchionne Picchionne, Luciana. "Oriana Fallaci, *Un uomo*." *Canadian Journal of Italian Studies* 4 (1979): 327–28.

"Monument to a Martyr." *Time*, 17 September 1979, 31.

Murphy, Kim. "Prima Donna of Press Sets Off Desert Storm." *The Guardian*, 28 February 1991, 5.

Nozza, Marco. "Guerra e amore nel 'suo' Libano." *Il Giorno*, 7 August 1990, 3.

Pasti, Daniela. "Italo sul trono se Oriana acconsente." *La Repubblica*, 12 May 1990, 2.

Peer, Elizabeth. "The Fallaci Papers." *Newsweek*, 1 December 1980, 53–54.

Petrignani, Sandra. "Oriana in guerra." *Panorama*, 5 August 1990, 90–94.

Pickering-Iazzi, Robin. "Designing Mothers: Images of Motherhood in Novels by Aleramo, Morante, Maraini, and Fallaci." *Annali d'Italianistica* 7 (1989): 325–40.

Rossella, Carlo. "Beirut, mon amour." *Panorama*, 5 August 1990, 92–93.

R. U. "Come Dio vuole e Oriana decide." *Epoca*, 24 July 1990, 18–19.

Scarpino, Salvatore. "Rambo, l'ultimo amore di Oriana." *Il Giornale*, 3 March 1988, 1.

Sereni, Silvia. "Una mezza critica." *Epoca*, 21 November 1990, 26.

———. "Se questo è un reato. . . . " *Epoca*, 16 January 1991, 50–53.

Serri, Mirella. "Oriana è antipatica e fa sognare." *La Stampa*, 25 July 1990, 12.

Turoldo, David M. "Viaggio nel vulcano 'Insciallah.'" *Corriere della Sera*, 2 August 1990, 3.

Vigorelli, Giancarlo. "Il racconto più umano sul dramma d'un popolo." *Il Giorno*, 7 August 1990, 3.

Natalia Ginzburg

Primary Works

Novels and Short Stories

La strada che va in città. Torino: Einaudi, 1942. (*The Road to the City.* New York: Arcade; Little, Brown, and Company, 1990.)
E' stato così. Torino: Einaudi, 1947. (*The Dry Heart.* New York: Arcade; Little, Brown, and Company, 1990.)
Tutti i nostri ieri. Torino: Einaudi, 1952. Reprint, 1975. (*All Our Yesterdays.* Translated by Angus Davidson. Manchester: Carcanet, 1985.)
Valentino. Torino: Einaudi, 1957. Includes "La madre" and *Sagittario.* (*Valentino and Sagittarius.* Manchester: Carcanet, 1987.)
Le voci della sera. Torino: Einaudi, 1961. (*Voices in the Evening.* New York: Arcade; Little, Brown, and Company, 1989.)
Cinque romanzi brevi. Torino: Einaudi, 1964. Includes *La strada che va in città, E' stato così, Valentino, Sagittario, Le voci della sera,* and the short stories "Un'assenza,", "Casa al mare," "Mio marito," and "La madre."
Caro Michele. Milano: Mondadori, 1973. (*Dear Michael.* London: Owen, 1975. *No Way.* New York: Harcourt Brace Jovanich, 1974.)
Famiglia. Torino: Einaudi, 1977. Includes *Borghesia.* (*Family.* Manchester: Carcanet, 1988.)
La città e la casa. Torino: Einaudi, 1984. (*The City and the House.* Manchester: Carcanet, 1986.)

Nonfiction

Le piccole virtù. Torino: Einaudi, 1962. (*The Little Virtues.* New York: Seaver Books, 1986.)
Mai devi domandarmi. Milano: Garzanti, 1970. (*Never Must You Ask Me.* London: Joseph, 1973.)
"Ecco un capitolo di *Caro Michele.*" *Epoca,* 29 April 1973, 118–22.
Vita immaginaria. Milano: Mondadori, 1974.
La famiglia Manzoni. Torino: Einaudi, 1983. (*The Manzoni Family.* Manchester: Carcanet, 1987.)
"Per Primo Levi." *Paragone Letteratura* 448 (1987): 3–4.
Serena Cruz o la vera giustizia. Torino: Einaudi, 1990.

Autobiographical Works

Lessico famigliare. Torino: Einaudi, 1963. (*Family Sayings.* Manchester: Carcanet, 1984.)

166   *Selected Bibliography*

Plays

Ti ho sposato per allegria e altre commedie. Torino: Einaudi, 1967.
Paese di mare e altre commedie. Milano: Garzanti, 1973.

Interviews

"Con molto sentimento." Interview by Oriana Fallaci. In *Gli antipatici*, 337–58. Milano: Rizzoli, 1963.
"Questo mondo non mi piace." Interview by Raffaello Baldini. *Panorama*, 3 May 1973, 129–36.
"Oggi i bambini vivono soffocati dalle troppe paure dei genitori." Interview by Luciano Simonelli. *Domenica del Corriere* 5 (1975): 49–51.
"Nove domande sul romanzo." Interview. *Nuovi Argomenti* 38 (1991): 77–78, 91–92.

Secondary Works

Barani, Valeria. "Il 'latino' polifonico della famiglia Levi nel *Lessico famigliare* di Natalia Ginzburg." *Otto/Novecento* 6 (1990): 147–57.
Bini, Luigi. "La 'semplice vocalità' di Natalia Ginzburg." *Letture* 18 (August/September 1963): 585–86.
Bisutti, Donatella. "L'artificio della lettera (Appunti in margine a *La città e la casa* di Natalia Ginzburg)." *Letteratura italiana contemporanea* 16 (1985): 67–72.
Bowe, Clotilde Soave. "The Narrative Strategy of Natalia Ginzburg." *Modern Language Review* 68 (October 1973): 788–95.
Bryfonski, Dedria, ed. *Contemporary Literary Criticism.* Vol. 11. Detroit, Michigan: Gale Research Company, 1979.
Bullock, Alan. "Maternità e infanzia nell'opera di Natalia Ginzburg." *Critica Letteraria* 7 (1979): 502–33.
———. "Uomini o topi? Vincitori e vinti nei *Cinque romanzi brevi* di Natalia Ginzburg." *Italica* 60, no. 1 (1983): 38–54.
———. *Natalia Ginzburg: Human Relationships in a Changing World.* New York and Oxford: Berg Publishers, 1991.
Calvino, Italo. "Natalia Ginzburg o le possibilità del romanzo borghese." *L'Europa Letteraria* 9–10 (June–August 1961): 132–38.
Clementelli, Elena. *Invito alla lettura di Natalia Ginzburg.* Milano: Mursia, 1972.
Del Greco Lobner, Corinna. "A Lexicon for Both Sexes: Natalia Ginzburg and the Family Saga." In *Contemporary Women Writers in Italy*, edited by Santo L. Aricò, 27–42. Amherst: University of Massachusetts Press, 1990.
De Tommaso, Piero. "Elegia e ironia in Natalia Ginzburg." *Belfagor* 17 (1962): 101–4.
———. "Una scrittrice 'geniale.'" *Belfagor* 18 (1963): 335–40.
———. "Natalia Ginzburg." *Letteratura Italiana. I Contemporanei* 3 (1969): 817–33.

Garzonio, Marco. "Ginzburg e Moravia, dalla letteratura al teatro." *Vita e Pensiero* 49 (December 1966): 1016–18.
Gordon, Mary. "Surviving History." *New York Times Magazine*, 25 March 1990.
Groppali, Enrico. "Natalia Ginzburg." *Rivista Italiana di Drammaturgia* 2, no. 6 (1977): 103–10.
Heiney, Donald. "Natalia Ginzburg: The Fabric of Voices." *Iowa Review* 1, no. 4 (Fall 1970): 87–93.
Kakutani, Michiko. "Two Italian Heroines Torn by Loyalties." *New York Times*, 17 April 1990.
Knapp, Bettina L. *Women in Twentieth-Century Literature: A Jungian View.* University Park and London: Pennsylvania State University Press, 1987.
Marchionne Picchione, Luciana. *Natalia Ginzburg.* Il Castoro 137. Firenze: La Nuova Italia, 1978.
Mazza, Antonia. "Natalia Ginzburg." *Letture* 395 (March 1983): 203–22.
O'Healy, Anne-Marie. "Natalia Ginzburg and the Family." *Canadian Journal of Italian Studies* 32 (1986): 21–36.
Pasti, Daniela. "La profondità di un cuore semplice." *La Repubblica*, 9 October 1991, 33.
Personè, Luigi. "Natalia Ginzburg." *Nuova Antologia* 2064 (1972): 539–61.
Quigly, Isabel. "The Low in Spirit." *Times Literary Supplement*, 2 June 1978, 607.
Sebastiani, Gioia. *Letteratura 1937–1947.* Milano: Franco Angeli, 1991.
Siciliano, Enzo. "Natalia Ginzburg: Il caso, la poesia." *Paragone Letteratura* 252 (February 1971): 125–28.
Spagnoletti, Giacinto. "Natalia Ginzburg (Nota bibliografica)." *Belfagor* 1 (1984): 41–54.
Stajano, Corrado, Salvatore Mannuzzu, and Natalia Ginzburg. "Ritratto: Natalia Ginzburg." *Leggere* 37 (1992): 27–35.
Szymusiak, Molyda. *Il racconto di Peuw, bambina cambogiana.* Translated with a preface by Natalia Ginzburg. Torino: Einaudi, 1986.
Wienstein, Jen. "La simbologia animale nelle opere di Natalia Ginzburg." *Quaderni d'italianistica* 2 (1987): 263–76.

Rosetta Loy

Primary Works

Novels and Short Stories

La bicicletta. Torino: Einaudi, 1974.
La porta dell'acqua. Torino: Einaudi, 1976.
L'estate di Letuqué. Milano: Rizzoli, 1982.
All'insaputa della notte. Milano: Garzanti, 1984.
Le strade di polvere. Torino: Einaudi, 1987. (*Dust Roads of Monferrato.* New York: Knopf, 1991.)
"Gli orecchini." *Paragone Letteratura* 468 (1989): 19–27.
Sogni d'inverno. Milano: Mondadori, 1992.

Nonfiction

"La collina delle fragole." *Paragone Letteratura* 450 (1987): 99–107.
"Christina Rossetti." *Paragone Letteratura* 454 (1987): 36–40.
"Scrittori a Toronto." *Paragone Letteratura* 494 (1991): 117–21.

Secondary Works

Bianchini, Angela. "Il vivere quotidiano." In *Scritture, scrittici*, edited by Maria
    Rosa Cutrufelli, 33–34. Milano: Longanesi, 1988.
Lapasini, Gabriella. "I gesti dell' amore." In *Scritture, scrittrici*, edited by Maria
    Rosa Cutrufelli, 66–67. Milano: Longanesi, 1988.
Lilli, Laura. "Premio Viareggio: La parte del leone tocca a Einaudi." *La Repub-
    blica*, 2 July 1988, 21.
Rusconi, Marisa. "Nuovi percorsi tra esprienza e scrittura." In *Scritture, scrittrici*,
    edited by Maria Rosa Cutrufelli, 23. Milano: Longanesi, 1988.
Serri, Mirella. "Una saga in Monferrato ispirata dalla foto della nonna." *La Stampa*,
    12 December 1987, 3.

Gianna Manzini

Primary Works

Novels and Short Stories

Tempo innamorato. Milano: Corbaccio, 1928. Reprint, Milano: Mondadori, 1973.
Incontro col falco. Milano: Corbaccio, 1929.
Boscovivo. Milano: Treves, 1932.
Forte come un leone. Roma: Documento, 1944. Includes "La lezione della Woolf."
    Reprint, Milano: Mondadori, 1947.
Lettera all'editore. Firenze: Sansoni, 1945. Reprint, Milano: Mondadori, 1946.
Ho visto il tuo cuore. Milano: Mondadori, 1947.
Il valtzer del diavolo. Milano: Mondadori, 1947.
Animale sacri e profani. Roma: Casini, 1953.
Cara prigione. Milano: Mondadori, 1958.
Arca di Noè. Milano: Mondadori, 1960.
Un'altra cosa. Milano: Mondadori, 1961.
Allegro con disperazione. Milano: Mondadori, 1965.

Nonficton

Confessioni di scrittori (Interviste con se stessi): Quaderni della Radio XI. Torino:
    Edizioni Radio Italiana, 1951.
Ritratti e pretesti. Milano: Il Saggiatore, 1960.
Album di ritratti. Milano: Mondadori, 1964.

Autobiographical-Fictional Works

La Sparviera. Milano: Mondadori, 1956.
Ritratto in piedi. Milano: Mondadori, 1971.
Sulla soglia. Milano: Mondadori, 1973.

Secondary Works

Accrocca, E. F. "Da Gide a Ungaretti, da Kafka a Sartre." *L'Europa Letteraria* 2, no. 7 (1961): 158.
Battaglia, Salvatore. "Le 'frantumate lontananze' di Gianna Manzini." *Il Dramma* 6 (1971): 101–6.
Bettarini, Rosanna. "*Ritratto in piedi.*" *Paragone Letteratura* 22, no. 258 (1971): 139–44.
Cecchi, Emilio. "Gianna Manzini." In *Storia della Letteratura Italiana: Il Novecento*, edited by Emilio Cecchi and Natalino Sapegno, 9:683–87. Milano: Garzanti, 1969.
Contini, Gianfranco. "Narratori di 'aura poetica' e Solariani: Gianna Manzini." In *La letteratura italiana: Otto-Novecento*, 4:361–62. Firenze: Sansoni, 1974.
Costa, Simone. "Ipotesi per un 'ritratto' di Gianna Manzini." *La Rassegna della Letteratura Italiana* 3 (1974): 467–79.
Debenedetti, Giacomo. "La Manzini, l'anima e la danza." In *Intermezzo*, 126–45. Milano: Mondadori, 1963.
De Tommaso, Piero. "La 'superiore vacuità' di Gianna Manzini." *Belfagor* 17 (1962): 466–69.
Fava Guzzetta, Lia. *Manzini*. Il Castoro 96. Firenze: La Nuova Italia, 1974.
———, ed. *Omaggio a Gianna Manzini*. Messina: Edizioni "Promoteo," 1986.
Ferri, Licinio. "Una testimonianza." *Galleria* 1–2 (1986): 52–56.
Finocchiaro Chimirri, Giovanna. *Due "solariani" altrove: Gianna Manzini—Elio Vittorini*. Catania: Cooperativa Universitaria Editrice Catanese di Magistero, 1986.
Forti, Marco, ed. *Gianna Manzini: Tra letteratura e vita*. Milano: Fondazione Mondadori, 1985.
Livi, Grazia. "Cinquant'anni dopo: Gianna Manzini." *Corriere della Sera*, 24 June 1971, 12.
Lombardi, Olga. "Gianna Manzini e il 900 letterario." *Nuova Antologia* (1974): 249–53.
Miceli-Jeffries, Giovanna. "Gianna Manzini's Poetics of Verbal Visualization." In *Contemporary Women Writers in Italy*, edited by Santo L. Aricò, 90–106. Amherst: University of Massachusetts Press, 1990.
Mutini, Claudio. "Ricordo di Gianna." *Galleria* 1–2 (1986): 49–51.
Nozzoli, Anna. "Gianna Manzini: Metafora e realtà del personaggio femminile." In *Tabù e conscienza: La condizione femminile nella letteratura italiana del Novecento*, 65–84. Firenze: La Nuova Italia, 1978.
Panareo, Enzo. *Invito alla lettura di Gianna Manzini*. Milano: Mursia, 1977.
Parsani, Maria Assunta, and Neria De Giovanni. *Femminile a confronto—Tre realtà*

della narrativa italiana contemporanea: Alba de Céspedes, Fausta Cialente, Gianna Manzini. Manduria: Lacaita, 1984.

Pomes, Mathilde. "Lectures difficiles." *Revue des Deux Mondes*, 1 May 1966, 107–8.

Rizzo, Gino. "L'*imago* paterna in G. Manzini." *Albero* 51 (1974): 22–36.

Robertazzi, Mario. "I racconti di Gianna Manzini." In *Scrittori italiani contemporanei*, 15–21. Milano: Leonardo, 1942.

Sergi, Pina. "Gianna Manzini, *La Sparviera*." *Belfagor* 12 (1957): 14–15.

Sobrero, Ornella. "Gianna Manzini." *Letteratura Italiana: I Contemporanei* 2 (1963): 1163–84.

———. "Gianna Manzini." *Letteratura italiana: I Contemporanei* 6 (1979): 5468–5495.

Stampa, Carla. "Il mondo magico di Gianna Manzini." *Epoca*, 11 July 1971, 71–74.

Ulivi, Ferruccio. "G. Manzini fra prosa e racconto." *Letteratura Italiana: I Contemporanei* 6 (1979): 5495–5501.

———. "Narrativa emozionale di G. Manzini." *Letteratura Italiana: I Contemporanei* 8 (1979): 7515–26.

Dacia Maraini

Primary Works

Novels and Short Stories

La vacanza. With a preface by Alberto Moravia. Milano: Lerici, 1962. (*The Holiday.* London: Weidenfeld and Nicolson, 1966.)

L'età del malessere. Torino: Einaudi, 1963. (*The Age of Malaise.* New York: Grove, 1963. *The Age of Discontent.* London: Weidenfeld and Nicolson, 1963.)

"Gita a Viareggio." *Paragone Letteratura* 176 (1964): 70–93.

A memoria. With an introduction by Renato Barilli. Milano: Bompiani, 1967.

Mio marito. Milano: Bompiani, 1968.

Memorie di una ladra. Milano: Bompiani, 1972. (*Memoirs of a Female Thief.* Levittown, New York: Transatlantic Arts, 1974.)

Donna in guerra. Torino: Einaudi, 1975. (*Woman at War.* Brightlingsea, Essex: Lighthouse Books, 1984. Reprint, New York: Italia, 1989.)

Lettere a Marina. Milano: Bompiani, 1981.

"Madre insanguinata." *Ridotto* 1–2 (1983): 28–40.

Il treno per Helsinki. Torino: Einaudi, 1984.

Isolina: La donna tagliata in pezzi. Milano: Mondadori, 1985.

La lunga vita di Marianna Ucrìa. Milano: Rizzoli, 1990. (*The Silent Duchess.* London: Peter Owen, 1992.)

Voci. Milano: Rizzoli, 1994.

Nonfiction

"Quale cultura per la donna." In *Donna, cultura e tradizione*, edited by Pia Bruzzichelli and Maria Luisa Algini, 60–66. Milano: Mazzotta, 1976.

Il bambino Alberto. Interview of Alberto Moravia. Milano: Bompiani, 1986.
La bionda, la bruna e l'asino: Con gli occhi di oggi sugli anni Settanta e Ottanta. Milano: Rizzoli, 1987.
"Ritorno al passato attraverso il ritratto di una donna." *Sette*, 24 February 1990, 15.
"Bruciare vivi davanti alla televisione." *L'Unità*, 3 February 1992, 1.
Cercando Emma. Gustave Flaubert e la Signora Bovary: indagini attorno a un romanzo. Milano: Rizzoli, 1993.

Autobiographical Works

Bagheria. Milano: Rizzoli, 1993.

Plays

Il ricatto a teatro e altre commedie. Torino, Einaudi, 1970.
Viva l'Italia. Torino, Einaudi, 1973.
Don Juan. Torino, Einaudi, 1976.
Lezioni d'amore e altre commedie. Milano: Bompiani, 1982.
Stravaganze. Roma: Serarcangeli, 1987.
Veronica, meretrice e scrittora. Milano, Bompiani, 1992.

Poetry

Crudeltà all'aria aperta, Milano: Feltrinelli, 1966.
Donne mie. Torino, Einaudi, 1974.
Mangiami pure. Torino, Einaudi, 1978.
Dimenticato di dimenticare. Torino, Einaudi, 1982.
Viaggiando con passo di volpe. With an introduction by Cesare Garboli. Milano: Rizzoli, 1991.

Interviews

Parlare con Dacia Maraini. Interview by Ileana Montini. Verona: Bertani, 1977.
"Scrivo inebriandomi con il basilico." Interview by Carla Stampa. *Epoca*, 2 May 1981, 118–23.
"Un nuovo linguaggio per il teatro italiano." Interview by Roberta Sibona. *La Repubblica*, 20 January 1983, 29.
"Questa città sembra un travestito con le calze a rete." Interview by Maria Stella Conte. *La Repubblica*, 8 March 1984, 24.
"Con Pasolini e altri amici in una città amata e odiata." Interview by Antonio Debenedetti. *Corriere della Sera*, 15 July 1984, 2.
La nuit de Tempaku-ryô. Interview by Ryôji Nakamura and René de Ceccatty. *Europe* 693–94 (1987): 140–54.
"Siamo sempre state donne, mai persone." Interview by Lidia Ravera. *Corriere della Sera*, 7 April 1987, 3.

"Il Settecento delle donne? Un secolo muto." Interview by Monica Ricci Sargentini. *L'Unità*, 7 March 1990, 15.
"Perché questa donna? Mi è venuta a cercare. . . . " Interview by Filippo Abbiati. *Il Giorno*, 10 September 1990, 3.
"Perché anch'io sono stata muta." Interview by Stella Pende. *Europeo*, 21 September 1990, 34–35.
"Scrivere da donna / Questione di punto di vista." Interview by Giulia Salvagni. *Avvenimenti*, 13 March 1991, 46.
"Dacia Maraini: 'La mia innata tendenza al nomadismo.' " Interview by Antonio Debenedetti. *Corriere della Sera*, 15 November 1991, 5.
"Nove domande sul romanzo." Interview. *Nuovi Argomenti* 38 (1991): 77–78, 101–3.
"Bestseller: Sebben che siamo donne. . . . " Interview by Isabella Bossi Fedrigotti. *Corriere della Sera*, 28 January 1992, 11.
"L'écriture a longtemps été pour les femmes la seule façon de dire non." Interview by Elisabeth Barillé. *Contemporaine*, June 1992, 132–33.
"We Are Artisans of Our Craft." Interview by H. Lee Bimm. *Wanted in Rome*, 13 October 1993, 10–11.

Secondary Works

Bernardi, Adria. "A Blossoming of Italian Writers." *Chicago Tribune*, 25 March 1990, 2.
Cambria, Adele. "Alberto senza segreti." *Il Giorno*, 27 October 1986, 5.
Ciotta, Mariuccia. "Un nuovo linguaggio poetico." *La Repubblica*, 20 January 1983, 29.
D'Amico, Arnaldo. "Nei segreti della mente: 'Il cervello? E' solo un naso iperevoluto.' " *La Repubblica*, 12–13 July 1992, 22.
Debenedetti, Antonio. "Povera Isolina, finita in fondo all'Adige." *Corriere della Sera*, 17 April 1985, 15.
Fano, Nicola. "Il linguaggio del silenzio di Dacia Maraini e la premiata ditta dei romanzi storici." *L'Unità*, 10 September 1990, 11.
Feinstein, Wiley. "Twentieth-Century Feminist Responses to Boccaccio's Alibech Story." *Romance Languages Annual* 1 (1989): 116–20.
Garbesi, Marina. "Sposate alla paura: Il marito le picchia nessuno si ribella." *La Repubblica*, 7 March 1992, 7.
Giovanardi, Stefano. "Armida va a Helsinki." *La Repubblica*, 1 September 1984, 20–21.
Green, Charlotte. "The Sounds of Silence." *The World and I*, January 1992, 482–89.
Jacobbi, Ruggero. "Per un teatro senza ricatto." *Il Dramma* 6 (1970): 88–99.
Lazzaro-Weis, Carol. "Gender and Genre in Italian Feminist Literature in the Seventies." *Italica* 65 (1988): 293–307.
———. "From Margins to Mainstream: Some Perspectives on Women and Literature in Italy in the 1980s." In *Contemporary Women Writers in Italy*, edited by Santo L. Aricò, 197–217. Amherst: University of Massachusetts Press, 1990.
Massie, Allan. "In the Shadows of an Enlightened Age." *Scotsman Weekend*, 23 May 1992, 3.

Pallotta, Augustus. "Dacia Maraini: From Alienation to Feminism." *World Literature Today* 58 (1984): 359–62.

Pasti, Daniela. "Dacia Maraini: Lunga vita al piccolo guerriero." *Il Venerdì di Repubblica*, 21 September 1990, 31.

Pickering-Iazzi, Robin. "Designing Mothers: Images of Motherhood in Novels by Aleramo, Morante, Maraini, and Fallaci." *Annali d'Italianistica* 7 (1989): 325–40.

Saladrigas, Robert. "La escritura nacida del silencio." *La Vanguardia*, 24 May 1991, 3.

Sereni, Silvio. "Una troupe femminile girerà *Donna in guerra*." *Paese Sera*, 11 April 1976, 7.

Sumeli Weinberg, Grazia. "All'ombra del padre: La poesia di Dacia Maraini in *Crudeltà all'aria aperta*." *Italica* 67 (1990): 453–65.

———. "Word and Commitment in the Works of Dacia Maraini." Ph.D. diss., University of South Africa, 1988. Abstract in *Dissertation Abstracts International* 50, no. 9:2886A.

Tamburri, Anthony J. "Dacia Maraini's *Donna in guerra*: Victory or Defeat?" In *Contemporary Women Writers in Italy*, edited by Santo L. Aricò, 139–51. Amherst: University of Massachusetts Press, 1990.

Tornabuoni, Lietta. "Maraini, l'amazzone azzurra." *La Stampa*, 19 July 1992, 17.

Venezia, Alessandra. "Il filo di Marianna." *Panorama*, 4 March 1990, 19.

Wis, Roberto. "La Dacia in fallo." *Il Giornale*, 14 April 1986, 3.

Elsa Morante

Primary Works

Novels and Short Stories

Menzogna e sortilegio. Torino: Einaudi, 1948. 1st ed. in the "Struzzi" series. Torino: Einaudi, 1975. (*House of Liars*. New York: Harcourt, Brace and Company, 1951.)

L'isola di Arturo. Torino: Einaudi, 1957. (*Arturo's Island*, Manchester: Carcanet, 1988.)

Lo scialle andaluso. Torino: Einaudi, 1963. Contains "Il ladro dei lumi" (1935), "L'uomo dagli occhiali" (1936), "Il gioco segreto" (1937), "La nonna" (1937), and other short stories.

La Storia. Torino: Einaudi, 1974. (*History: A Novel*. Translated by William Weaver. New York: Knopf, 1977.)

Aracoeli. Torino: Einaudi, 1982. (*Aracoeli*. Translated by William Weaver. New York: Random House, 1984.)

Nonfiction

"Una lettera inedita del febbraio 1957 a Giacomo Debenedetti." *Corriere della Sera*, 26 November 1985, 3.

"Due lettere." Letter addressed to Goffredo Fofi. *Linea d'ombra* 13 (1986): 5–6.

Pro o contro la bomba atomica e altri scritti. Torino: Einaudi, 1987.

Autobiographical Works

"Pagine di diario." *Paragone Letteratura* 456 (1988): 3–16.
Diario 1938. Edited by Alba Andreini. Torino: Einaudi, 1989.

Poetry

Alibi. Milano: Longanesi, 1958.
Il mondo salvato dai ragazzini. Torino: Einaudi, 1968.

Fables

"La casa dei sette bambini." *Corriere dei Piccoli* 44 (1933). Reprint, *Linea d'ombra* 66 (December 1991): 45–47.
"Qualcuno bussa alla porta." *I Diritti della Scuola,* 25 September 1935–15 August 1936.
Le bellissime avventure di Caterì dalla trecciolina. Torino: Einaudi, 1941.

Interviews

"Nove domande sul romanzo." Interview. *Nuovi Argomenti* 38–39 (1959): 1–2, 17–38.

Secondary Works

Bayley, John. "Off the Map." *New York Review of Books,* 12 May 1994, 23–24.
Capozzi, Rocco. "Elsa Morante: The Trauma of Possessive Love and Disillusionment." In *Contemporary Women Writers in Italy,* edited by Santo L. Aricò, 11–25. Amherst: University of Massachusetts Press, 1990.
Castelli, Ferdinando. "Elsa Morante nell'inferno della solitudine." *La Civiltà Cattolica* 3184 (1983): 337–47.
Cordati, Bruna. "*Menzogna e sortilegio*: Lo spazio della metamorfosi." *Paragone Letteratura* 450 (1987): 77–87.
Debenedetti, Giacomo. "L'isola della Morante." In *Intermezzo,* 101–25. Milano: Mondadori, 1963.
Evans, Annette. "The Fiction of Family: Ideology and Narrative in Elsa Morante." In *Theory and Practice of Feminist Literary Criticism,* edited by Gabriela Mora and Karen S. Van Hooft, 131–37. Ypsilanti, Michigan: Bilingual, 1982.
Filippelli, Fiammetta. "L'ultima Morante e la storia come memoria: *Aracoeli.*" *Annali Istituto Universitario Orientale: Sezione Romanza* 31 (1989): 397–415.
Finucci, Valeria. "The Textualization of a Female 'I': Elsa Morante's *Menzogna e sortilegio.*" *Italica* 65 (1988): 308–28.
Fofi, Goffredo. "La pesantezza del futuro." *Paragone Letteratura* 450 (1987): 88–92.
Forti, Marco. "*Aracoeli* fra romanzo e simbolo." *Nuova Antologia* 2147 (1983):209–310.

Galey, Mathieu. "Elsa Morante, la madone des beatniks." *Réalités* 257 (1967): 105–15.

Giordano, Emilio. "Due casi letterari degli anni settanta: *La Storia* di Elsa Morante, *Horcynus Orca* di Stefano d'Arrigo." *Misure Critiche* 78–79 (1991): 99–115.

Girard, René. *Deceit, Desire, and the Novel*. Translated by Yvonne Freccaro. Baltimore, Maryland: Johns Hopkins University Press, 1965.

Guj, Luisa. "Illusion and Literature in Morante's *L'isola di Arturo*." *Italica* 65 (1988): 144–53.

Jeuland-Meynaud, Maryse. "Le identificazioni della donna nella narrativa di Elsa Morante." *Annali d'Italianistica* 7 (1989): 300–24.

Marras, Emma. "The Island Motif in the Works of Grazia Deledda, Elsa Morante, and Anna Maria Ortese." In *Proceedings of the XII Congress of the International Comparative Literature Association*, 275–80. Munich: Iudicium, 1990.

Moi, Toril. "The Missing Mother: The Oedipal Rivalries of René Girard." *Diacritics* 12 (1982): 21–31.

Morante, Marcello. *Maledetta benedetta: Elsa e sua madre*. Milano: Garzanti, 1986.

Pampaloni, Geno. "Menzogna e sortilegio." *Il Ponte* 4 (1949): 544–45.

Pasolini, Pier Paolo. "Il mondo salvato dai ragazzini." *Paragone Letteratura* 224 (1968): 120–26; 230 (1969): 136–42.

Pickering-Iazzi, Robin. "Designing Mothers: Images of Motherhood in Novels by Aleramo, Morante, Maraini, and Fallaci." *Annali d'Italianistica* 7 (1989): 325–40.

Pizzocaro, Massimo. "Saffo nell'isola di Arturo." *Belfagor* 45 (1990): 198–201.

Poeti, Alida. "Time, Tense, and Symbol in Elsa Morante's *Aracoeli*." *Studi d'Italianistica nell'Africa Australe* 2 (1989): 1–11.

Pupino, Angelo R. *Strutture e stile della narrativa di Elsa Morante*. Ravenna: Longo, 1968.

———. "Elsa Morante." *Letteratura Italiana: I Contemporanei* 3 (1969): 715–43.

Pupino, Angelo R., Enzo Siciliano, and Enzo Golino. "Elsa Morante." *Letteratura Italiana. Novecento. I Contemporanei* 8 (1979): 7565–7605.

Ragni, Eugenio. "Elsa Morante." *Letteratura Italiana Contemporanea* 2 (1979): 767–81.

Ravanello, Donatello. *Scrittura e follia nei romanzi di Elsa Morante*. Venezia: Marsilio, 1980.

Ricci, Graziella. "*L'isola di Arturo*." *Nuovi Argomenti* 62 (1979): 237–75.

Sanjust, Margherita. "Dall'isola alla storia." *Paragone Letteratura* 450 (1987): 93–98.

Schifano, Jean-Noël. "Barbara e divina." *L'Espresso*, 2 December 1984, 122–33.

Sergi, Pina. "Elsa Morante, *L'isola di Arturo*." *Belfagor* 12 (1957): 595–97.

Sgorlon, Carlo. *Invito alla lettura di Elsa Morante*. 3d ed. Milano: Mursia, 1978.

Stefani, Luigina. "Elsa Morante." *Belfagor* 26 (1971): 290–308.

Venturi, Gianni. *Morante*. Il Castoro 130. Firenze: La Nuova Italia, 1977.

Wood, Sharon. "The Bewitched Mirror: Imagination and Narration in Elsa Morante." *Modern Language Review* 86 (1991): part 2, 310–21.

Zago, Esther. "Il carattere di stampa come segno ne *Lo scialle andaluso* di Elsa Morante." *Il lettore di provincia* 81 (1991): 33–40.

Lalla Romano

Primary Works

Novels and Short Stories

Le metamorfosi. Torino: Einaudi, 1951.
Maria. Torino: Einaudi, 1953. Reprint, Torino: Einaudi, 1973.
Tetto Murato. Torino: Einaudi, 1957.
L'uomo che parlava solo. Torino: Einaudi, 1961.
Opere. Edited by Cesare Segre. Vol. 1. I Meridiani. Milano: Mondadori, 1991. Includes the poems *Fiore*, *L'autunno*, and *Giovane è il tempo*, and the narratives *Le metamorfosi*, *Maria*, *Tetto Murato*, *Diario di Grecia*, *L'uomo che parlava solo*, and *La penombra che abbiamo attraversato*.

Nonfiction

"Vi racconto una storia. Itinerari della narrativa italiana contemporanea." In *Scuola e Territorio*, document 20, 155–66. Rimini: n.p., 1985.
Un sogno del Nord. Torino: Einaudi, 1989. Contains occasional pieces.
Le lune di Hvar. Torino: Einaudi, 1991.

Autobiographical Works

La penombra che abbiamo attraversato. Torino: Einaudi, 1964.
Le parole tra noi leggere. Torino: Einaudi, 1969.
L'ospite. Torino: Einaudi, 1973.
Una giovinezza inventata. Torino: Einaudi, 1979.
Inseparabile. Torino: Einaudi, 1981.
Nei mari estremi. Milano: Mondadori, 1987.
Un caso di coscienza. Torino: Bollati Boringhieri, 1992.

Interviews

"Gli scrittori a casa loro." Interview by Grazia Livi. *Corriere della Sera*, 13 January 1972, 12.
" . . . Che cosa ci aspettiamo anche dal linguaggio dell'arte, se non verità, che vuol poi dire ricerca dell'autentico?" Interview. *Uomini e libri* 15, no. 76 (1979): 58.
"Lalla Romano: In punta di penna il sapore delle cose." Interview by Maria Pia Bonante. *Madre* 11 (1987): 126–28.
"Intervista a Lalla Romano." Interview by Alfredo Barberis. *Millelibri* 2, no. 8 (1988): 62–70.

"Appunto e a capo." Interview by Grazia Cerchi. *Panorama*, 4 August 1991, 103–4.
"Ogni mio amore è un libro." Interview by Simonetta Fiori. *La Repubblica*, 22–23 September 1991, 33.
"Intervista a Lalla Romano per *Le lune di Hvar.*" Interview by Claudio Toscani. *Otto/Novecento* 15, no. 6 (November/December 1991): 143–45.

Secondary Works

Antonielli, Sergio."Lalla Romano." *Paragone Letteratura* 232 (1969): 104–6.
———. "Lalla Romano, *L'ospite.*" *Belfagor* 29 (1974): 228–31.
Banti, Anna. "Lalla Romano." *Paragone Letteratura* 178 (1964): 96–98.
Brizio, Flavia. "The Photographic Novels of Lalla Romano." Paper presented at the ninth annual conference of the American Association for Italian Studies at the University of Lowell, Lowell, Massachusetts, 13–16 April 1989.
———. "Memory and Time in Lalla Romano's Novels, *La penombra che abbiamo attraversato* and *Le parole tra noi leggere.*" In *Contemporary Women Writers in Italy*, edited by Santo L. Aricò, 63–75. Amherst: University of Massachusetts Press, 1990.
Catalucci, Annamaria. *Invito alla lettura di Lalla Romano.* Milano: Mursia, 1980.
Catalucci, Annamaria, and Anna Maria del Sole. "*Le metamorfosi* di Lalla Romano." *Paragone Letteratura* 216 (1968): 160–61.
Cattanei, Luigi. "Mastronardi, Berto, Romano: La condizione della coppia." *Otto/Novecento* 5–6 (1987): 5–27.
Ferrata, Giansiro. "L'infanzia memorata di L. Romano." *Letteratura italiana. Novecento. I Contemporanei* 8 (1979): 7650–57.
Frassica, Pietro. "Lalla Romano, *Nei mari estremi.*" *Autografo* 5, no. 13 (1988): 109–11.
Grassano, Giuseppe. "L'ultimo libro di Lalla Romano: *Nei mari estremi.*"*Otto/Novecento* 12, no. 2 (1988): 179–86.
Lector [Claudio Marabini]. "Lalla Romano parla di *Inseparabile.*" *Resto del Carlino*, 5 September 1981, 8.
Manacorda, Giuliano. *Storia della letteratura contemporanea (1940–1975).* 4th ed. Roma: Editori Riuniti, 1977.
Montale, Eugenio. "Non mettetela nell'apartheid." *L'Espresso*, 21 April 1991, 115.
Morabito, Pierfrancesco. "Lalla Romano: *Un sogno del Nord.*" *Il Verri* 2–3 (1991): 145–47.
Onofri, Massimo. "Lalla Romano: *Opere*, Volume I." *Nuovi Argomenti* 40 (1991): 121–24.
Petrignani, Sandra. "Bricciole di gloria." *Panorama*, 13 October 1991, 151–57.
Serri, Mirella. "L'orgoglio di Lalla." *L'Espresso*, 21 April 1991, 114–19.
Sgorlon, Carlo. "Enigma tra le pareti." *Il Giornale*, 4 October 1981, 4.
Tesio, Giovanni. "Ritratti critici di contemporanei: Lalla Romano." *Belfagor* 6 (1980): 671–86.
Vincenti, Fiora. *Lalla Romano.* Il Castoro 94. Firenze: La Nuova Italia, 1974.
———. "Lalla Romano." *Letteratura italiana. Novecento. I Contemporanei* 8 (1979): 7634–50.

Matilde Serao

Primary Works

Novels and Short Stories

[Tuffolina, pseud.]. *Opale*. Napoli: De Angelis, 1878.
Dal vero. Milano: Perussia e Quadrio, 1879.
Cuore infermo. Torino: Casanova, 1881.
Leggende napoletane. Milano: Ottimo, 1881.
Fantasia. Torino: Roux e Favale, 1883.
La virtù di Checchina. Catania: Gianotta, 1884. Reprint, with an introduction by Natalia Ginzburg, Milano: Emme Edizioni, 1974.
La conquista di Roma. Firenze: Barbera, 1885.
Il romanzo della fanciulla. Milano: Treves, 1886. Reprint, edited by Francesco Bruni, Napoli: Liguori, 1985. Contains "Telegrafi dello Stato," "Per monaca," "Nella lava," "Scuola normale femminile," "Non più," and "La virtù di Checchina."
Vita e avventure di Riccardo Joanna. Milano: Galli, 1887. Reprint, Milano: Garzanti, 1939.
Addio, amore!. Napoli: Gianni, 1890.
Il paese di cuccagna. Milano: Treves, 1891. Reprint, Milano: Treves, 1928.
Castigo. Torino: Casanova, 1893.
Telegrafi dello Stato. Roma: Perino, 1895.
La ballerina. Catania: Giannotta, 1899.
Suor Giovanna della Croce. Milano: Treves, 1901.
O Giovannino o la morte!. Napoli: Perrella, 1912.
Mors tua. . . . Milano: Treves, 1926.
L'occhio di Napoli. Edited by Anna Banti. Milano: Garzanti, 1962.

Nonfiction

Il ventre di Napoli. Milano: Treves, 1884.
Nel paese di Gesù (Ricordi di un viaggio in Palestina). Napoli: Tocco, 1899.
Il Giornale. Napoli: Perrella, 1906.
Lettere di una viaggiatrice. Napoli: Perrella, 1908.

Secondary Works

Accolti Gil, Mario, and Mimma De Leo. "Matilde Serao: La giornalista, la scrittrice, la donna." *Mond-Operaio* 10 (1988): 71–84.
Banti, Anna. *Matilde Serao: Con 13 tavole fuori testo*. Torino: Unione Tipografica Editrice Torinese, 1965.
———. "La Serao a Roma (1882–84)." *Paragone Letteratura* 182 (1965): 36–55.
Caccia, Ettore. "Appunti sullo stile di Matilde Serao." *Humanitas* 14 (1959): 35–46.

Croce, Alda, and Elena Croce, eds. *Narratori meridionali dell'Ottocento*. Torino: Unione Tipografica Editrice Torinese, 1970.

De Giovanni, Neria. *L'ora di Lilith: Su Grazia Deledda e la letteratura femminile del secondo Novecento*. Roma: Ellemme, 1987.

Eco, Umberto, Marina Federzoni, Isabella Pezzini, and Maria Pia Pozzato, eds. *Carolina Invernizio, Matilde Serao, Liala*. Il Castoro 145. Firenze: La Nuova Italia, 1979.

Fanning, Ursula. "Sentimental Subversion: Representations of Female Friendship in the Work of Matilde Serao." *Annali d'Italianistica* 7 (1989): 273–86.

Ginzburg, Natalia. "Scrittori della realtà." *Leggere* 37 (1992): 32–35.

Infusino, Gianni, ed. *Matilde Serao tra giornalismo e letteratura*. Napoli: Guida Editori, 1981.

Kroha, Lucienne. "Matilde Serao: *Il romanzo della fanciulla*." *Quaderni d'italianistica* 11 (1990): 152–57.

Lepri, Laura. "Serao, Matilde." In *Dizionario critico della letteratura italiana*, edited by Vittore Branca, 2d ed., 4:163–65. Torino: Unione Tipografica Editrice Torinese, 1986.

Lilli, Laura. "Perché Matilde perse il Nobel." *La Repubblica*, 1 July 1988, 30.

Pezzini, Isabella. "Matilde Serao." In *Carolina Invernizio, Matilde Serao, Liala*, edited by Umberto Eco, Marina Federzoni, Isabella Pezzini, and Maria Pia Pozzato, Il Castoro 145, 61–94. Firenze: La Nuova Italia, 1979.

Prisco, Michele. "Matilde Serao." *Terzo Programma* 3 (1963): 57–95.

Romanzi e racconti italiani dell'Ottocento: Serao. Vol. I. Milano: Garzanti, 1946.

Schilardi, Wanda de Nunzio. *Matilde Serao giornalista (con antologia di scritti rari)*. Lecce: Milella, 1986.

Tench, Darby. "Gutting the Belly of Naples: Metaphor, Metonymy, and the Auscultatory Imperative in Serao's City of *Pietà*." *Annali d'Italianistica* 7 (1989): 287–99.

General Bibliography

Amoia, Alba. *Women on the Italian Literary Scene: A Panorama*. Troy, New York: Whitston Publishing Company, 1992.

Aricò, Santo L., ed. *Contemporary Women Writers in Italy*. Amherst: University of Massachusetts Press, 1990.

Aspesi, Natalia. "Alla ricerca delle Grandi Madri." *La Repubblica*, 1 May 1992, 31.

Bàrberi Squarotti, Giorgio. *La narrativa italiana del dopoguerra*. Bologna: Cappelli, 1968.

Belotti, Elena Gianini. "Letteratura femminile: Quattro campioni di erotismo." *Paragone Letteratura* 478 (1989): 86–99.

Birnbaum, Lucia Chiavola. *Liberazione della donna: Feminism in Italy*. Middletown, Connecticut: Wesleyan University Press, 1986.

Blelloch, Paola. *Quel mondo dei guanti e delle stoffe. . . .* Verona: Essedue Edizioni, 1987.

Bosetti, Gilbert. *Le mythe de l'enfance dans le roman italien contemporain*. Grenoble: Ellug, 1987.

Carrano, Patrizia. *Le signore "grandi firme."* Rimini and Firenze: Guaraldi, 1978.

Cecchi, Emilio. *Ritratti e profili*. Milano: Garzanti, 1957.

Cecchi, Emilio, and Natalino Sapegno, eds. *Storia della letteratura italiana: Il Novecento*. 10 vols. Milano: Garzanti, 1979.

Contini, Gianfranco. *La letteratura italiana: Otto-Novecento*. Firenze: Sansoni, 1974.

Croce, Benedetto. *Le letteratura della nuova Italia*. Vol. 3. Bari: Laterza, 1964.

Cutrufelli, Maria Rosa, ed. *Scritture, scrittici*. Milano: Longanesi, 1988.

de Michelis, Cesare, ed. *Studi Novecenteschi: Quadrimestrale di Storia della Letteratura Contemporanea*. 13 vols. to date. Università di Padova, 1972–.

Dizionario critico della letteratura italiana. Edited by Vittore Branca. 2d ed. 4 vols. Torino: Unione Tipografica Editrice Torinese, 1986.

Dizionario generale degli autori contemporanei. Edited by Enzo Ronconi and Vallecchi editors. 2 vols. Firenze: Vallecchi, 1974.

Knapp, Bettina L. *A Jungian Approach to Literature*. Carbondale and Edwardsville: Southern Illinois University Press, 1984.

Livi, Grazia. *Le lettere del mio nome*. Milano: La Tartaruga, 1991.

Manacorda, Giuliano. *Storia della letteratura italiana contemporanea (1940–1975)*. Roma: Editori Riuniti, 1977.

Merry, Bruce. *Women in Modern Italian Literature: Four Studies Based on the Works of Grazia Deledda, Alba de Céspedes, Natalia Ginzburg, and Dacia Maraini*. Townsville, Australia: Department of Modern Languages, James Cook University of North Queensland, 1990.

Morandini, Giuliana. *La voce che è in lei: Antologia della narrativa femminile italiana tra '800 e '900*. Milano: Bompiani, 1980.

Nozzoli, Anna. *Tabù e coscienza: La condizione femminile nella letteratura italiana del Novecento*. Firenze: La Nuova Italia, 1978.

Peritore, G. S., ed. *Letteratura italiana: I Contemporanei*. Vol. 3. Milano: Marzorati, 1970.

Petronio, Giuseppe, and Luciana Martinelli. *Il Novecento letterario in Italia*. Palermo: Palumbo, 1974.

Rasy, Elisabetta. *Le donne e la letteratura: Scrittrici eroine e ispiratrici nel mondo delle lettere*. Roma: Editori Riuniti, 1984.

Testaferri, Ada, ed. *Donna: Women in Italian Culture*. Toronto: Dovehouse, 1989.

West, Rebecca, and Dino S. Cervigni, eds. "Women's Voices in Italian Literature." *Annali d'Italianistica* 7 (1989): 4–429.

Zecchi, Barbara. "Il corpo femminile trampolino tra scrittura e volo. Enif Robert e Biancamaria Frabotta: settant'anni verso il tempo delle donne." *Italica* 69 (1992): 505–18.

INDEX

Alba Amoia lives in Rome, Italy, where she is engaged in research and writing, after her retirement from the Department of Romance Languages at Hunter College of the City University of New York.

She received her bachelor of arts degree from Barnard College and then went on to Columbia University to earn her master of arts, master of international affairs, and doctorate. She also studied at the Université d'Aix-Marseille in France as a Fulbright scholar and has taught at Barnard College, Columbia University, and the United Nations.

Her book publications include *Jean Anouilh* (1969), *The Italian Theatre Today* (1975), *Edmond Rostand* (1978), *An Anthology of Modern Belgian Theatre* (coedited, 1982), *Albert Camus* (1990), *Thomas Mann's "Fiorenza"* (1990), *Women on the Italian Literary Scene: A Panorama* (1992), and *Feodor Dostoevsky* (1993).